From Homer to Joyce:

A STUDY GUIDE TO THIRTY-SIX GREAT BOOKS

From Homer to Joyce:

A STUDY GUIDE TO THIRTY-SIX GREAT BOOKS

J. Sherwood Weber
Jules Alan Wein
Pratt Institute

Arthur Waldhorn
Arthur Zeiger
College of the City of New York

HOLT, RINEHART AND WINSTON, INC.
New York — Chicago — San Francisco — Toronto — London

September, 1965

Library of Congress Card Catalog Number: 58-6316
29272-0129
Printed in the United States of America

To all our parents.

Preface

In recent years, more and more people—of all sorts and conditions—have been reading and discussing the world's great books. Their reasons? The great books stimulate, move, enlarge—and, not least, entertain. They search man's purposes, illuminate his ways, measure his accomplishments, gratify his hunger for beauty.

The generations of man have agreed to call only a handful of books "great"—the vital record of the best that has been thought and said in the world. Our guide considers thirty-six such masterworks, those most often included in Great Books, Comparative Literature, and Humanities courses. It tries to do two things: to help readers understand and appreciate thirty-six great books; and to help them develop critical techniques that will encourage independent perception and evaluation.

Our chapters have a simple format. First, a brief introductory essay provides the minimum background necessary for reading the great work with full understanding. While noting the pertinent biographical data as well as the special literary and social traditions, we have avoided (sometimes painfully) attempting the kind of interpretation and analysis each reader should undertake for himself. Second, a list of core questions establishes the basis for extended study and systematic discussion of theme, plot, structure, setting, language and style, character, tone, relationship to other great books, and impact on man's intellectual and cultural development.

Two additional sections follow each essay and set of questions. One is a selective, annotated bibliography of critical materials. The works cited—articles, chapters, and books—aid the reader to explore more widely and penetrate more deeply than the limits of group discussion allow. The notations describe the scope, readability, and special point of view of each reading. The final section is a critical list of inexpensive translations and editions. Wherever possible we have recommended the translations currently regarded as most effective.

Although each chapter is largely the product of a single author, all reflect our combined experience and judgment. J. Sherwood Weber prepared Chapters 1-5, 8, 17-18; Arthur Waldhorn, Chapters 7, 12, 20, 25-26, 28-29; Jules Wein, Chapters 1, 6, 11, 13-16, 19; and Arthur Zeiger, Chapters 21-24, 27, 30. Chapters 9 and 10—on the *Aeneid* and the *Divine Comedy*—were written respectively by Mario DiCesare and Rolf Fjelde of Pratt Institute. Mr. Fjelde and Edwin B. Knowles, also of Pratt Institute, contributed generously to the study questions and to the bibliographies.

The librarians at Pratt Institute, particularly Pauline Pfeifer, were variously helpful. Dorothy L. Parker aided in preparing the manuscript. Finally, our students assisted in ways they can never know. To them we are especially grateful.

Pratt Institute

College of the City of New York

J. S. W.
J. A. W.
A. W.
A. Z.

December 21, 1958

Contents

From Homer to Joyce:

A STUDY GUIDE TO THIRTY-SIX GREAT BOOKS

1

Homer: ILIAD and ODYSSEY

I. Background of Homer (*c.* 9th century B.C.)

We shall probably never be certain whether the *Iliad* and the Odyssey were written by the same man, by two different men, or by a number of men in collaboration. Both epics are generally credited to Homer, a court poet who lived on the Ionian coast of Asia Minor in the 8th or 9th century B.C. Homer apparently drew not only from myth and legend but also from sagas composed before his day. Certainly, both heroic epics represent the highest stage in the development of Greek narrative poetry. In each, several traditional stories have been shaped by a master hand into a structurally unified work of surpassing power. Composed several centuries after the events they narrate took place—or might have taken place—these poems must be understood as syntheses of tradition and legend rather than as authentic history.

The *Iliad* focuses on a single climactic event during the siege of Troy, a series of battles which Greek tradition places in the 12th century B.C. The *Odyssey* relates the adventures and misadventures of a Greek hero trying to return home from the war. Though there may have been a Trojan war, the events and characters celebrated in the epics are probably legendary.

The historical period reflected in these poems (variously calculated as from the 15th to the 10th centuries B.C.) was characterized by intense social distress—by frequent mass migrations, by wars of conquest and plunder, by the subjugation or forced displacement of settled populations, by political chaos, and by collapsing cultures. Each major upheaval gave rise to tales of prowess and adventure; these, in time, were fused into a rough sort of unity. Thus, the *Iliad* and the *Odyssey* are thought to telescope an age of looting expeditions and maritime raids into the artistically manageable proportions of a single catastrophe and its sequel.

Both epics were composed for oral delivery to an aristocratic audience—the rulers and nobles of small agricultural kingdoms, the relatively peaceful descendants of the rude chieftains who had fought at places like Troy. Both poems glorify the ancestry of these people as well as rationalize and codify some of their contemporary social values, economic practices, and religious convictions. The human drama of the epics is so absorbing that we must be especially alert to grasp the system of ideas that underlies the story. To the ancients, art was much more than entertainment: it was a fascinating mode of education, combining philosophical abstractions, religious dogma, and traditional history in esthetically attractive and emotionally persuasive form. The *Iliad* and the *Odyssey* embodied so much of the heritage of the Greeks that Homer was regarded for centuries as their foremost preceptor, even after changed conditions and values required that his works be interpreted allegorically.

Sociologically, the *Iliad* and the *Odyssey* embody the ideals and preoccupations of a rather primitive society whose wealth derived mainly from livestock, small-scale agriculture, and plunder, and whose social unit was the patriarchal household. The *Odyssey* describes such a household, idealizing its domestic relationships. In the *Iliad* the tribe is still the basis of political organization, but evidence of its decline appears in dissension between rulers and ruled. The *Odyssey* offers even more striking evidence of advancing social stratification and of the rise of centralized monarchies. Both works express an aristocratic world view, dealing largely with kings and nobles, only incidentally glancing at the life of the common people. The universality of both epics lies not in their restricted social scope, but in their exploration of problems and motives common to all men.

From the ancient myths and legends he inherited, Homer

(along with Hesiod, an 8th-century B.C. Greek poet, whose *Theogony* is also fundamentally important in the study of Greek religion) standardized Greek Olympian theology for generations. His gods—disarmingly human but divinely powerful—lack that ethical awareness and involvement that readers of the Bible expect of divinity. But their very indifference to moral behavior may have helped to encourage man's trust in himself and to spur the development of humanism—Greece's noblest contribution to Western thought. Like all primitive peoples, the early Greeks expressed their experience of life in mythological form. Even so sordid an adventure as the destruction of a flourishing center of civilization for booty and slaves found justification and glorification in myth and legend. The fictional background of the Trojan War, involving the story of the Judgment of Paris and the abduction of Helen, is just such a version of history.

Although much of Homer's narrative style is lost even in the best translations, enough survives to deserve comment. Two plot devices heighten the dramatic intensity: he begins *in medias res*, in the middle of things—that is, he starts each story after the precipitating event—and supplies the background through flashbacks; and he proceeds through digression—that is, he interpolates long episodes that usually reinforce the theme of the main story, but do not necessarily advance the plot. The oral delivery of the poems or the demands of a rigid meter account at least partially for stylistic devices such as the repetition of whole speeches, phrases, and allusions; the Homeric simile (an extended comparison in which the unfamiliar is likened in detail to an event or procedure or object drawn from common experience); the catalogue (a long list of things, persons, or gods); the stock epithet (a compound descriptive and adjective—"grey-eyed Athene," "wine-dark sea"—used repeatedly, and not always pertinently, to refer to some person or thing; and elaborate parallelism (the balancing of phrase against phrase, clause against clause, thought against thought).

In the *Iliad* and the *Odyssey* Homer fused and expanded naive tales and legends into an epic version of human life, permeated by a profound conviction of the meaningfulness of man's adventure and exalted by that twofold sense of joy and doom which all thoughtful mortals share but which only the great artist can memorably express.

II. Questions for Study and Discussion

Iliad

1. What is the theme of the *Iliad?*
2. Describe the organization of the *Iliad.* Is it a loose chronicle? Has it structural unity? What seems effective or ineffective about the plot arrangement?
3. What of importance to the whole story is accomplished through the meeting of Achilles and Priam at the end?
4. What aspects of Greek life are emphasized as a result of the setting of the events? Which areas of life are slighted or ignored?
5. Cite several examples of Homeric similes. From what specific areas of life does Homer draw the material for these similes?
6. What other figures of speech or stylistic devices does Homer regularly use? Which of these seem particularly attuned to oral delivery of the poem? Why and how?
7. Identify and explain Achilles' motivations. How many exist, and in what order do they appear? Which are emotional, which rational in origin?
8. Describe Homer's concept of the hero and of heroic virtue. Which of the opposing heroes, Achilles or Hector, is most appealing to you? Why? Which does Homer seem to regard as the greater hero? On what do you base your opinion?
9. Characterize each of the other principal characters. What traits in each have been idealized, and why?
10. Describe the qualities of the Achaean king, of the Trojan king. Define the social and political position of each. Explain how their roles and functions differ from those of the kings depicted in the *Odyssey.*
11. Characterize the social structure pictured in the *Iliad.* What social values seem to be most respected?
12. Identify the evidence which indicates that the Homeric Greeks placed a high value on material things.
13. Describe the function of the priest in this society. How does the Homeric priest differ from the Old Testament prophet?
14. What can you infer about the status of women? About mar-

riage? About sexual relationships? In what ways are women (mortal or immortal) the causes of dissension? What is Homer's attitude toward women?

15. What is the attitude of the Greeks toward war? Of the Trojans? What seems to be Homer's view?
16. Discuss the behavior of the gods as a group—toward each other as well as toward men. Characterize the religion they embody.
17. According to Homer, to what extent do men shape and bear responsibility for their own actions? To what extent are they motivated and controlled by the gods? By Fate? By chance? To what extent is Homer consistent in his position on personal responsibility?
18. What is the Greek view concerning the presence of pain in life? Can suffering be avoided? What makes life worth living?
19. Explain the Homeric view of sin. How does it differ from the Old Testament view? From the New Testament view?
20. What qualities does Homer seem to admire in the Greeks? In the Trojans? To what degree is he objective in depicting both sides in this epic struggle?
21. As a narrative about war, how does the *Iliad* compare with or differ from other war stories with which you are familiar?
22. What has been preserved and what has been lost in the film and television versions of the *Iliad* and the *Odyssey*?

Odyssey

1. What is the theme of the *Odyssey*?
2. How many major story lines can you trace in the plot of this poem? Which character dominates each? Explain how these plot lines are finally integrated.
3. Explain how structure illuminates theme in the *Odyssey*.
4. How much time elapses from the beginning to the end of the story? Explain the dramatic value of the flashback technique of plotting.
5. Homer often digresses from the main narrative to tell a tan-

gential story. What do these digressions indicate about the Homeric outlook on life? About the audience for whom the poem was intended? Which digressions are closely related to the theme. How are they related?

6. Describe the societies in which the Odyssey is set. What are the basic social values of each? Which of these values do we still respect in America?
7. What can you infer about the attitude toward marriage in this society? About the status of women? About the role of family life?
8. Characterize the economic basis of life in the Homeric Age. (Consider the attitude toward property, hospitality, gift-giving, distribution of wealth, etc.)
9. Describe such characteristics of Homer's poetic style as survive in translation. Which of these devices probably enhanced the oral delivery of the poem?
10. Describe each of the major characters. In what respects has each been idealized or typified?
11. Which characters change significantly during the course of events? What do the answers to this question suggest about the Homeric code of values and the intent of the poem?
12. To what degree are Homer and (presumably) his audience interested in psychology? How is motivation treated in the poem?
13. Characterize the Homeric hero. What ideals of conduct are encompassed in heroic virtue?
14. Why must Odysseus be tested? Can you think of other works in which a hero is variously tested before he can win his goal?
15. Which of Odysseus's problems are not satisfactorily resolved at the end of the story?
16. How would you explain the appeal of the Odyssey to modern authors such as James Joyce, Ezra Pound, Nikos Kazantzakis, and others?
17. What might each of Odysseus' experiences symbolize? Of these encounters—with the Ciconians, Lotus-eaters, Cyclops, Aeolus, Laestrygones, Circe, Hades, Sirens, Scylla and Charybdis—which have become traditional metaphors for certain life situations? Why?

18. Characterize the gods in their relationships with each other and in their dealings with men.
19. Describe the relationship of the hero to the gods. Of the hero to other nobles. Of the hero to the common man.
20. To what extent does Homer hold the individual responsible for his own destiny? To what extent the gods in general? To what extent Zeus? To what extent Fate? Is Homer's position always consistent?
21. For Homer, what is the highest good for man in life? What is Odysseus' view on this point? What is Homer's view concerning life after death?
22. In what ways are the values (social, political, personal) of the *Odyssey* different from those of the *Iliad*? What significance can you infer from these differences?
23. What influence might the omnipresence of the sea exert on a national literature in process of formation?

III. Readings in Background and Criticism

Auerbach, Erich, *Mimesis* (Doubleday Anchor Books, 1957). An illuminating study of the representation of reality in Western literature. The first chapter, "Odysseus' Scar," is a superb analysis of typical passages from the *Odyssey* and from *Genesis* as illustrating opposing but basic concepts of reality. According to Auerbach, Homer heightened reality without violating it; the Old Testament writers strove to transcend sensual reality.

Baldry, H. C., *Greek Literature for the Modern Reader* (Cambridge University Press, 1951). A handbook of background facts for the understanding of Homer's epics (as well as other Greek classics). Answers many questions commonly raised by students about both epics.

Bowra, C. M., *Heroic Poetry* (Macmillan, 1952). The fullest modern study of the literary type to which Homer's epics belong.

Cook, Albert, *The Dark Voyage and the Golden Mean* (Harvard University Press, 1949). An ingenious study of the nature of comedy. The final chapter explores the tragic complexity of the *Iliad* and the comic implications of the *Odyssey*.

Finley, M. I., *The World of Odysseus* (Meridian, 1959). The best popular introduction to the world and works of Homer. Particularly good on the social organization, the economy, the customs, and the moral values of the Homeric Age.

Graves, Robert, *The Greek Myths*, 2 vols. (Penguin Classics, 1955). A fascinating retelling of the myths of the gods and heroes in the light of modern anthropological knowledge. Though Graves has vast learning and often provides fresh insights, some of his interpretations are at least dubious. Pages 259-376 of Volume 2 are devoted to the myths and legends incorporated into the Homeric poems.

Hadas, Moses, *History of Greek Literature* (Columbia University Press, 1950). A comprehensive discussion of Greek literature. Chapter 3, "Homer," considers the *Iliad* as a reflective poem, the *Odyssey* as an entertainment indicating the decline of the heroic tradition.

Hamilton, Edith, *The Greek Way* (New American Library, 1948). A gracefully written and sound introduction to ancient Greek life, thought, and literature. Chapter 15, "The Religion of the Greeks," suggests that artists like Homer—not theologians—defined the function of Greek religion: "To make the visible express the invisible."

Jaeger, Werner, *Paideia*, Vol. 2 (Oxford University Press, 1939). Chapters 1 to 3 discuss the Homeric epics on the stimulating but controversial assumption that they were consciously designed to codify and cultivate aristocratic ideals.

Lord, George De F., "The *Odyssey* and the Western World," *Sewanee Review* (Summer 1954). Expounds and augments the interpretive approach of Denton Snider (below) as an alternative to both allegorical and realistic readings of the *Odyssey*.

Lorimer, H. L., *Homer and the Monuments* (Macmillan, 1950). A meticulous, exhaustive resumé of the last 75 years of archeological research into the world of the Homeric poems.

Nilsson, M., *Homer and Mycenae* (Methuen, 1933). A lucid summary of Homeric Age culture, particularly enlightening on mythology, on the origin and transmission of epic poetry, on Mycenaean social structure, and on the language and style of Homer.

Platnauer, Maurice, editor, *Fifty Years of Classical Scholarship* (Basil Blackwell, 1954). Chapter 1, "Homer," reviews the contributions of twentieth-century scholarship to a field alive with controversy and fresh discovery. Evaluates books and theories and suggests further secondary reading.

Rose, H. J., *A Handbook of Greek Literature* (Methuen, 1950). A manual, supplying the background facts in more detail than Baldry's handbook cited above.

Snider, Denton J., *Homer's Odyssey: A Commentary* (William Miner, 1895). A penetrating study of the *Odyssey*, book by book, as the account of the moral and spiritual restoration of Odysseus after "the grand estrangement caused by the Trojan Expedition."

Stanford, W. B., *The Ulysses Theme* (Basil Blackwell, 1955). A Dublin editor of the *Odyssey* examines classic as well as modern variations of the Odyssean prototype. Chapter 14 on Dante and Tennyson and Chapter 15 on Joyce and Kazantzakis are especially interesting.

IV. Translations and Editions

In the past men often regarded the Greek classics as almost sacred texts; to approach them as living literature (though they were often bursting with vitality) seemed a profanation. Almost without exception, therefore, pre-20th-century translations of the *Iliad* and *Odyssey* are stiff, archaic, remote, abstract, or ornate. Reading either Homeric epic in an old translation generally entails sacrificing much of its potential impact.

Within the present generation, fortunately, scholar-writers have created very readable versions of both poems in accurate, idiomatic prose, and even in effective poetry, employing language alive with the force of contemporary speech. Two new prose versions of the epics are especially good and very inexpensive: W. H. D. Rouse's (New American Library) and E. V. Rieu's (Penguin). Both are faithful to meaning and lively in phrasing. The Rouse *Odyssey* is vivid, plain, even racy at times; the Rieu *Iliad*, colloquial and clear, captures much of the dignity of the tragic story. The verse translation of the *Iliad* by Richmond Lattimore (University of Chicago Press; paperbound) is superior to any prose version. And the T. E. Shaw prose *Odyssey* (Oxford University Press) is impressive for its economy, vividness, and pleasantly archaic flavor.

Other readily available translations—too often still recommended —may seriously reduce the reader's enjoyment of either narrative. These include standard, but dated, prose versions by E. G. Derby (Everyman's), Lang, Leaf, and Myers (Modern Library), and Butcher and Lang (Modern Library). Two couplet translations—of the *Iliad* by Pope (Heritage Press) and of the *Odyssey* by Cowper (Everyman's)—are faithful to Homer in neither style nor tone.

2

Aeschylus: ORESTEIA

Background of Greek Tragedy

In the 5th century B.C. the small city-state of Athens, at the height of its material and cultural prosperity, produced one of the two most impressive bodies of dramatic literature the world has ever seen (the other is Elizabethan drama). Yet surprisingly little is known (though much has been written) about the origin and evolution of drama before it flowered so magnificently in the tragedies of Aeschylus (c. 525 - 455 B.C.), Sophocles (c. 496 - 405 B.C.), and Euripides (480 - 406 B.C.).

The roots of drama stretch back in time beyond the evidence of archeological and literary research. The main root seems to have been the worship of a god in a ritual dance. This dance ritual, a form of primitive magic designed to increase fertility, developed partly from man's compelling need to worship powers beyond his control but obviously affecting his daily life; partly from the awe with which he viewed the cycle of death and resurrection; and partly from his instinctive urge to express his deepest feelings in physical movement, in mime, and in song. So long as a group of men representing the community danced in supplication to a god, they enacted merely a prayer in dance. Imitation or impersonation began when one dancer portrayed the god. The spoken word was added when the dancer god chanted. From this ritual, primitive drama was born. Neither the conjectures nor the counterconjectures of scholars have established how these things happened or the approximate dates to be assigned them; but tradition, a fragile substitute for history, credits the final synthesis to Thespis of Athens (c. 535 B.C.), "Father of the Drama."

The god whose celebration gave birth to drama was Dionysus. He was a popular god, for as bull or goat he incarnated the fecundity principle. Because of him, the vines yearly renewed themselves, the crops gave their yield, the cattle multiplied. In the spring and fall, at planting and harvest, men worshiped him in dances of supplication and thanksgiving. The celebration of Dionysus became so important that Pisistratus, a late-6th-century Athenian ruler who helped lay the foundations of his city's future greatness, established the Festival of Dionysus in 534 B.C. as an official state holiday. For these festivals, which lasted three or four days, the tragedies of Thespis (unhappily lost) were written.

By the 5th century tragedy had developed clearly recognizable characteristics. In keeping with its ritual origin, its prime function was religious and moral: its themes mirrored man's endless conflicts both with the nonhuman forces controlling his destiny and with himself—with the inner forces keeping him from happiness. The conflicts—external and internal—were embodied in stories already familiar to Greeks, in the myths and legends that constituted their cultural heritage; and from them the dramatists drew most of their plots. Similarly reflecting its origin in dance ritual, the form of early tragedy was choric and lyric rather than dramatic: theme overwhelmed character; narrative and interpretive elements overshadowed the limited action of the protagonists.

The circumstances of production were also affected by tradition. Staged at public expense as a function of state religion, plays were presented principally during the spring religious holidays that became known as the Great Dionysia. The *orchestra*, or dancing ground, was the central feature of the theater. On or adjoining the *orchestra* was the altar of Dionysus, where sacrifices were made before the plays began. Production was stylized: movements were slow and mannered; sets and costumes were simple and suggestive; the actors, using masks, elevated shoes, and padded costumes, appeared bigger than life. The audience attended the huge, open-air theaters (admission was free until late in the 5th century) not only to be entertained, but also to be edified, enlightened, perhaps even inspired.

Plays were written, selected for production, and staged in groups of four—three tragedies and one satyr-play (a short, grotesque, often obscene comedy). Frequently the satyr-play dealt with the phallic side of Dionysus, thus reminding the audience of the patron god of the festival. The tetralogies of three dramatists were chosen, each tetralogy to be presented in one day. A jury of citizens awarded prizes to the best playwright and to the star actor, as well as to the wealthy sponsor of the winning play. Sometimes, as in the *Oresteia*, the plots were drawn from a single legend and developed a unified theme; sometimes the three tragedies used separate subjects, with or without related motifs.

Structurally, Greek tragedies are rigidly conventional, again attesting their ritualistic origin. They contain two elements: the choral and the dramatic. Plays begin with a prologue *(prologos)* that sets forth the subject and situation of the drama, continue with alternating long choral odes *(stasima)* and acted scenes *(epeisodia)*, and conclude with a denouement *(exodus)*. Generally there are four acted scenes. Thus through long choral lyrics, a Greek tragedy often presents as much comment on and interpretation of action as it unfolds action itself. As drama evolved during the 5th century, the choric element diminished and the enacted scenes assumed new and greater importance.

While in form classical Greek tragedies adhere to structural conventions, evolving very slowly from Thespis to Euripides, in conception they often differ markedly. Yet a basic pattern emerges. Almost always centering on a person of heroic stature who is flawed by some human weakness, the plays portray his struggle to adjust to an inevitable but not wholly unmerited doom. Such a situation enabled the playwright to express dramatically his perception of the relationship of man to himself, to other men, or to the moral laws of the universe. Usually, but not always, the tragic hero, through his courage, strength, and intelligence, arouses the admiration and sympathy of the audience. But a flaw in character *(hamartia)* leads to a moral transgression *(hubris)* that begets retribution *(nemesis)*. Without the tragic flaw, the spectacle of unmerited suffering would be harrowing without being illumining.

The dramatic impact of a Greek tragedy usually results from the playwright's skillful employment of three devices: recognitions, reversals, and dramatic irony. All three rely to a degree on the audience's previous knowledge of the plot. In a recognition scene the protagonist learns an important truth about himself and his circumstances. This knowledge precipitates a reversal of situation, in which the action changes direction completely. Because the audience knows the truth before it is unfolded to the hero, dramatic irony is compact with plot structure: aware that things are the reverse of what they seem to be to the hero, the audience sits enthralled, awaiting the protagonist's awful recognition of the truth. Consequently the audience pities the hero and fears for his future before the hero himself recognizes his own tragic predicament.

Further dramatic compression and impact are achieved through sharp restriction of time, place, and action. By beginning the stage action just before the crisis and filling in background through flashback narratives, many Greek dramas achieve *unity of time;* that is, they span a period not much longer than performance time. By centering the action in one place (or in places near one another), they maintain *unity of place.* And by developing intensively only one simple sequence of events, without digressions, they preserve *unity of plot.* The concentration on a single, narrow line of action and the absence of subplots heighten the tragedy, make it taut and tense. Though rigid adherence to these unities often impeded convincing character development, it afforded concentration, speed, and inevitability to the tragic action.

Why does a Greek tragedy—so unremittingly painful—excite the esthetic response of audience and reader alike? Because we are moved by significant experiences—our own or another's—even when they are harrowing? Because we are deeply relieved that we are untouched while someone better than ourselves suffers? Because we admire a courageous struggle against overpowering odds? Because (to paraphrase Aristotle's famous definition in the *Poetics*) having been excited to pity and terror, we experience purgation (*catharsis*) of these emotions and feel purified, strengthened, perhaps exalted? Though the sufficient answer is shrouded in ambiguity, the dramatic effect is overwhelmingly clear: the great tragedies, it is true, rack and depress us; but they also restore, refresh, and recreate us.

I. Background of Aeschylus (*c.* 525 - 455 B.C.)

The flourishing of Greek tragedy during the 5th century B.C. coincides with the period of highest Athenian political and economic development. Early in the century the powerful Persian empire attempted to conquer the city-states of the Greek mainland. Bolstered mainly by the splendid Athenian fleet, the Greeks routed the Persians first at Thermopylae, then at Salamis, finally at Plataea. Because of her control of the seas, Athens after 480 B.C. headed a naval confederacy which became virtually an economic (but not a political) empire. Exacting tribute from neighboring city-states and deriving huge profits from her slave-worked silver mines, Athens prospered greatly. Athenian citizenship was limited to 40,000 free males of her 300,000 population. These freemen had much leisure, which they devoted to politics, to beautifying the city, and to practicing and promoting the arts of architecture, sculpture, oratory, and drama. By 470 B.C. Athens had become the intellectual as well as the commercial capital of Greece.

Yet not all was harmonious. Athenian merchants grew richer while Athenian workers, in competition with slave labor, became poorer. Free to think and to express their thoughts, some men challenged tradition, the old religion, even democratic procedures. Neighboring city-states, particularly military Sparta, resented Athenian economic dominance. By 431 B.C. cumulative antagonism led to the Peloponnesian War, which was partly a revolt against Athenian control of trade routes and partly an ideological struggle between democracy and oligarchy. Lasting until 404 B.C., this long war sapped Athens financially and started her economic, and eventually cultural, decline.

However, between 480 B.C. (the final defeat of the Persians) and the death of the great statesman Pericles (429 B.C.), Athens enjoyed almost continuous peace and prosperity. Their happy state, many Athenians believed, reflected the favor of the gods, the rightness of tradition, and the triumph of civilization over barbarism. In this intellectual climate, literature and the arts flourished—drama perhaps beyond the others. And the milieu nurtured the genius of Aeschylus, the first great Greek tragedian.

Aeschylus played an important part in the Persian defeat and lived during the period of Athenian ascendancy. Before his death in 455 B.C. he saw Athens develop into the center of Greek civilization. The moral conflicts stimulated by the struggles and crises of his age became the raw materials of his plays. Finding tragedy in a relatively primitive form, he advanced the art of drama by introducing a second actor, thus extending the scope of action; by reducing the size of the chorus, making it manageable in a dramatic episode; and by elaborating on staging and costuming techniques. Although he wrote more than seventy plays and won first prize at the Great Dionysia at least a dozen times, only seven of his plays survive.

Aeschylus' sole extant trilogy (indeed, the only surviving trilogy in Greek drama) is the *Oresteia*, which won first prize in 458 B.C. The *Oresteia* unfolds a succession of offenses against marriage culminating in a series of barbaric blood revenges—of brother against brother, wife against husband, son against mother. In this legend of three generations of retributive murders of kinsmen, Aeschylus dramatized the historical transition from primitive tribal institutions of justice to civilized communal justice. His purpose was to reveal god's ways to man by showing the relationship between Fate and the will of Zeus.

In his trilogy Aeschylus dramatized three pivotal events of the long, involved legend of the House of Atreus: the murder of Agamemnon in *Agamemnon*; the murders of Clytemnestra and Aegisthus in *The Libation Bearers*; and the trial and expiation of Orestes in

The Eumenides. In the many long choral lyrics, Aeschylus developed the legend, analyzing its meaning and exploring the motives of its characters.

The symbolic meaning of a myth that touched on so many aspects of the problem of evil obviously intrigued Aeschylus. In the 5th century B.C., Greek religion was undergoing a basic change—emerging from tribalism and moving toward universalism, shedding barbaric and reaching for humanistic ideals. The gods of Homer and Hesiod—often immoral beings, motivated by whim and caprice—were proving inadequate; they scarcely served as models for ethical human behavior. In the *Oresteia* Aeschylus re-examined the traditional gods and the old moral codes (especially that of the family vendetta). In the actions of his heroes and gods he projected his convictions about the relationship between divine law and human justice, the source and nature of evil and suffering, and the extent of man's responsibility for his behavior.

Though complex, the tragedies of the *Oresteia* constitute a unified and impressive whole. One theme, with its numerous corollaries, is explored to its conclusion. The theme is of more compelling interest than the protagonists, whose tragic flaws resemble one another's, epitomizing Aeschylus' views on the relationship between divine fate and individual guilt. In method, lyric elements overshadow enacted scenes, with the chorus playing a large narrative and interpretive role throughout. And through the reiteration of key metaphors (for example, the net and the web) Aeschylus achieved unity of imagery.

Several aspects of Aeschylus' dramatic technique may offer difficulties to a reader unfamiliar with the formal characteristics of Greek tragedy. The entire story of the House of Atreus is told in the trilogy, but neither chronologically nor in one place; it must be pieced together through flashback narratives contained in long choral odes. Although this story is replete with violent action, very little physical energy is expended on the stage; Aeschylus reveals the results of action rather than action itself. His highly compressed and metaphorical style, largely responsible for his greatness as a poet, is often difficult to follow. Moreover, the contemporary reader may react unsympathetically to the Old Testament severity of the Aeschylean moral code, which is not unlike that of the Book of Job.

But the reader can hardly overlook the epic scale of the action, the universality of the theme, or the skill of its development. Nor should he fail to perceive that Aeschylus, like the writers of the Old Testament, affirms a positive relationship between suffering and wisdom.

II. Questions for Study and Discussion

1. What is the over-all theme of the trilogy?
2. State the themes and subthemes of each play. Explain how all these themes are related in a unified trilogy.
3. What do the settings contribute to each play?
4. What must the audience know about the entire House of Atreus legend to comprehend the specific events portrayed in each tragedy? How, if at all, does Aeschylus present this knowledge? To what extent does he assume audience familiarity with the entire legend?
5. Who is the central character, the protagonist, of each play? Defend your choice. Characterize this person, explaining how, if at all, he or she changes during the course of action.
6. Describe the dilemma (the forced choice of one of two almost equally unpleasant alternative courses of action) confronting each protagonist. How does his choice reveal his tragic flaw? What relationship exists between the dilemma and the tragic flaw it helps reveal?
7. Identify the external and internal conflicts in each play. Which is central—in each play and throughout the trilogy? Which conflicts are explained to the audience? Which are developed dramatically in the action of the play? How do these conflicts unfold the tragic flaw of each hero?
8. Who constitute the chorus in each play? Why are these people

appropriate? What are the specific functions of the chorus in each *stasimon* (long choral passage)?

9. Identify the recognition and reversal scenes in each play. Explain the nature of the dramatic irony resulting from each such scene.
10. Identify the climax of each play.
11. Comment on Aeschylus' imagery. What repeated images, other than those of the web and net, contribute to the unity of the plays?
12. What is the prevailing tone or mood of each tragedy? Describe the shift in tone from play to play.
13. What is Aeschylus' attitude toward the old practice of retribution through the vendetta?
14. What significance attaches to Aeschylus' attribution of the murder to Clytemnestra? (*Note:* In most versions of the legend Aegisthus is the murderer of Agamemnon.)
15. What ethical and religious views are implicit in the plays?
16. What political and social views are implicit in the plays?
17. How does the concept of Zeus evolve through the three plays?
18. How do Aeschylus' gods and ethical views differ from Homer's?
19. Devise a definition of tragedy that will fit this trilogy.
20. What elements generally found in plays are missing in these tragedies? What does Aeschylus offer instead? How is he more or less dramatic as a result?
21. Which of the unities (time, place, action) does Aeschylus observe in each play? What seem to you to be the dramatic values and disadvantages of observing the unities?
22. What meaning does Aeschylus find in human suffering? What other conclusions about human wisdom does he reach? Where in literature have you encountered similar ideas?
23. Summarize Aeschylus' position on fate and human responsibility. How paradoxical is his position? How is this paradox related to his view of life?
24. What did Aeschylus wish his Athenian audience to learn from his plays? What of value does he have to say to you?
25. Describe your emotional responses to each tragedy. Which moved you most? Why did you react as you did? Why do such plays give pleasure?

III. Readings in Background and Criticism

Baldry, H. C., *Greek Literature for the Modern Reader* (Cambridge University Press, 1951). A handbook for the nonspecialist, presenting Greek literature against its historical background. Chapter 6, "Drama and Democracy," explains the civic function of drama in Athens and analyzes Aeschylus' plays.

Graves, Robert, *The Greek Myths*, 2 vols. (Penguin Classics, 1955). Pages 43-83 of Volume 2 summarize, analyze, and interpret the myths and legends on which Aeschylus based the *Oresteia*.

Hamilton, Edith, *The Greek Way* (New American Library, 1948). Chapter 12, "Aeschylus," credits Aeschylus with creating Attic tragedy and argues that his perceptive portrayal of both the beauty and mystery of suffering makes him the most tragic of the tragedians.

Harsh, P. W., *A Handbook of Classical Drama* (Stanford University Press, 1944). Unusually complete in supplying the facts and summarizing the scholarship that the intelligent reader of Greek tragedy should know.

Kitto, H. D. F., *Greek Tragedy* (Doubleday Anchor Books, 1955). Contains stimulating analyses of all the Greek tragedies. Chapter 3, "The *Oresteia*," explains how the themes of the plays determined dramatic form and style; and Chapter 4, "The Dramatic Art of Aeschylus," contrasts the Aeschylean tragic conception (based on man's violation of fundamental moral principles) with the Sophoclean (based on the imperfections of human nature).

Lattimore, Richmond, *Oresteia* (University of Chicago Press, 1953). In a masterful introduction to his new verse translation, Lattimore summarizes the Atreus legend, explains the themes of the trilogy, analyzes Aeschylus' poetic imagery and symbolism, and describes the structural form of the tragedies.

Macgowan, Kenneth, and Melnitz, William, *The Living Stage*. (Prentice-Hall, 1955). The first two chapters lucidly trace the origin and development of drama and the theater in ancient Greece.

Murray, Gilbert, *Aeschylus, Creator of Tragedy* (Oxford University Press, 1940). A detailed study of the dramatic development of the father of tragedy. This excellent scholarly work should not be read as an introduction.

Smyth, H. Weir, *Aeschylean Tragedy* (University of California Press, 1924). A thorough, informed, perceptive full-length study to be read after the student is familiar with all of Aeschylus' plays.

Thomson, G. D., *Aeschylus and Athens* (Lawrence and Wishart, 1941). A Marxian version of the social evolution of Athens through matriarchy, feudalism, tyranny, and democracy. Contains an illuminating explanation of the relationship of the *Oresteia* to the developing ideology of the Periclean Age.

Vellacott, Philip, *The Oresteian Trilogy* (Penguin Classics, 1956). In an informative essay prefacing his excellent translations, Vellacott recounts the House of Atreus story, explains the historical and intellectual background of the plays, and explores their meaning.

IV. Translations and Editions

Although many translations of individual plays of the *Oresteia* trilogy are available in anthologies, few volumes contain all three plays, and fewer still offer first-rate versions. Because the tragedies of Aeschylus are lyrical and narrative rather than dramatic, and because his style is compounded of tight, complex metaphors, he suffers in translation more than Sophocles and Euripides. Most of the older versions can be avoided without serious loss.

Two excellent new translations have recently been published in inexpensive editions. The most readable is by Philip Vellacott (Penguin). Using many of the Greek verse forms, Vellacott recaptures much of Aeschylus' lyric genius in clear and effective verse. The Richmond Lattimore versions, available paperbound as well as in hard cover (University of Chicago Press), are accurate but less graceful. A third translation, by George Thomson—competent but inferior to those of Vellacott and Lattimore—is published with three other Greek tragedies in *Six Greek Plays in Modern Translation* (Dryden Press).

3

Sophocles: THE THEBAN PLAYS

I. Background of Sophocles (*c.* 496 - 406 B.C.)*

Aeschylus justified the ways of the gods to man; Sophocles, in addition, justifies the ways of man to man himself. Based on the ultimate triumph of moral law—divine and unchangeable—the Aeschylean conception of tragedy demands punishment (generally death) as the wages of sin. Two-dimensional creations, Aeschylus' protagonists epitomize single sins (blasphemy, presumption, hate, envy). Sophocles, in contrast, envisions man's tragedy as largely self-caused, arising from his humanity, not descending from the gods: character determines fate—man is doomed because he is man, because the human condition involves doom, not because of the divine imperative. Complex in personality and motivation, his heroes, in failing to achieve lasting happiness, become paradigms of man's limitations.

In small measure, at least, this striking difference in world-view can be explained by chronology: Aeschylus died just before the middle of the 5th century B.C. and Sophocles at nearly its end. Maturing while Athens was achieving greatness, Aeschylus died before economic decline and intellectual skepticism had shattered

* For a general essay on Greek tragedy see pages 10-14.

Athenian security. Convinced that all was right in this world, Aeschylus systematically justified the divine order. But after his death, Athens slowly changed—economically, politically, culturally.

The history of Athens in the 5th century B.C. has been traced in the introduction to Aeschylus (see page 14). After the final defeat of the Persians in 480 B.C., Athens prospered, becoming the center of trade, the banker, and the naval protector of all Greece. But her economic pre-eminence involved Athens in responsibilities of empire, obligations she was neither politically nor militarily equipped to assume. City-states under Athenian protection resented their subservience. Athenian plutocrats, grown rich from trade, lamented democracy's failure to solve current problems and proposed oligarchy. The spirit of free thought and inquiry fostered by Athenian democracy stimulated a challenging of values and beliefs previously held sacred. The Sophist stimulus (see page 39), too, added to the intellectual ferment: hallowed standards were questioned, criticized, often assailed; in fact, many Sophists held that no standard, no value, ought to be considered true, save provisionally. Then the Peloponnesian War (431 - 404 B.C.) sapped Athens' financial and human resources. Demoralization and disorder set in: revolutions and counterrevolutions left Athens weak and confused.

Sophocles lived through the early decades of Athens' decline. He saw cynicism triumph over the old verities. Few among the articulate had a good word to say for democracy. Philosophers scarcely concealed their contempt for the old religion. And of course the Sophists were still at work transvaluing values. But Sophocles did not lose faith in the traditional. Prominent citizen, popular playwright, general, and priest, he defended the *status quo* and became a bulwark of conservatism. Like all great playwrights, he shaped his plays to express his convictions: the tragedies dramatize his deepest thoughts and feelings through the characters he imagined. In them he affirms that a moral order governs the universe, that man creates his own problems, but that finite man cannot always grasp infinite purpose. Over all his generations arches the inscrutable divine; and man must endure, act piously, walk humbly.

By all accounts the most revered tragedian in his own day,

Sophocles was born about 496 B.C., when Athens was emerging as the strongest city-state; he died in 406, just before Athens lost the war that exhausted her materially and wrecked her spiritually. His dramatic genius and his services to the government applauded by his contemporaries, he led a predominantly happy and rewarding life. Inspired and informed by the example of Aeschylus, Sophocles led tragedy in new directions and brought it to new heights. He wrote 123 or more plays and won first prize in at least 24 Dionysian contests—victories that perhaps indicated the general popularity of his moral and religious conservatism quite as much as the excellence of his dramas.

Only eight of his plays survive—three of them on the Oedipus myth. These Theban plays are not a trilogy like the *Oresteia.* While adapted from a single myth, they were neither conceived nor executed at the same time, nor do they fulfill a single purpose or develop a common theme. According to the sequence of the myth, their order should be *Oedipus the King, Oedipus at Colonus,* and *Antigone;* but Sophocles wrote *Antigone* first (c. 441 B.C.), *Oedipus the King* second (c. 430 B.C.), and *Oedipus at Colonus* shortly before his death (c. 406 B.C.). Obviously, since he turned to the same story on three widely separated occasions, Sophocles found the myth compelling; it revealed continually new significances, becoming the symbol of man lost, chartless, but persevering to find his path.

Sophocles constructs his tragedies around three climactic episodes of the myth: Oedipus' self-discovery of his identity and of his crimes in *Oedipus the King;* the last days and semi-deification of Oedipus in *Oedipus at Colonus;* and the conflict between Creon and Antigone in *Antigone.* Successively, he illuminated the myth's social and ethical implications about tyranny, divine moral law, oracles and prophets, kinship, sin and punishment, and individual responsibility.

Written when the shortcomings of democracy were already being debated, *Antigone* dramatized the conflict between the primitive religious ties of family and the newer claims of the city-state and its ruler. The issue broadens to encompass other fundamental and related conflicts. Though in following their psychological bents, both Antigone and Creon behave unreasonably, displaying that excessive pride that the Greeks called *hubris*, one's defeat is noble, the other's victory empty. But both central characters have choices: had they not chosen as they did, they might have come to different ends.

Even though Sophocles wrote *Oedipus the King* about twenty-five years before *Oedipus at Colonus*, the tragedies have a basic thematic unity. In the earlier play—often regarded as the greatest tragedy ever written—Oedipus resembles Creon of *Antigone*, but with a crucial difference: his error in judgment involves more than a human weakness. The prototype of human intelligence and achievement (notice the metaphors that characterize him: helmsman, liberator, doctor), Oedipus also symbolically represents human ignorance. Thus the play defines the limits both of man's intelligence and of divine justice. In demonstrating, through Oedipus, that man's place is somewhere below that of the gods, Sophocles answered the widely held Sophist position that "man is the measure of all things."

Oedipus at Colonus, the final statement of an old man revaluing his convictions, softens the hard doctrine of the earlier play without fundamentally altering it. The innocent sinner, through suffering, arrives at a blessed end. In the manner of Oedipus' death Sophocles creates a new myth: Oedipus, illumined by the gods and by suffering with the suprahuman vision of the oracle and of the prophet he had once despised, is now almost equated with the gods. Yet even thus transformed, he symbolizes both the limitations and the potentials of man and the power of the gods.

In these plays, as in others, Sophocles altered and refined the art of drama. Idealizing his protagonists, he nevertheless created believable men and women who speak a language realistic in its brevity, colloquialness, and freedom from involved metaphor. By introducing a third actor, he extended and complicated stage action, dramatized rather than narrated story, and, by showing the protagonist in a variety of situations, developed rounded, convincing characterization. He both decreased and expanded the role of the chorus. Although his choruses still utter brief lyric comment between episodes, only rarely do they narrate a story that can be enacted on the stage. But within episodes he handled the chorus originally, integrating it into the action so that it functioned as a character. He advanced the art of stagecraft by designing elaborate scenery and costumes, thus enhancing the spectacle appeal of a production. A painstaking craftsman, keenly alert to dramatic as well as human values, he adapted myths freely to fit his needs, constructing plots that are theatrically effective, symbolically compelling, and emotionally gripping.

Sophocles' life-view was colored by his perception of the fundamental irony of life, and his dramatic technique was shaped to express it. The awesome discrepancy between the way things seem and the way they are, between what the audience knows and what the characters perceive, is exploited by Sophocles to its extreme. Dramatic irony gives his tragedies their distinctive form and flavor. Irony permeates the imagery (particularly that of sight and blindness, of light and darkness), appears abundantly in the double meanings of lines, and structures the reversal scenes. Sophocles employed irony so masterfully that "irony of fate" and "tragic irony" have become almost synonymous with Sophoclean tragedy.

II. Questions for Study and Discussion

1. What is the central theme of each play? What are the secondary themes? How are the plays thematically unified?
2. What do the settings contribute to each play?
3. Locate the climax of each play.
4. Identify the external and internal conflicts developed in each play. Which is central? Which are merely explained to the audience and which are dramatically developed?
5. Which dramatic unities does Sophocles observe? What does each play gain by having unity of time, place, or action?
6. Who is the protagonist in each tragedy? Characterize this person, explaining how, if at all, he changes or develops during the play's action.
7. Describe the dilemma (forced choice of one of two equally unpleasant alternative courses of action) confronting each protagonist. How does his choice illumine his tragic flaw? What

relationship exists between the dilemma and the human limitation it exposes?

8. What must the audience know about the Oedipus myth to comprehend fully the events portrayed in each play? How, if at all, is such knowledge presented?
9. Who constitute the chorus in each play? Why are these people appropriate? What are the dramatic functions of the chorus?
10. Compare and contrast Sophocles' and Aeschylus' uses of the chorus.
11. Locate the recognition and reversal scenes in each tragedy. What is recognized or reversed in each? How is dramatic irony explicit in each reversal scene?
12. What are the major nondramatic ironies in each play?
13. Comment on Sophocles' imagery. Find metaphors that unify the plays. Compare and contrast Aeschylus' and Sophocles' use of imagery.
14. What is the prevailing tone or mood of each play? How, if at all, does the tone shift from play to play?
15. In *Oedipus the King,* why does Oedipus suffer? Is he justly punished? How is the punishment altered in *Oedipus at Colonus?*
16. On one level *Oedipus the King* is a detective story; on another, a deep psychological study; on a third, a penetrating life-view. Explain each.
17. Explain the role of the tension between illusion and reality in *Oedipus the King.* In *Antigone.*
18. What is Sophocles' attitude toward each central character? Toward the nature of his choice? Toward the human condition?
19. What ethical, political, and social views are implicit in each play? Are the plays mainly religious or political statements?
20. What Christian analogies do you discern in *Oedipus at Colonus?* Cite other ritualistic parallels.
21. Define Sophoclean tragedy. How do Sophoclean and Aeschylean tragedy differ?
22. What conclusions about human wisdom does Sophocles reach? Where have you encountered similar ideas?

23. Define Sophocles' position on man's responsibility for his own actions and destiny.
24. What of value does Sophocles say to you? Wherein lies his universal appeal?
25. Describe your emotional responses to each tragedy. Which moved you most? Why did you react as you did? Why do such tragedies give pleasure?

III. Readings in Background and Criticism

Bowra, C. M., *Sophoclean Tragedy* (Oxford University Press, 1944). An impressive scholarly study of the mind and art of Sophocles, with perceptive discussions of the Theban plays.

Fergusson, Francis, *The Idea of a Theater* (Doubleday Anchor Books, 1953). Chapter 1, "*Oedipus Rex*: The Tragic Rhythm of Action," a stimulating short essay on one of the Theban plays, finds the clue to its form in the tragic rhythm of "Purpose, Passion (Suffering), Perception."

Graves, Robert, *The Greek Myths*, 2 vols. (Penguin Classics, 1955). Pages 9-21 of Volume 2, which recount the versions of the Oedipus myth, are useful for a study of how Sophocles altered and adapted myth.

Green, W. C., *Moira: Fate, Good, and Evil in Greek Thought* (Harvard University Press, 1944). A chapter on Sophocles compares the relative importance of character and fate in his tragedies, and finds them in harmonious balance.

Hamilton, Edith, *The Greek Way* (New American Library, 1948). In a short but illuminating appreciation, a distinguished scholar explains Sophocles' world-view: though men are helpless to alter their fates, they can choose the good; suffering and death then have meaning and significance.

Harsh, P. W., *A Handbook of Classical Drama* (Stanford University Press, 1944). An extremely useful volume. A long chapter on Sophocles provides the facts about his life, dramatic technique, sources, and themes, and contains a helpful critical analysis of each play.

Jaeger, Werner, *Paideia*, Vol. 1. (Oxford University Press, 1945). A chapter on Sophocles places the dramatist against his times and argues that "dramatic action is for Sophocles the process by which the true nature of a suffering human being is unfolded, by which he fulfills his destiny and through it fulfills himself."

Kitto, H. D. F., *Greek Tragedy* (Doubleday Anchor Books, 1955). A notable study, containing several chapters of fresh insights into Sophocles' philosophy, tragic conception, and dramatic art. Each Theban play is analyzed at length.

Knox, Bernard, "Sophocles' Oedipus," *Tragic Themes in Western Literature*, edited by Cleanth Brooks (Yale University Press, 1955). In a persuasive, graceful essay on the meaning of the Oedipus plays, Knox views them as religious statements, Oedipus as a symbol of the inadequacy of man's intelligence.

Webster, T. B. L., *Introduction to Sophocles* (Oxford University Press, 1936). In this clear, lively approach to Sophocles, the author contends that the fundamental theme of the Theban plays is the survival of human nobility even in disaster.

Whitman, C. H., *Sophocles: A Study in Heroic Humanism* (Harvard University Press, 1951). A detailed, scholarly study, emphasizing Sophocles' idealistic humanism. Difficult, but extremely rewarding.

IV. Translations and Editions

Sophocles' three tragedies on the Oedipus theme have been frequently translated, but few collections of Greek drama include all three of them; most of the available translations, moreover, are deficient in clarity and disastrous to Sophocles' poetry. Happily, five new translations—two of them excellent, and three very good indeed—have recently appeared in inexpensive paperbound books. The best (and cheapest), by E. F. Watling (Penguin), combines dignity, clarity, grace, and accuracy. Of almost equal merit are the versions by Dudley Fitts and Robert Fitzgerald, first published in 1939 and reissued in 1949 (Harvest Books). (Both the Watling and Fitts-Fitzgerald adaptations have been staged with notable success.) A third impressive one-volume collection, with translations of *Oedipus the King* by David Grene, of *Oedipus at Colonus* by Robert Fitzgerald, and of *Antigone* by Elizabeth Wyckoff, was published in 1954 (University of Chicago Press). The most recent translations are by Theodore H. Banks (Oxford University Press) and by Paul Roche (New American Library). The reader is advised to select from these five.

4

Euripides:

ALCESTIS
MEDEA
HIPPOLYTUS

I. Background of Euripides (*c.* 480 - 407 B.C.)*

Euripides was to late-5th-century Athens what Ibsen was to late-19th-century Europe. Rebel, individualist, satirist, defier of convention and champion of the dispossessed, he was hated and feared by all who opposed change and revered the *status quo*, respected and admired by the intellectual and social radicals (that is, the Sophists and the rising middle class). Author of about ninety plays, he competed in at least twenty-two Dionysian competitions, gaining first prize only five times (once posthumously). Yet shortly after his death, his modern temper and theatrical explosiveness combined to make him more popular in revival than either Aeschylus or Sophocles. Because Euripides' plays appealed so strongly to succeeding generations, eighteen have survived—more than all of Aeschylus and Sophocles combined.

Though contemporaries, Euripides and Sophocles do not seem to be addressing a common audience. Reading Sophocles, one

* For a general essay on Greek tragedy see pages 10-14.

scarcely suspects that his tragedies were composed when the Athenian economic empire was toppling, when the tenets of the traditional religion were being seriously challenged, when criticism of the Athenian brand of democracy was intense, when the spirit of free thought fostered by the Sophists (see page 39) was producing widespread skepticism, and when the Peloponnesian war was sapping Athens' finances and decimating her manpower. Sophocles' confident orthodoxy in the face of prevailing doubt contrasts sharply with Euripides' critical questioning.

Thus the plays of Euripides mirror their times more clearly than do those of Sophocles. Translating into his medium the Sophist attitude of determined skepticism and free inquiry, Euripides dramatized the questions that troubled his age, but provided no firm answers. Like the Sophists, too, he tried to sweep away the superstitious fears and the conventional taboos that blocked the light. He wanted man to develop all his powers, an endeavor that required free and untrammeled intelligence.

Born about forty-five years after Aeschylus and fifteen after Sophocles, Euripides was subject more intensely than they to the prevailing spirit of doubt; unlike them, he did not resist. He approached the problems with which his tragedies deal as a humanitarian and even more as a rationalist, respecting no idea simply because it was old. The Athenian concept of the gods, the notion of male superiority, the institution of slavery, the distinctions of birth, the status of women, the idealization of war—he scrutinized all with unobstructed vision, as a sociologist and as a psychologist who had as well the gift of dramatic genius.

The extent of the Euripidean dramatic revolution can hardly be overstressed. Into the theater of Athens—the city's greatest religious manifestation—he introduced agnosticism. He took the ancient and venerated myths and refashioned them so that they became vehicles for his new and destructive religious criticism. Yet he did not function as a propagandist: assailed by doubt, he could find no comfortable certainties to offer. He had broken with the past, but he saw no bright future. He rejoiced over the good in the life of man, admired his heroic struggle to rise above his circumstances, but most he lamented the evil which he discovered everywhere.

However, Euripides never wavered in his sympathy for human beings suffering in an unreasonable world. Intelligent, sensitive, imaginative, he profoundly understood human psychology. Although Aristotle in the *Poetics* labeled Euripides "the most tragic of the poets," he seems instead the most provocative of pathos and compassion. In the world of his dramas the innocent suffer with the guilty, the cowards prosper with the courageous. His faith in the worth of every mortal, man or woman, aristocrat or slave, is unique in Greek tragedy. Though they bear the names of men and women from myth and legend, his protagonists are of human rather than heroic dimensions. Sophocles recorded his awareness of Euripides' realism when he reportedly said, "I portray men as they ought to be portrayed, but Euripides portrays them as they are."

The few known facts about Euripides profile a man detached and aloof from life, an observer rather than a participant. He rarely accepted a civic assignment, and he studied and wrote in seclusion. Like Socrates, he was publicly disgraced as a corrupter for questioning convention and advocating nonconformity. Unlike Socrates (but like the later Aristotle), he fled Athens, and he spent his last years in the court of Archelaus, King of Macedon. But immediately after news of his death reached Athens, his star began to ascend; even Sophocles allegedly joined in the public mourning.

Over the years, Euripides has been called many things: atheist and religious reformer, rationalist and romantic, realist and formalist, poet and rhetorician, feminist and misogynist. In his inconsistency, Euripides was at times all of these. As represented in *Alcestis, Medea,* and *Hippolytus,* he seems agnostic, pessimistic, and humanitarian. Occasionally taking the gods seriously, he more generally mocked them. Convinced of the injustice of natural law, he portrayed man as morally superior to the universe. Aware that men are often impelled by instinct and emotion rather than by reason, he nevertheless pitied them. Developing character realistically, he handled plot formally and even artificially. Though at times he wrote dialogue that is prosy or rhetorical, he frequently composed beautiful choral lyrics, especially on the subject of nature's loveliness.

Structurally, Euripides' plays are often disconcerting. More preoccupied with his protagonist's motivations than with situation, Euripides constructed plots episodically, supplying prologues to present the exposition quickly and epilogues to tie together hastily the loose ends. His plays abound with coincidences, and he employed the *deus ex machina* (god from the machine) to achieve a facile denouement. His choruses often lack integration, serving instead as interlude entertainments. Euripides tended to manipulate secondary characters like puppets. And his fondness for rhetorical debate (a predilection probably acquired from the dialectical methods of the Sophists) often resulted in forensic eloquence rather than dramatic movement.

But Euripides' apparent indifference to structure was counterbalanced by his undeniable dramatic and poetic genius. He motivated his chief characters purposefully and perceptively. His coincidences and violent reversals of fortune can be interpreted as symbolic of his themes as well as indicative of his impatience with technical matters. Though obsessed with morbid or taboo subjects, Euripides pitied his abnormal heroes and heroines and adopted a radically new position concerning their responsibility. Adapting myths and legends to contemporary events, he reduced heroic figures to the level of the everyday world and developed through them sermons for his times. Though characteristically he failed to integrate the chorus into the dramatic action with the skill of Aeschylus and Sophocles, he put it to new and equally effective uses, making it a lyric adjunct, a source of beauty in itself.

The three recommended plays illustrate the variety and scope, the strengths and limitations of Euripides' art. *Alcestis*, produced in 438 B.C. as a substitute for the satyr-play in a tetralogy, is neither comedy nor tragedy. The subject of Alcestis (a favorite in ancient art though not in the drama) is the story of a woman willing to die so that her husband might live. Euripides' interest lies in the effect of Alcestis' sacrifice on her husband, not in her character (her decision to sacrifice herself precedes the action of the play). In taking a fundamentally tragic story and resolving it happily, Euripides apparently created tragicomedy.

With *Medea*, his best known play today, Euripides won only third prize in 431 B.C. This revenge tale about a woman motivated by successive unbridled passions was well-known, but Euripides was probably the first to add the deliberate murder of her children to the traditional details of the myth. While fascinated by the lurid aspects of Medea's retribution, the dramatist concentrates chiefly on her internal conflict. Euripides often wrote plays to develop a social thesis, but despite the space given to Medea's and the chorus' feminist pleadings, he did not portray Medea solely as a symbol of the persecuted sex. Neither idealizing nor admiring her, he approached Medea as a subject for analysis and pity. His handling of the chorus is unusual: he lets it start as a detached observer, but draws it into the excitement of the action until the chorus functions almost like another character.

Like *Medea, Hippolytus* demonstrates the overwhelming power of natural instincts and the ironic consequences of opposing them. For the group of plays including *Hippolytus*, produced in 428 B.C., Euripides was awarded first prize. Again breaking away from the classic tragic pattern, Euripides centered attention on typical, though exaggerated, human weaknesses; and, as in the previous plays, he was intrigued by the woman's side of a case, taking a typically unconventional view of Phaedra's moral problem.

Together, Aschylus, Sophocles, and Euripides reflect the drift of 5th-century thought from orthodoxy to radicalism, from sublime confidence to disillusionment; the evolution of the drama from an adjunct of religious ritual to a secular art. Aeschylus was as orthodox in theme as he was traditional in form. Sophocles, though he initiated significant changes in form that served to divorce drama from ritual, upheld conventional moral and religious views. Euripides, superficially almost reactionary in adherence to ritual structure, even when this obviously inconvenienced him, completely secularized the substance of tragedy. As a group, these dramatic giants help us recreate the Golden Age of Athens—the Age they themselves helped make golden.

II. Questions for Study and Discussion

1. What is the theme of each play?
2. What do the settings contribute to each play?

3. Explain how, if at all, the protagonist changes or develops during the course of the play's action.
4. How does the dilemma of each protagonist reveal his typical human weakness or tragic flaw? What is the relationship between the dilemma and the tragic flaw? How does Euripides' use of the tragic flaw differ from Sophocles'?
5. What are the major external and internal conflicts in each play? Which is central?
6. Who constitutes the chorus in each play? Why are these people appropriate? What dramatic functions does the chorus fulfill?
7. Identify the recognition and reversal scenes in each play. Explain the specific nature of the dramatic irony resulting from each such scene. Explain how Euripides' use of coincidences and violent reversals symbolizes his themes.
8. Discuss Euripides' use of imagery.
9. What is the prevailing tone or mood of each play? How is mood related to theme?
10. Describe Euripides' attitude toward each central character, toward the nature of this person's problem, toward the human condition in general.
11. What social, political, and religious views are implicit or explicit in each play?
12. Characterize Euripidean tragedy. How does Euripides' tragic concept differ from that of Aeschylus? That of Sophocles?
13. What conclusions about human wisdom does Euripides reach? To what extent does he hold man responsible for his destiny?
14. Discuss the judgment that Euripides created psychological tragedy.
15. In what respects is *Alcestis* a tragedy? In what respects a comedy?
16. Who are the brave, who are the cowards in *Alcestis?* Discuss Euripides' attitude toward courage and cowardice.
17. Is the central character in *Alcestis* Admetus or Alcestis? Defend your choice.
18. How does the Greek ideal of hospitality figure in *Alcestis?*
19. What comment on the general nature of man and on the human condition is Euripides making in this play?

20. What social views does Euripides attack in *Medea?*
21. Is the central conflict in *Medea* internal or external? Defend your interpretation.
22. What is the function of Aegeus? Of the *deus ex machina?*
23. Why does Euripides make so much of the primitive-sorceress aspect of Medea?
24. How does the theme of immortality through children lend unity to *Medea?*
25. In *Hippolytus,* why does Euripides shift his focus from Phaedra to Hippolytus midway through the play?
26. Identify the typical, though exaggerated, human weaknesses of Phaedra, Hippolytus, Theseus.
27. How do you explain Euripides' preoccupation with the problems of women in these plays? To what extent is he sympathetic to women and their problems, to what extent critical and unflattering?
28. What of value does Euripides say to you? Wherein lies his universality?

III. Readings in Background and Criticism

Decharme, P., *Euripides and the Spirit of His Dramas* (Macmillan, 1906). A lively survey for the general reader. The first half of the study, summarizing Euripides' views on contemporary social, political, and moral issues, is especially useful.

Dodds, E. R., "Euripides the Irrationalist," *Classical Review* Vol. 43 (1929, 97-104). A spirited attack on scholars (Verrall, Murray) who have overpraised Euripides as doctrinaire. Dodds finds him a romantic emotionalist rather than a critical rationalist.

Graves, Robert, *The Greek Myths,* 2 vols. (Penguin Classics, 1955). Ably retells the stories of Alcestis, Hippolytus, and Medea, embodying the conclusions of modern anthropology and archeology. Useful as background for a study of how Euripides humanized and secularized myth.

Greene, W. C., *Moira: Fate, Good, and Evil in Greek Thought* (Harvard University Press, 1948). A balanced chapter on Euripides concludes that his thought is so varied and inconsistent that he took no clear position on the role of fate in human life: "Euripides is baffling because he himself is baffled."

Grube, M. A., *The Drama of Euripides* (Metheun, 1941). Contains an illuminating chapter on Euripides' art as well as detailed, fresh analyses of each of his plays.

Hamilton, Edith, *The Greek Way* (New American Library, 1948). In a short, appreciative essay Miss Hamilton finds Euripides the most modern Greek tragedian because of his fearless questioning of tradition and his compassionate understanding of suffering.

Harsh, P. W., *A Handbook of Classical Drama* (Stanford University Press, 1944). Chapter 3, "Euripides," details thoroughly the facts about each play (legend, sources, theme, influence) and analyzes critically the dramatic technique of each.

Jaeger, Werner, *Paideia*, Vol. 1 (Oxford University Press, 1945). Explains clearly and convincingly how Euripides used ancient myths to interpret contemporary problems: war and peace, convention and reason, the rights of individuals, the status of women.

Kitto, H. D. F., *Greek Tragedy* (Doubleday Anchor Books, 1955). In several chapters—on Euripides' concept of tragedy, dramatic technique, and tragicomedies—Kitto supplies many fresh insights, frequently makes provocative analyses. He argues that Euripidean tragedy results from the exposure of ordinary people to situations far beyond their human capacity to handle.

Murray, Gilbert, *Euripides and His Age* (Henry Holt, 1913). An important short introduction to the times and art of Euripides. Always stimulating, often controversial, tending to overstress the consciously doctrinaire aspect of the dramatist's genius.

IV. Translations and Editions

Because the eighteen surviving plays of Euripides include neither a trilogy nor a group of tragedies using a single myth or legend, he must be approached through individual plays. All of his dramas have been translated; every anthology of Greek or world drama contains one or more. Fortunately, a paperbound edition of four of Euripides' most highly regarded plays—each in a superior new version by a different translator—has recently been published (University of Chicago Press): it contains *Alcestis*, translated by Richmond Lattimore; *Medea*, translated by Rex Warner; *Heracleidae*, translated by Ralph Gladstone; and *Hippolytus*, translated by David Grene. Philip Vellacott has prepared (for Penguin) two volumes of excellent new translations: one includes *Alcestis* and *Hippolytus*, but neither contains *Medea*. *Medea* and *Hippolytus*, translated by Rex Warner, are available in *Three Great Plays of Euripides* (New American Library). A powerful free adaptation of *Medea* has been written by Robinson Jeffers, but many scholars frown on it as un-Euripidean and even un-Greek. All Euripides' plays are included in a two-volume collection, *The Complete Greek Drama* (Random House).

5

Plato:
REPUBLIC

I. Background of Plato (*c.* 428 - 347 B.C.)

As an intellectual discipline, philosophy was born in early 6th century (B.C.) Greece, when a few men, skeptical of the hallowed mythological explanations concerning the nature of man, especially his origin and destiny, sought to arrive at truth through the free play of reason. Asking the basic question, "What, in an ever-changing world of physical phenomena, is permanent?" many early thinkers advanced answers grounded on natural science. By the 5th century philosophy had taken the two main directions it has followed ever since. One trend, exemplified by Leucippus of Miletus (early 5th century B.C.) and Democritus of Abdera (c. 460 - c. 370 B.C.), was materialist. Rejecting religious and mythological explanations of the origin and purpose of the universe, the materialists developed scientific rationales based on sense perception and logical deduction. Early materialists, concerned with the physical universe rather than with man and his institutions, attempted to locate the ultimate substance of reality in a single element—water, air, earth, fire, or even the atom. A second trend, illustrated by Pythagoras (c. 582 - c. 507 B.C.), was idealist. Mistrusting the evidence of the senses, idealists sought absolute, nonmaterial truths—fundamental abstract principles that transcended sense experience. Like their antagonists in philosophy, they were more interested in metaphysics than in psychology and ethics.

The shift in philosophy from preoccupation with natural science (the cosmological period of philosophy) to concentration on man and the state (the anthropological period) was made jointly by the Sophists and by Socrates. The Sophists (who flourished in Athens after 450 B.C.), analyzing human experience rationally, insisted on the tentative quality of "right" and "wrong," argued the relativity of "knowing" and "not knowing," and urged that philosophy be harnessed to practical living. Protagoras, perhaps the greatest name among the Sophists, implied their whole ethos in his famous apothegm, "Man is the measure of all things." Prodicus proposed that practical consequences were the basic test of conduct: if successful, an action was "right"; if not, then it was "wrong." Subsidiary articles of belief, held by many though not by all Sophists, included the notions that laws are made by the strong and must be obeyed by those too weak to disobey; that when made by the many, laws restrain the powerful few, but when made by the few, laws enslave the many; and that happiness results not from obedience to laws but from shrewdly calculated self-interest.

The idealist position of Pythagoras was further developed by Socrates, a great 5th-century Athenian philosopher who was the teacher of Plato. Like the Sophists, Socrates was interested in ethics (the study of the moral life of man) rather than in metaphysics. Unlike the Sophists, he sought to separate the essence of things from their transient manifestations, holding that right, rather than subsisting as a function of time, place, and social conditions, has an absolute and eternal warrant. In large part Plato's philosophy is the product both of his revolt against Sophist moral flux and of his extension of the Pythagorean (later the Socratic) notion that whereas the phenomenal world is illusory, truth remains one and the same always.

But Plato's thought, especially as propounded in the *Republic*, was also shaped by Greek social and political conditions. As a result of the Peloponnesian War (431 - 404 B.C.) with authoritarian Sparta (see page 14), Athenian democracy suffered disastrous change. Internally, economic and class gaps between rich and poor widened; the ideal of citizenship, of loyalty to the city, was corrupted by rapacious individualists; the specialist and the professional superseded the Periclean man of wide attainment. Externally, powerful autocrats wrested control in many neighboring city-states and labored to undermine the economic dominance of Athens. From within and from without, the democratic forms and traditions of Athens were under attack. Influenced by the successful examples of autocratic Sparta and Persia, some late-fifth- and early-fourth-century critics of democracy projected utopian schemes for social reform, schemes that hinged on developing authoritarian rulers, albeit enlightened ones. Most important of the antidemocratic manifestoes, Plato's *Republic* expounded the objectives of just government and the modes of realizing them.

The dialogue form of the *Republic*, like its thought, was a reflex of Plato's age. With labor performed mainly by the large slave population of Athens, free citizens had plentiful leisure. When not performing civic duties, men gathered—in gymnasiums, in the market place, in private homes—to discuss affairs, personal and general. This habit of conversation, as well as the spirit of inquiry it stimulated, was nurtured by the Sophists, the professional teachers of the day, who encouraged the arts of discussion, of question and answer, of disputation. But while the Sophists, consistent with their contention that truth is relative, developed these arts for the practical purpose of winning a case or downing an adversary, Socrates, convinced of the existence of absolute truth, used dialectic as an instrument to discover it. The dialogue—a literary convention used by other Greek writers as well as by Plato—attempts to record an idealized Socratic conversation. Because he was seeking a wide audience in the hope of influencing political action, Plato chose a form with which most educated Athenians were familiar.

The dialogue was shaped as well by the drama, particularly by the species called the "mime." In his *Poetics* Aristotle classified the Socratic conversation as a form of prose drama, a quasi-dramatic conversation marked by some attempt to characterize the speakers. After his death Socrates was made the central character in many dialogues written by Plato and others, though often he acted mainly as a convenient spokesman for the author. Because Socrates wrote nothing but was much written about, scholars ever since his time have tried to distinguish what he believed from what the writers who employed him as their surrogate believed (the "Socratic problem"). It is widely agreed, however, that in the *Republic* most of the ideas are Plato's.

Plato was Socrates' outstanding disciple. Born about 428 B.C. into a wealthy, aristocratic Athenian family in a time of social and political ferment, Plato received the best education available. His youthful experiences in politics—witnessing the excesses of the oligarchical rule of the Thirty Tyrants in Athens and the trial and conviction in 399 B.C. of his mentor Socrates—disillusioned him with both oligarchy and democracy as practiced in Athens and caused him to remain aloof from practical political activity. After Socrates' death, Plato visited Megara, possibly Egypt, and definitely Italy, where he came under the influence of Pythagoreanism. Returning to Athens about 386 B.C., he soon founded "the world's first university," the Academy, in which he taught until his death in 347 B.C. Because of the close relationship of life and politics in Athenian democracy, Plato made political science the central study of the Academy. He abandoned political theory for practical politics only once—in an extended but unfruitful effort to guide Dionysius II of Syracuse in reforming the government of that city.

From time to time Plato wrote the philosophic dialogues on which his fame and influence rest. The dialogues not only fall short of presenting a systematic philosophy, but at times argue for principles inconsistent with one another. They may be divided into three groups. Those in the first, generally short—for example, *Apology* and *Crito*—highlight the personality and ideas of Socrates and depict him overthrowing the opinions of others rather than advancing views of his own. Vividly they create the Athenian "gadfly," master inquisitor, and unsurpassed ironist, yet urbane and modest quester for truth—the figure that has fascinated generations since. In the second group, still speaking through the character Socrates but apparently advancing his own concepts, Plato attempted to establish positive doctrines, often embodying them in myths. These dialogues, generally long—for example, *Phaedo*, *Symposium*, and *Republic*—develop the core of Plato's transcendentalism. The dialogues of the third group are also long—for example, *Laws*—and often feature someone other than Socrates.

What did Plato, as distinct from Socrates, believe? A skeletal statement deprives his metaphysic of its subtleties and shadings, of its poetry and harmony—more, of its living essence. But these principles are fundamental: that the soul of man is immortal; that man is born with all knowledge, and "learning" is simply recalling (the doctrine of *anamnesis*); and, most important, that every material object, even man himself, is an imperfect copy of a perfect archetype (the Doctrine of Ideas). From Socrates Plato derived both his faith in the significance of the individual soul and his absorption with abstract moral qualities—justice, wisdom, temperance, love. From Pythagoreanism he acquired his belief in the soul as a fallen spirit, temporarily imprisoned in the body but destined to return to a higher state.

Informing and animating these views with his own insights, Plato synthesized a new idealism. In it ideas or forms become the ideals toward which men can aspire, and such abstract ideas—not the world of sensation and action—constitute the true reality. It is the Platonic paradox that the only reality is unreal. The aim of philosophy, Plato held, is to recollect the ideal truths possessed by the soul before its embodiment in the flesh; to disengage the universals from their incomplete, accidental representation in the world of sense phenomena; to peel off error and reach the core of truth. To Plato the aim of philosophy coincides with the goal of education—to learn what is really wise and good. For Plato, compelled by the logic of his assumptions, believed that misconduct and evil results from ignorance rather than from willful choice—that once man learns what is the wise and good course of action he will follow it undeviatingly.

On this metaphysic Plato founded the political theory of his masterpiece, the *Republic*. Convinced that Athens had fallen from greatness because she had deserted rational ideals, he prescribed his cure for her restoration by answering four questions: Who should rule? How should rulers be trained? What would an ideal society be like? And how would a just society promote individual virtue?

Though the *Republic* describes Plato's utopian state, it ranges over his entire philosophy. Indeed, on casual reading, much of the book seems to be a digression. Hence the development of his thought is often elusive. In Book I he begins by discussing and rejecting various popular definitions of justice. From Books II through VII he tries to discover the nature of justice by setting up an ideal republic. In the process he explains the theoretic bases of his metaphysic, outlines his theory of education (advancing a number of daring proposals), and describes the operation of his government. Books VIII and IX characterize states and rulers who fall short of the ideal, and set forth his cyclical theory of government. By explaining how various existing systems are unjust, Plato arrives at a final definition of justice in the state and in the individual. A kind of appendix, Book X contains Plato's views on censorship and reincarnation and closes with a vision (through a myth) of the rewards and punishments of the soul after death.

Although the *Republic* develops Plato's thought more fully and more tightly than any other dialogue, it is seldom read in its entirety. Some passages are better known and more widely studied than others. These include the analysis of the cardinal virtues—wisdom, courage, temperance, justice—in Book IV; the figurative explanations of the Theory of Ideas in Books VI (the simile of the divided line) and VII (the allegory of the cave); the sharply etched portraits of corrupt rulers and states that fill Book VIII; and the glowing mythic vision of the soul's destiny that closes Book X.

Platonic idealism, at once profound and poetic, has had an incalculable effect on subsequent thought. On the one hand, perhaps to Plato's discredit, the repudiation of experience implied in his theory of ideas helped retard the development of natural science begun by the early Greeks. Not until modern times did the empiric method of arriving at truth replace revelation or intuition. Again, his justification of absolutism has been said to provide a basis for modern totalitarianism. On the other hand, Plato's apparent devotion to the common good of humanity has helped shape modern democratic political theory. Perhaps most important, his emphasis on the primacy of the nonmaterial elements in civilization—his contention that society has a duty beyond providing animal comforts, beyond creating a "city of happy pigs"—has done much to encourage man to envision and seek the good life.

But our attention to Plato's often difficult, sometimes absurd, though always stimulating ideas should not blind us to his achievement as a stylist. An incomparable dialoguist, he writes with conversational ease. He bites, shimmers, soars—fusing sharp irony with poetic phrasing and mythopoeic power. Urbane in his approach to philosophy, he develops controversy dramatically. His greatness derives not only from the cogency of his thought, but, perhaps as much, from the eloquence of his language.

II. Questions for Study and Discussion

1. What is the theme of the *Republic?*
2. What basic assumptions (beliefs that he makes no attempt to prove) underlie Plato's thought in this dialogue?
3. Compare the form of the *Republic* with that of Greek tragedies.
4. Describe the Socratic method of seeking truth.
5. What definitions of justice are advanced in Book I? How does Socrates criticize each? How valid is his reasoning?
6. Why does Plato believe it easier to arrive at a notion of justice in the city-state than in individual man?
7. How does Plato explain the origin of the state? What kind of state has he in mind? What assumption about human nature underlies this theory?
8. Describe the structure of Plato's ideal state and the functions of each class in it. How is this related to the structure and function of the human soul?
9. Why does Plato believe wars necessary? Would our technological advance have made him alter this contention?
10. Describe the good ruler. How should he be trained?

11. Why does Plato urge censorship? What would he censor? What conception of God emerges out of the discussion?
12. Outline Plato's theories of education.
13. How does Plato answer the criticism that the ruler's lot in his state would be unhappy? What assumption about the nature of happiness does Plato make here?
14. Explain how, and why, Plato uses myths to reinforce his arguments. Discuss the morality of the "edifying lie."
15. Describe the role of women in Plato's state.
16. Explain, and comment on, his eugenic theories.
17. What are the cardinal virtues in the state? In the individual? How are these related to class structure? How sound is the analogy?
18. Explain in detail Plato's final definition of justice.
19. What, to Plato, is ultimate reality? What status and responsibility does the allegory of the cave give the philosopher? How does his theory of ideas explain Plato's ordering of the state?
20. Explain the cyclical theory of government advanced in Book VIII.
21. According to Plato, can the ideal state exist? If not, why has he taken such pains to describe it?
22. How does Plato relate art to ultimate reality? Describe the poet's place in the *Republic*. Is Plato's view confirmed by his own practice?
23. Explain the view of the soul with which Plato concludes the *Republic*.
24. What seems to be Plato's political and social biases?
25. What does Plato imply about individualism, free will, individual responsibility, the perfectibility of man?
26. Describe the "true philosopher." Who can become such a person?
27. Socrates is Plato's hero. Compare him with Odysseus, Achilles, Orestes, Oedipus. How had the concept of heroism developed or changed?
28. How can you refute Plato's conclusions about the weaknesses of democracy? What virtues of democracy, as we understand it, has Plato slighted or overlooked?

29. In what ways, and to what extent, do Plato's views foreshadow dictatorship, fascism, communism?

III. Readings in Background and Criticism

Buchanan, Scott, *The Portable Plato* (Viking Press, 1948). The "Introduction" provides an illuminating short discussion of Plato's debt to previous philosophers, to the 5th-century tragedians, and to the social and political conditions of his time.

Burnet, John, *Greek Philosophy* (Macmillan, 1914), *Part I: Thales to Plato*. A readable scholarly history of the evolution of man's thought up to and including Plato.

Cornford, Francis M., "Introduction," *The Republic of Plato* (Oxford University Press, 1942). A lucid, informed examination and evaluation by a distinguished scholar and translator of Plato.

Durant, Will, *The Story of Philosophy* (Simon & Schuster, 1926). A popular, generally sound survey. Chapter 1, "Plato," outlines the main concepts of Plato's idealist thought, with special attention to his Theory of Ideas.

Fite, Warner, *The Platonic Legend* (Scribner, 1934). Contains a provocative, though often controversial, analysis of the unfortunate aspects of the Platonic heritage, particularly of the distortions of Platonism embodied in Neo-Platonism.

Jaeger, Werner, *Paideia*, Vol. 2 (Oxford University Press, 1942). The second half of this volume contains an excellent analysis of the main ideas of the *Republic*.

Nettleship, R. L., *Lectures on the Republic of Plato* (Macmillan, 1936). A thorough study of organization, style, and thought in the *Republic*. Each major concept receives a separate chapter, which can be understood without reference to the others.

Shorey, Paul, *What Plato Said* (University of Chicago Press, 1933). A chapter on the *Republic* summarizes the dialogue, interjecting explanations of the more difficult doctrines.

Taylor, A. E., *Plato, the Man and His Work* (Dial, 1926). A gracefully written introduction to Plato. One chapter contains an unusually helpful analysis of the *Republic*.

Wild, John, "Plato," *Collier's Encyclopedia*, Vol. 16. A short, useful digest of the major ideas encompassed by the term Platonism.

Winspear, A. D., *The Genesis of Plato's Thought* (S. A. Russell, 1940). Traces the social evolution of Greece from Homer to Plato in order to illuminate the social and political concepts of the *Republic.* A stimulating companion to Plato's masterpiece.

IV. Translations and Editions

Many translators of the Platonic dialogues have accurately enough reproduced the thought; none has yet transferred into English the varied poetic qualities of the Greek original. The best translation of the *Republic* —now available in a paperbound edition—is by F. M. Cornford (Oxford University Press); it contains an excellent introduction and full notes. Perhaps the most eloquent, and certainly the most widely read, version is by Benjamin Jowett, available in many reprint series and other inexpensive editions (for example, Modern Library, Living Library, Viking Portable); however, Jowett sometimes deliberately mistranslated—for example, "true love" instead of "boy love" for *paedophilia*—to avoid offending. Paul Shorey's line-by-line version printed side-by-side with the Greek, is in a two-volume (Loeb Classical Library) edition. A "basic English" version by I. A. Richards (Norton), using a highly restricted vocabulary, is thoroughly readable. Finally, a spirited new translation has been made by W. H. D. Rouse for *Great Dialogues of Plato* (New American Library).

6

Aristotle:

NICOMACHEAN ETHICS

I. Background of Aristotle (384 - 322 B.C.)

Aristotle was one of the most prodigious and influential thinkers of all time. The body of his work which has survived is but a fragment of his breathtaking effort to systematize, extend, and interpret in the light of a unified world view the whole range of science and philosophy available to the Greeks of the 4th century B.C. Each of Aristotle's extant treatises—including essays on meteorology, metaphysics, logic, biology, rhetoric, psychology, ethics, politics, and poetry—has an important place in the history of ideas. But no single work, except perhaps the *Poetics*, has proved as enduringly attractive and fertile as his *Nicomachean Ethics*, a study in the modes, methods, and values of human conduct.

In Aristotle's day, moral philosophy was a relatively new field of formal inquiry—not more than a century old. The Greek philosophers of the 6th century B.C. (see page 38), convinced that human life is determined by uncontrollable external forces, attached little intrinsic importance to human action; therefore, they produced no significant body of ethical doctrine. It remained for the Sophists, in the following century, to breach the walls of philosophical determinism. By insisting that man is capable of controlling his social fortunes even if he is helpless to affect his ultimate destiny, the Sophists established the first philosophical basis for a theory of ethics.

Most Sophists considered traditional moral standards as arbitrary conventions, anticipating Machiavelli (see Chapter 13) by more than two millennia in declaring success the only valid criterion of action. The moral anarchy to which such precepts led provoked Socrates to re-examine the whole problem of purposes and values in human life. His conclusions, later amplified and systematized by Plato, identify man's highest happiness with the maximum detachment from worldly pleasures and preoccupations. Although both Socrates and Plato recognized that a normal life moderated by reason is more practicable for most people, contempt for the world of flesh and secular ambition pervades the philosophy of both men and colors their ethical doctrines. Arguing from ideal principles, they tended to preach superhuman virtues.

Because our knowledge of other Greek philosophical tendencies before the 4th century B.C. is fragmentary, little firm information can be added to this summary of pre-Aristotelian ethical theory. Democritus of Abdera, a contemporary of Socrates and Plato, characterizing the good life as a state of cheerful tranquility, advocated the temperate enjoyment of natural pleasures. Other philosophers variously believed that pleasure is the highest good or the greatest evil. Ideals of reasonableness, moderation, and fair dealing were of course current in Greek social thought at least as far back as the time of Homer, and were doubtlessly widely shared. But as far as we know, the major problems of ethics—problems centering on the goal of life, the nature of the good life, and the proper criteria of right and wrong in social intercourse—received no scientific analysis before Aristotle.

The thoughtful reader of the *Ethics* will be struck by Aristotle's common-sense approach to human conduct as well as by his consistent effort to relate theory to observation and experience. These characteristics, so divergent from the Socratic-Platonic method of reasoning from abstract principles, surely owe much to Aristotle's early education. Born at Stagira (and hence often called "the Stagirite"), Aristotle was the son of the court physician to the king of Macedon. Some scholars have supposed that the boy was apprenticed to the medical profession; his scientific interests and methods in later years lend credence to this view and suggest, at the very least, the influence of his father's vocation.

In his late teens Aristotle settled at Athens, embarking upon two decades of philosophical studies at Plato's Academy (sometimes referred to as "the world's first university"). While he was mastering and reflecting upon the principles of Platonic thought, his scientific inclinations must have been strengthened by the presence at Athens, and for a time at the Academy, of Eudoxus of Cnidus, the great Greek astronomer, geographer, mathematician, and physician.

After Plato's death in 347 B.C. Aristotle left Athens and continued his studies abroad. In 343 B.C., at the invitation of Philip II of Macedon, he moved to the Macedonian capital at Pella to become tutor to Philip's son, Alexander, then a boy of thirteen. Soon after Alexander became king, in 336 B.C., Aristotle returned to Athens, where he established his own school ("the world's second university") in the Lyceum. Perhaps because of his custom of lecturing in the covered walk (*peripatos*) of the Lyceum, the school acquired the name *Peripatetic*, and its disciples were known as *peripatetics*. Aristotle remained in Athens—teaching, writing, and conducting scientific research—until the death of Alexander in 323 B.C. precipitated a wave of anti-Macedonian feeling that placed his life in jeopardy. Accused of heresy, as Socrates had been before him, he thought it prudent to leave the city lest the Athenians "sin twice against philosophy." He died at Chalcis, on the island of Euboea, in the following year.

Aristotle's works effect a brilliant synthesis of science and rationalism, bridging the gap between the two central—and long divergent—tendencies of Greek philosophy. Nowhere is this achievement more impressive than in the *Ethics*. Combining moral principle with penetrating psychological and social insight, Aristotle produced a theory of conduct more practicable than Plato's and more idealistic than the Sophists'. In so doing, he raised moral philosophy to a new height.

Although its structure may not be apparent at first glance, the *Ethics* is carefully organized and logically developed. Basing his argument on an essentially Platonic view of the nature of man, Aristotle moves efficiently through sequential analyses of the human virtues and their personal and social prerequisites. Unlike earlier ethical theorists, he analyzed human behavior empirically and practically. Where Plato, for example, was content with precept, exhortation, and visions of utopia, Aristotle offered an effectual guide to virtuous conduct: the famous Doctrine of the Mean. Although the concept itself was not new to Greek thought, it had never before been systematically interpreted or concretely applied to specific life problems. Naive as Aristotle's solutions may sometimes appear, they bear the stamp of creative originality.

A viable approach to moral philosophy was sorely needed in Aristotle's time. The preoccupation of Greek thinkers of the 4th and 5th centuries B.C. with standards of behavior was largely motivated by social chaos (see page 14)—as typical of Greece in that period as was the unprecedented flowering of political and esthetic culture. Aristotle's lifetime coincided with a series of exhausting wars among the Greek city-states, with bitter class conflict in the cities themselves, and with the gradual extinction of Greek independence by Philip of Macedon. In Aristotle's ethics, as in Plato's, one senses a desperate search for stability in the face of crumbling values and a general cheapening of life. Because Aristotle, like Plato, was an aristocrat, his search, too, ended in a theory more suited to a social elite than to the generality of men. Yet his attitudes were so civilized that they have permeated ethical thought on all social levels ever since his death.

Aristotle's early dialogues, unfortunately lost, were apparently of considerable literary merit. The extant treatises, perhaps worked up from lecture notes by one or more of Aristotle's students, are rarely polished or graceful. But the power of their author's intellect commands attention, and at their best the essays are perspicuous and incisive. The *Ethics*, in which Aristotle is often at the top of his bent, is a stimulating essay as well as a basic document in the history of western thought.

II. Questions for Study and Discussion

1. What is the subject of the *Ethics*?
2. Describe Aristotle's general method of argumentation. How far is it deductive? How far inductive? Illustrate. Compare his method with Plato's.
3. Characterize Aristotle's prose style.
4. Why, according to Aristotle, can ethics not be an exact science? To what extent is he scientific in this work?
5. Upon what basic assumptions about man does the *Ethics* rest? Compare Aristotle's view of man with Plato's.
6. Summarize the process of reasoning by which Aristotle determines the highest good for man.
7. What is that good? How, according to Aristotle, may it be achieved? Compare Aristotle's view of the highest good with Plato's.
8. To what authority does Aristotle appeal in support of his notions of the good? Explain the circularity involved in his reasoning.
9. Explain Aristotle's attitude toward ethical systems based on transcendental (a priori) standards.
10. What is his position on the relationship of pleasure and amusement to true happiness? What is his criterion of true pleasure?
11. Explain Aristotle's theory of the constitution of the human soul. How is this related to his ethics? Compare his theory of the soul with Plato's.
12. How does Aristotle define virtue? What two classes of virtue does he distinguish? Which does he regard as higher? Why? With which is the *Ethics* more concerned? Why?
13. What is his theory of the relationship between heredity and environment in character formation?
14. Where does Aristotle stand on the question of Fate, Fortune, and Free Will in relation to human responsibility for conduct?
15. Define his position on the subject of human perfectibility. Compare it with the Christian view. What seems to be Aristotle's religious position?
16. Explain the Doctrine of the Mean as a guide to virtuous be-

havior. How, according to Aristotle, may the Mean be achieved in practice?

17. Describe the complete Aristotelian gentleman. What do you think of him?
18. How does Aristotle define justice? Compare his definition with Plato's.
19. Why does Aristotle devote so much space to friendship in a treatise on ethics?
20. Under what circumstances, according to Aristotle, is friendship most likely to be rich and enduring? Why?
21. What does Aristotle consider the proper function of education? Explain his position on private versus public education.
22. How, according to Aristotle, are ethics and politics related? Which is the higher discipline? Why?
23. Compare Aristotle's ethics with those of Homer, the Greek tragedians, Plato, the Old Testament, the New Testament.
24. What social attitudes and implications do you find in Aristotle's ethics?
25. What does Aristotle offer the modern reader?

III. Readings in Background and Criticism

Allan, D. J., *The Philosophy of Aristotle* (Oxford University Press, 1952). An admirable introduction to Aristotle for the general reader. Chapter 13 provides a brief exposition of the ideas set forth in the *Ethics* and opposes the view that Aristotle's ethical doctrine is inconsistent.

Burnet, John, "Introduction," *The Ethics of Aristotle* (Methuen, 1910). A fine presentation of the relationship of Aristotle's *Ethics* to his *Politics* and of both to his general philosophy. One section compares and contrasts Aristotle's views with Plato's.

Case, Thomas, "Aristotle," *Encyclopaedia Britannica*, 11th ed. (1910-1911). At once both scholarly and readable, this essay (in Vol. II, pages 501-522) is still the best short account of Aristotle's life and works and of the relationship of Aristotelianism to Platonism.

Gomperz, Theodor, *Greek Thinkers: A History of Ancient Philosophy*, 4 vols. (John Murray, 1905-1920). A basic work in its field. Chapters 20-25 of the fourth volume give a detailed explication and criticism of the *Ethics*.

Jaeger, Werner, *Aristotle* (Oxford University Press, 1934). An advanced and scholarly study of the history of Aristotle's development. Chapter 15 discusses the place of his *Ethics* in intellectual history.

Kelsen, Hans, "The Philosophy of Aristotle and the Hellenic-Macedonian Policy," *International Journal of Ethics*, XLVIII (October 1937, 1-64). A brilliant analysis of the relationship of the *Ethics*, *Politics*, and *Metaphysics* to each other and to the Greek political situation in Aristotle's time.

MacCunn, John, "The Ethical Doctrine of Aristotle," *International Journal of Ethics*, XVI (1905-1906, 288-311). An unusually creative and illuminating exploration of some of the central ideas in the *Ethics*.

Ross, William D., *Aristotle* (Meridian Books, 1959). Pages 187-234 explain and critically examine the main features of Aristotle's ethical doctrine.

Russell, Bertrand, *History of Western Philosophy* (Simon & Schuster, 1945). Chapter 20 contains a clear and concise summary and evaluation of the main ideas of the *Ethics*, which are contrasted with Christian and modern ethical theories.

Stocks, John L., *Aristotelianism* (Longmans, Green, 1927). A simple, straightforward exposition of the essence of Aristotle's ethical doctrine appears in Chapter 2.

Taylor, A. E., *Aristotle* (Dover, rev. ed., 1955). A superb introduction, for the general reader, to Aristotle's method, physics, metaphysics, ethics, and politics. Chapter 5 deals with the ethical theories.

Zeller, Eduard, *Aristotle and the Earlier Peripatetics*, 2 vols. (Longmans, Green, 1897). Chapter 2 of Volume II provides a short but valuable exposition and analysis of the *Ethics*. Chapter 4, Volume I, compares and contrasts Aristotle and Plato.

IV. Translations and Editions

Inexpensive editions of the *Ethics* are available in translations by D. P. Chase (Everyman's), Harris Rackham (Loeb Classical Library), Richard McKeon (Modern Library), and J. A. K. Thomson (Penguin). The Modern Library version is included in a volume of selections from Aristotle, entitled *Introduction to Aristotle*. The advantage of the Loeb Library edition, for students of Greek, is its presentation of the literal translation along with the Greek text. The Penguin edition is recommended for its clarity, unobtrusive style, judiciously placed explanatory comments, and low cost.

7

THE BIBLE

I. Background of the Bible

Baruch Spinoza, a noted 17th-century Dutch philosopher, was the first to discuss the Bible as a work of imaginative literature; he suffered excommunication. But the Bible, the most sacred book of the Western world, has survived partly because it is literature. Though the Testaments differ in tone and intention—the Old Testament primarily records national, the New Testament other-worldly aspirations—together they integrate thousands of years of human experience. They epitomize historical, philosophical, and sociological, as well as theological, developments leading to ethical monotheism; and they detail the trials and achievements implicit in man's emergence from primitive fear of the supranatural to courage, integrity, and dignity before the unknown. Though its authors dedicated the Bible to God, they wrote poignantly and understandingly about the human problems and emotions that concerned them as men. From such material, literature emerges; in the prose and poetry of the Bible its quality is ennobled by lofty and metaphoric style and by simple, concrete, and emotive language.

The Old Testament, written chiefly in Hebrew over a period of about a thousand years (to about 250 B.C.), addressed Hebrews; the New Testament, written in Greek in less than a century (c. A.D. 60 - 150), addressed all mankind. As literature, however, the Old

Testament yields the more abundant harvest. Its thirty-nine books, encompassing nearly every literary type, may be separated into three large divisions: the Pentateuch or "The Law," the Writings, and the Prophets. The Pentateuch, including Genesis, Exodus, Leviticus, Numbers, and Deuteronomy, narrates the story of the creation of the world and of man, describes the prehistorical patriarchal fathers of Israel, and enunciates the religious and legal code that unified the Hebrew people. Immediately following the Pentateuch are the books of the Former Prophets (including Joshua, Judges, Samuel, and Kings), which dramatically trace the history of the Hebrews through the reigns of Saul and David, the founders of the kingdom, and the years of exile and captivity following Israel's destruction by Assyria and Babylon.

History, biography, fiction, and poetry, however tangential to the theology, animate the pages of the Pentateuch and the Former Prophets. Though more conscious of creed than of characterization, the authors embody in their writing memorable portraits of legendary and historical leaders—from Abraham to Moses and from Samson to Solomon—whose lives afford exciting reading and probing insights into human experience and understanding. Their narratives delineate characters within plots forthrightly simple, concretely detailed, and deeply felt. In the poetry of these early books—and in the later ones as well—the intense personal emotion of the Hebrews may be most fully admired and enjoyed. Although variant forms of parallelism, balanced lines, and incremental repetition help technically to identify poetry in the Old Testament, the surge of lyric expression that culminates in songs of anguish, supplication, or triumph obviates for the nonspecialist any need for close rhetorical analysis.

The fifteen Latter Prophets, whose writings fill half the pages of the Old Testament, range historically from the breakup of the kingdom in the middle of the 8th century B.C. to the return to Jerusalem four hundred years later. Ethics and eloquence highlight their able though futile attempts to urge church and state toward an ideal beyond lip-service ritualism or legalistic orthodoxy. Their impassioned attacks upon the exploitation of the underprivileged, profoundly influential upon Western social thought, contributed the opening chapter to the literature of class struggle. The best-known among them—Amos, Isaiah, Ezekiel, and Jeremiah—were sharply different in background, and strikingly dissimilar in style, language, and tone. But with all of the Prophets they shared a dedication to God and man: "forth-tellers" rather than foretellers, they preached to an afflicted people the message of moral righteousness, courage, and hope.

Under the broad, inclusive heading of Writings are grouped all other books of the Old Testament. Here are skillfully wrought prose stories like those of Ruth, Esther, Jonah, and Daniel, all thoroughly enjoyable as fiction, but important also because they exemplify principles of religious doctrine. Psalms and the Song of Solomon —containing some of the most exquisite poetry in the Bible—also belong to Writings, as do the saws of Proverbs, the dirges of Lamentations, and the unorthodox pessimism of Ecclesiastes. The most stirring of all, however, is the Book of Job, whose poetic grandeur and dramatic statement of man's dignity remain unsurpassed in the Bible and rarely matched anywhere in literature.

By the time anonymous Hebrew scribes began, during King Solomon's reign, to copy onto rolls of papyrus (called *biblia* or "little books") the lore of their people, they had inherited more than a thousand years of oral tradition. Contradictions between myth or legend and history did not deter them. To establish a continuity from Creation to David's kingdom of Israel, the scribes unhesitatingly mingled authentic historical events with myths and legends acquired during centuries of nomadic travel. In the generations after Solomon, more sophisticated scribes tried to modify the primitive myths; but, proscribed by Hebrew law from expunging what had already been written into the sacred rolls, they either emended earlier texts or simply added their own versions. Unfamiliar with such procedures, modern readers may be confused, especially in the Pentateuch, by conflicting accounts of a single episode. To avoid confounding that confusion, readers must understand that the early Hebrews' historical perspective differed from ours significantly. Religion rather than a detached recording of events spurred Hebrew historians: they sought only to unify their people in a common belief in one God and in a sure destiny under His law. Myth enhanced that unity by helping the Hebrews to envisage a power greater than themselves: a power that dominated the world of man and nature; a power whose omnipotence they feared, whose justice and mercy they sought. Not only each of the several books in their Testament but the Hebrew people as well became unified through continuing awareness of single divine guidance.

The personality of God, however, changes and develops: the God of the Pentateuch is not ultimately the God of the Old Testament. In his earliest appearances God is frequently awesome and tyrannical. Like Zeus, He resembles a jealous mountain god whose strong magic enables Him to arouse violent storms, to destroy entire cities, or, in milder temper, to "walk in the garden" or to become a burning bush. Such examples of magic, anthropomorphism, and animism—common to all primitive religions—abound in the earlier books of the Old Testament. Centuries passed before God became the "still, small voice" Elijah heard within his spirit. Throughout the Old Testament, nevertheless, despite refinements of His nature, God always remains a dynamic presence the Hebrews experience personally. Never an abstraction, an Essence, God appears ever as a vital, dramatic personality, actively guiding His "chosen people" toward the fulfillment of their destiny.

The Old Testament, as already indicated, is a book about man as well as God. From the outset it breathes forth the spirit of humanism, endows man with both reason and responsibility. The pragmatic laws codified in the Pentateuch, though often harshly retributive, instilled in the Hebrews a respect for justice rarely evident in the moral anarchy of primitive society. As myth stirred their sense of responsibility to God, the law rallied their esteem for the rights of their fellows. Yet realistically the writers candidly acknowledged and detailed human weakness. Hebrew kings and commoners err, their foibles enlivening the narrative, their punishment accenting the Old Testament's insistence upon man's moral obligations. Even beyond the discipline of law, the Old Testament concerns itself with problems central not only to the Hebrews but to all men: freedom of will, the dilemma of good and evil coexisting, the reasons and justifications for human suffering. Though God's will ultimately prevails, man attains nobility and dignity in the Old Testament, is shown as capable of meeting human experience with conscience and decency, of encountering the unknown with humility and courage.

The New Testament shifts attention from a whole people to a single man—Jesus; from life on earth to eternal life in the hereafter. Long oppressed by political, economic, and religious injustice, the underprivileged Jews of Palestine yearned for the prophesied deliverer or messiah. In parables and epigrams Jesus brought to them a simple message—faith and good works: the promise of a better life in Heaven, the continued moral responsibility of man on earth. A devout Jew, a learned student and skillful teacher of the Old Testament, Jesus synthesized those religious and ethical precepts of the earlier book most suitable for his time. He did so, however, with such imagination and intensity that his "new dispensation" of love, mercy, and compassion has since influenced millions and altered social and political as well as religious patterns throughout the world.

Three of the four parts of the New Testament—Gospels, Acts, and Epistles—relate the life and teachings of Jesus, the missionary labors of his apostles, and the letters, chiefly by Paul, to early converts. A final book, the apocalyptic Revelation of John, closes the New Testament with an allegorical and rhapsodic prophecy of the New Jerusalem in heaven and the imminent doom of Roman tyranny. Written almost entirely in prose, the New Testament lacks the literary variety and impact of the Old. But its twenty-seven books often provide intense drama, stirring narrative, and impassioned eloquence. Furthermore, its portraiture—of Jesus and Paul especially—constitutes the finest biographical writing in the Bible.

Whether inspired by the chemistry of his body or by his soul, man has ever pursued meaningful experience and correspondence with God, his fellow man, and himself. Because the Bible, perhaps more than any other book, searchingly and compassionately expresses the intricacy of that complex and often frustrating quest, it belongs not only to Jews and Christians but to all humanity.

II. Questions for Study and Discussion

General

1. What is the theme of the Old Testament? Of the New Testament? Enumerate several points of similarity and of dissimilarity between their central purposes.
2. What are the basic differences between the two Testaments in structure? In language? In imagery? Select passages from each to illustrate your answer.
3. Compare as examples of narrative the stories of Genesis with the parables of Jesus. What literary qualities does each possess? Which is your favorite narrative in the Old Testament? In the New Testament? Explain your choice.
4. Which character in the Old Testament most deeply impressed you? In the New Testament? Why? Which Testament provides the more effective characterization? Explain your choice.
5. What examples of father-son relationship appear in the Old Testament? How do they compare with the God-Jesus relationship in the New Testament?
6. Contrast the Hebrew attitude toward God with that of the Greeks (as reflected in the writings of Homer, Aeschylus, Plato, and Sophocles). Do the same with the Christian attitude.
7. How do the two Testaments differ in their approach to the problem of human dignity? Of good and evil? Of justice and mercy?

The Pentateuch

1. What questions about the ultimate purpose of the universe and about man's place in it are raised here? What answers are given? How, for example, do you interpret the story of Adam, Eve, the serpent, and the apple?
2. Cite examples of anthropomorphism, animism, myth, legend.
3. What religious and/or ethical ideas does each story in Genesis develop?
4. Describe the concept of God. How does it relate to the image modern man has of Him?
5. Characterize Abraham, Jacob, and Joseph. How do they differ? Which characterization is the most realistic? Explain.

6. How do the stories of Genesis compare as literature with the myths of the *Odyssey*?
7. Compare Moses with Joseph as a leader.
8. Can one live meaningfully today by the Ten Commandments? Why?

The Prophets (Former and Latter)

1. Characterize Saul and David. Who is the more interesting? Why?
2. What is the Hebrew attitude toward kings as expressed in Samuel and Kings? What does this attitude tell us about Hebrew ideas of the relationship between church and state?
3. What changes in the Hebrew attitude toward God occur during the reigns of Saul, David, and Solomon?
4. Describe Isaiah's concept of God. Compare it with Amos's, Ezekiel's, Jeremiah's.
5. What was the real function of the prophet? What problems did he encounter in fulfilling that function?
6. What are some of the poetic characteristics of Isaiah? Compare his style with that of several other prophets.
7. What is Isaiah's attitude toward women? How do you account for it?

The Writings

1. What are the major themes lyricized in Psalms?
2. Which poetic devices appear most commonly?
3. Which psalm is your favorite? Justify your choice.
4. What is the basic human problem dramatized in Job?
5. How do Job's friends try to explain his suffering? How does Job answer them? Why does God punish Job's comforters?
6. In the *Book of Job*, what is the poet's solution of the problem of human suffering? What modern explanation of this problem is quite different?
7. What general similarities and differences do you find between Job and Greek tragedy? Job and the Platonic dialogues?
8. What is the basic theme of Ecclesiastes? What does the Preacher mean by "vanity"?
9. What similarities exist between Ecclesiastes and Job?

10. Why might the author of Ecclesiastes be called a "kindly cynic"? Would you think a different word more appropriate? Why?
11. What does Ecclesiastes indicate about the social, religious, and political situation of its time?

The Gospels

1. Characterize the writing of each of the books of the Gospel. How does the Gospel of St. John differ from the others?
2. Characterize Jesus. Compare him with Moses as a leader of men and as a teacher.
3. What qualities does Jesus expect of an ideal Christian? To what extent are his expectations justifiable?
4. Characterize Paul. Compare him with Jesus as a leader and as an ethical philosopher. Compare him with the other disciples as a personality.
5. What was Paul's major contribution to Christianity?
6. What literary qualities does The Acts of the Apostles possess? Why has it generally been attributed to Luke?
7. What are Paul's views on marriage and virginity (Corinthians)? Compare them with Solomon's.
8. What is Paul's attitude toward love or charity (Corinthians)? Compare his view with those of Plato and Aristotle.
9. What are Paul's ideas about the application of Christian doctrine to everyday living (Romans)?
10. What is Paul's position on the relationship between church and state (Romans)?
11. What is Paul's estimate of the value of the Ten Commandments (Romans)?

III. Readings in Background and Criticism

Albright, William F., *From the Stone Age to Christianity* (Doubleday Anchor Books, 1957). An important and readable account of the origins of monotheism and its fullest expression in Judaism and Christianity. Particularly valuable are the chapters on Moses, the Prophets, and Jesus.

Auerbach, Erich, *Mimesis*. See Readings for Homer, page 7.
Branscomb, B. Harvie, *The Teachings of Jesus* (Abingdon-Cokesbury, 1931). A clear and helpful discussion—especially in the first seven chapters—of the historicity of Jesus and His teaching methods.
Buttrick, George, *et al.*, editors, *The Interpreter's Bible*, 12 vols. (Abingdon-Cokesbury, 1952- —). The most elaborate and thorough of all commentaries on the Bible. In addition to line-by-line explications, it contains first-rate general articles, notably in Volumes 1 and 7. For more common use, readers will find serviceable the one-volume *Abingdon Bible Commentary*, edited by F. C. Eiselen, *et al.* (Abingdon-Cokesbury, 1929).
Enslin, Morton S., *Christian Beginnings* (Harper, 1938). An historical and textual study of the New Testament. With Pfeiffer's study of the Old Testament (see below), it makes a comprehensive study of the Bible easier for advanced students.
Frazer, Sir James G., *Folklore in the Old Testament*, abridged ed. (Tudor, 1923). A famed anthropologist examines and evaluates the significance of parallels to several Old Testament stories—the Creation, the Fall, the Flood, the Witch of Endor, and the like.
Freud, Sigmund, *Moses and Monotheism* (Vintage Books, 1955). Freud's brilliant and controversial thesis suggests that Moses was an Egyptian monotheist, murdered by the Hebrews he sought to convert. The Hebrew "children" have since retained their sense of guilt for this unexpiated crime against their "father." Christians, on the other hand, have become reconciled to the Oedipal situation, for Jesus, the "son," has done penance for the original crime.
Gaster, Theodor H., *The Dead Sea Scriptures in English Translation* (Doubleday Anchor Books, 1956). Among several excellent books about the Dead Sea scrolls, Gaster's is perhaps most useful for beginners. A brief but informative introductory essay and lucid notes provide needed background for his translations of the texts. An intricate but thoroughly absorbing book.
Goodspeed, Edgar J., *The Story of the Apocrypha* (University of Chicago Press, 1939). A clear, simple, and useful introduction to the fourteen books usually omitted in Hebrew and Protestant versions of the Bible. Goodspeed's translation, *The Apocrypha: An American Translation* (University of Chicago Press, 1938), is excellent.
Keller, Werner, *The Bible as History* (William Morrow, 1956). A popular archeological study of the places and events significant in the Bible. Though many will dispute his conclusions, few will put Keller's book aside: it is exciting, informative, and readable.
Klausner, Joseph, *Jesus of Nazareth* (Macmillan, 1943). Though unsympathetic to notions of Jesus as divinity, messiah, or prophet, Klaus-

ner, one of the most esteemed Hebrew scholars of our century, brings sincere appreciation and admiration to his study of Jesus.

———, *From Jesus to Paul* (Macmillan, 1943). Although his approach is controversial, Klausner provides original and perceptive insights into the great leaders of early Christianity.

Pfeiffer, Robert H., *An Introduction to the Old Testament* (Harper, 1948). A scholarly and encyclopedic analysis of each book of the Old Testament. (See Enslin, above.)

Watts, Harold H., *The Modern Reader's Guide to the Bible* (Harper, 1949). A superb introduction to the literary, intellectual, and religious problems of the Bible. Expertly written, Watts's book clarifies the impact of "The Other"—the force of the unknown—on Western culture.

IV. Translations and Editions

Translations

Long before the classic translation of the Bible, the King James Version of 1611, each of the Testaments had been translated into a language other than its original. About 280 B.C., the Hebrew text of the Old Testament appeared in Greek, and for centuries thereafter this version, called the *Septuagint*, served as the Scripture throughout Mediterranean countries. At the end of the 4th and beginning of the 5th centuries A.D., Jerome, a Roman scholar, translated the entire Bible into Latin. His version, known as the *Vulgate*, remained the only complete Bible for more than a thousand years and remains today the official text of the Roman Catholic Church; it is Englished in the Rheims-Douay version.

With the Reformation and the invention of the printing press (Gutenberg printed his first book—the Bible—in 1455), several Continental and English Protestants undertook translations. Among the most significant were the Wycliffe translation of the Bible into English (1383) and Luther's German translation (1534), based on the original Hebrew and Greek rather than on Jerome's Latin version. In 1611, after four years of intense work by a large group of scholars, the superbly graceful and perennially readable King James Bible appeared and has since remained the most widely read of all editions.

Recent scholars, aware of textual errors in the King James Version or conscious of a need for stylistic modernization, have produced important new translations of the Bible. James Moffatt's *A New Translation of the Bible* (Harper) and J. M. P. Smith and Edgar Goodspeed's *The Bible: An American Translation* (University of Chicago Press) have "modernized" the language and style with considerable success. Monsignor Ronald Knox has done an authorized Catholic translation, *The Holy Bible* (Sheed & Ward), that is conservative, scholarly, but admirably readable. *The American Revised Standard Version* (Thomas Nelson), begun in 1901 and completed in 1952, is unquestionably the most accurate version of the Bible now available. Though it lacks the sublimity of the King James version, it possesses excellent literary qualities and deserves a place on every bookshelf.

Editions

Beyond the recent versions noted above, readers may of course choose among innumerable editions of the complete King James Version. Of these perhaps the most attractive is *The Reader's Bible* (Oxford University Press), printed in large, clear type and in simple and convenient format. Ernest S. Bates' *The Bible Designed to Be Read as Living Literature* (Simon & Schuster) rearranges the materials (omitting some and altering spelling and punctuation) of the Bible to effect a modern "literary" reading suitable for leisurely enjoyment.

Among the abridgments of the Bible, *The Dartmouth Bible*, edited by R. B. Chamberlin and H. Feldman (Houghton Mifflin), is easily the best, its selections generous, its introductions and notes splendid. For less advanced students, *A Bible for the Humanities*, edited by J. C. Thirlwall and A. Waldhorn (Harper), will prove useful. It contains ample reading selections and helpful introductory essays. Abridgments in inexpensive paperbacks are available in Mentor, Pocket Book, Rinehart, and Penguin editions.

8

Lucretius: ON THE NATURE OF THINGS

I. Background of Lucretius (*c.* 99 - *c.* 55 B.C.)

The supreme literary statements of idealist thought were made by a Greek, Plato, and by the Hebrew authors of the Old Testament. But the materialist view—although originated by Greeks and refined, expanded, and popularized by a Greek, Epicurus (342 - 271 B.C.)—lacked a classic statement until a Roman disciple of Epicurus, Titus Lucretius Carus, composed *De rerum natura* in the 1st century B.C.

We know next to nothing of the life and personality of Lucretius, but a great deal about the philosophical and historical background of his long, eloquent didactic poem. The early development of materialism—the doctrine that the ultimate stuff of the universe is finally reducible to matter, that not only the physical world but also the mind of man, his thought and aspirations, can be sufficiently explained by naturalistic data, by the evidence of the senses and the free use of reason—has been sketched in a previous chapter (see page 38). One 5th-century materialist theory, formulated by Democritus, led to atomism, which argued that the atom—in infinitely varied combinations, both visible and invisible—is the ultimate substance of all matter. A century later Epicurus adopted atomism as the metaphysical basis of a practical philosophy for living. Two centuries after Epicurus, Lucretius wrote his hexameter poem both as an adaptation of Epicureanism and as a panacea for the political and social evils of Rome.

Epicurus believed that sense experience and reason, not intuition or revelation, point the way to truth. Because no sense evidence indicated to him the survival of body or soul after death, Epicurus maintained that he had liberated his mind from fear, the debilitating fear that there existed another world dedicated to punishing those whom the gods deemed worthy of punishment. Though he did not deny the gods' existence, he reasoned that they interfered neither with man's destiny nor with the course of nature. Rejecting equally the notions of supernatural intervention and materialistic necessitarianism, Epicurus concluded that man was free—and freer because he had no cause to worry about future rewards and punishments. Because the register of his senses tells him plainly that pleasure is good and pain evil, man should seek pleasures free from accompanying pains. This hedonistic calculation implied moderation, not the "Epicurean" slogan "Eat, drink, and be merry." Indeed, Epicurus espoused an almost ascetic life of calm, uncluttered existence based on intellectual companionship.

Epicurus worked for intellectual freedom, not for political reform. However, the ruling classes in Greece and, later, in Rome vigorously opposed his teaching because, by attacking superstition, it undermined any government that exploited superstition as a means of political control. To the established rulers Epicureanism was subversive of law and religion.

Lucretius had lived through the Marian and Sullan massacres (a series of brutal political purges) and the first part of Caesar's consulship. He knew intimately the infinitude of woes that Romans endured: how they suffered from cruel depredations of power, from ubiquitous corruption, from the repetitive civil wars, and, no less, from the emotional paralysis and distortions bred by fear and uncertainty. In the strife-ridden Rome of the 1st century B.C. Lucretius sought peace in a philosophical system able to satisfy both intellect and soul, and he aspired to liberate the masses from political constraint. He found his answer in Epicureanism. By promoting it in a society disciplined by tradition, Lucretius attained the reputation of a religious heretic and, by implication, of a revolutionist.

A frontal assault on the stultifying effects of popular superstitution in general, *De rerum natura* indirectly attacks the state as the bulwark and propagator of superstition. Designed to foster free and independent thought, the poem was part of an unsuccessful minority movement to curb the police function of religion. Lucretius exploded the Roman version of the "edifying lie" (the myth, in Plato's ideal state, devised by the rulers to control the masses). He assailed also the prevailing Stoic philosophy, with its mood of resignation and its belief in the expediency of religious deception.

Scholars still debate whether Lucretius was trying primarily to induce others to accept Epicureanism or whether the poem is a massive effort to argue himself into accepting a world-view that might bring him inner peace. Certainly, no evidence points to his popularity or influence in his day; on the contrary, the fact that his poem survived in only one battered manuscript suggests that it was effectively suppressed. Christians, too, found Lucretius and Epicureanism pernicious. Not until the 18th century, in fact, did this philosophy find eagerly receptive disciples.

Today, *On the Nature of Things* is widely regarded as one of the two great poems (the *Aeneid* being the other) produced by Romans. Its six books are loosely organized and the thought is often tenuously developed. Book VI ends rather abruptly, suggesting that Lucretius died before completing the poem. After a long introduction almost deifying Epicurus, Lucretius expounds in Books I and II his postulates about the nature of matter and space and about the properties, shapes, and movements of atoms. In several digressions he attacks the theory of divine creation, explains nature's pattern of mutation and recurrence (of creation balancing destruction), and defends Epicurus against the charge that he ruled out free will. In Book III, which applies the atomic structure to man's body and soul, Lucretius marshals the empirical and deductive evidence of the soul's mortality. Book IV explains Epicurus' speculations on the nature of sensation, concluding with Lucretius' provocative views on sex. Book V is anthropological, setting forth a theory of creation and social evolution. And Book VI, on meteorology and geology, gives rational, if sometimes fantastic, causes for celestial and terrestrial phenomena.

Yet the method and spirit of poetry inform and illuminate this seemingly unpoetic—even antipoetic—scientific discussion and disputation. For Lucretius infused the scientist's earnest search for truth with his own compassion for oppressed mankind and his lyrical enthusiasm for the sensuous delights of physical nature. The fullest statement of the atomic theory of Democritus and the philosophy of Epicurus, an impressive fusion of poetic awe and scientific matter and method, and a rare example of liberalism in Latin literature, *On the Nature of Things* has become the bible of materialists. Its poetically charged defense of the Epicurean gospel of salvation by common sense often speaks more directly to the mid-20th century reader than does any other work of classical antiquity. And even if Lucretius' philosophy offends the devout, his fertile mind, humane ethics, and poetic genius can scarcely fail to compel their admiration.

II. Questions for Study and Discussion

1. What is the theme of the poem?
2. On what basic assumption is the philosophy of Lucretius (and of Epicurus) based? How can you argue for or against this assumption?
3. According to Lucretius, what is the goal of life? How can it be achieved?
4. What is materialism? Name some modern materialists. In what ways is Lucretius materialistic? In what respects is he not materialistic?
5. Why does Lucretius attack superstition?
6. What kinds of proofs and what types of reasoning does Lucretius employ to argue his points? How consistent is his method?
7. Summarize his basic propositions about the nature of matter and space.
8. What modern scientific and anthropological theories does Lucre-

tius anticipate? How does his atomic theory differ from that in vogue today? Which of his theories has science rejected?

9. How does Lucretius distinguish between a property and an accident of matter?
10. Describe Lucretius' theory of color. Is it physiologically or psychologically sound?
11. What, according to Lucretius, is the relationship between mind and spirit?
12. Outline Lucretius' conclusions about the nature of the senses and of sense perception.
13. State Lucretius' position on sex and marriage. Compare his views with those of Paul in the New Testament.
14. How does Lucretius explain the origin and nature of human society? How do we label this theory today?
15. Explain Lucretius' views on progress.
16. According to Lucretius, what is the fundamental evil of traditional religion? How does this evil lead to others?
17. Compare and contrast Plato, Aristotle, and Lucretius in terms of their reasoning methods and their conclusions.
18. Comment on Lucretius' poetic style, particularly on his imagery. On what subjects does he write most eloquently and imaginatively?
19. Explain Lucretius' position on free will and on individual responsibility.
20. What hope does Lucretius offer for the future? Do materialism and pessimism go hand in hand? Why, or why not?
21. What of value does Lucretius say to you?

III. Readings in Background and Criticism

Duff, J. Wight, *The Literary History of Rome* (Barnes & Noble, 1953). In academic style, one solid chapter discusses various aspects of Lucretius: sources, ideas, influence.

Farrington, Benjamin, *Head and Hand in Ancient Greece* (G. Allen & Unwin, 1947). The chapter on "The Gods of Epicurus" is an excellent summary and defense of the philosophy incorporated into *On the Nature of Things.*

———, *Science and Politics in the Ancient World* (G. Allen & Unwin, 1939). Despite the author's Marxian bias, perhaps the most cogent study of the effects of science, particularly its attacks on superstition, on Greek and Roman politics. Chapter 14, "Lucretius," argues that his poem was mainly an attack on the state cult as the mainstay and propagator of superstition to keep the people under control.

Hadas, Moses, *A History of Latin Literature* (Columbia University Press, 1952). Half of Chapter 5 sketches the life, sources, and basic ideas of Lucretius.

Hadzsits, G. D., *Lucretius and His Influence* (Longmans, Green, 1935). A sympathetic, shrewd, and revealing account of Lucretius' thought and influence, arguing that Lucretius was neither atheist nor hedonist, but an early humanist and ethical idealist with a vision of a brave new world to be founded on truth.

Santayana, George, *Three Philosophical Poets* (Doubleday Anchor Books, 1955). A graceful, informed, short essay on the sources and characteristics of Lucretius' naturalism. Appreciative of Lucretius as a poet of nature.

Sikes, E. E., *Lucretius, Poet and Philosopher* (Macmillan, 1936). A short, incisive study of Lucretius' thought and of his influence on modern philosophy and science. Contains especially valuable chapters on Epicureanism and on Lucretius' distinctive poetic genius.

Stanley, C., *Roots of the Tree* (Oxford University Press, 1936). Pages 75 to 90 discuss Lucretius' stature as a political and religious subversive.

Thomson, J. A. K., *The Greek Tradition* (Macmillan, 1915). Chapter 8, "Lucretius," analyzes the descriptive and lyric qualities of a poem too often analyzed solely for its thought. Thomson finds *On the Nature of Things* intensely religious despite its devastating attack on the evils of Roman religion.

IV. Translations and Editions

Most translations of *De rerum natura (On the Nature of Things)* make Lucretius seem too difficult to read pleasurably. In trying to transfer Latin grammatical structure and idiom into English, they guide the student of the Latin text but block everyone else. Among these—and not recommended to the contemporary reader—are prose translations by two distinguished Latin scholars: W. H. D. Rouse (Loeb Classical Library) and Cyril Bailey (Oxford University Press).

R. E. Latham has prepared (for Penguin) a new prose version—*The Nature of the Universe*—that expresses clearly Lucretius' thought and conveys something of his spirit in current, idiomatic English. The majority of readers will probably find this translation most satisfactory. Those who like to read a poem as a poem may prefer the often effective, but uneven, version by the distinguished poet and scholar William Ellery Leonard (Everyman's).

9

Vergil: AENEID

I. Background of Vergil (70 - 19 B.C.)

Though we know only a few facts about the life of Publius Vergilius Maro, they shed a revealing light on much of his work. Born in 70 B.C. near Mantua in northern Italy, he spent his life as student, thinker, and poet. Maecenas, the prototype of literary patrons, welcomed him into the circle around Augustus Caesar, and the emperor himself showered favors on this shy, brilliant poet. Though patronized and sometimes lionized, Vergil generally kept to himself, preferring to devote his time to reflection and poetry. His total output was slight, in quantity at least: the *Bucolics*, or *Eclogues*, ten short pastorals; the *Georgics*, four long didactic poems on farming; and the *Aeneid*, an epic which he had not finished revising when he died, in 19 B.C., while on a journey with Augustus. He had intended to devote the rest of his life to philosophy.

To Romans until the end of their civilization, Vergil was the voice of living Rome as no other Roman was—not Cicero or Horace or Livy or Seneca. Ignoring Vergil's immense respect for Homer, his contemporaries considered the *Aeneid* superior to the *Iliad*. Generations of Roman school children studied his works as textbooks; poets modeled their work upon his; soldiers and statesmen looked to him for inspiration—all this, not only because of the excellence of his poetry but also because his works epitomized the age in which he lived. The *Fourth Bucolic* evoked the great hope for the return of the Golden Age; the *Georgics* recalled strife-weary Italians to their loved but long-neglected fields; the *Aeneid* inspired the Romans to greatness, enshrining for them their heritage and responsibility. What Augustus and the Romans wanted most, Vergil celebrated: lasting peace and order. It was a dream Roman civilization died still holding; but while Rome lived, the *Aeneid* was its epic, a national epic that fitted the Roman sense of grandeur.

The age through which Vergil lived was one of the most savage and revolutionary in recorded history; but its end brought the "bright, fresh beginning of a new era of peace." We recall those men whose names, for good or ill, resound in that first century before Christ: Marius and Sulla, Pompey, Julius Caesar, Antony, Brutus, Cassius, and finally Octavian Augustus. Their world was a battleground, civil war after civil war ruthlessly draining Rome of much of her noblest blood. Many who survived the fighting were butchered in the subsequent purges. The Civil War between Julius Caesar and the Republican forces led by Pompey (49 - 46 B.C.) seemed to be the end, but Caesar's murder on the Ides of March in 44 B.C. signalled new violence. Even after Brutus and the Republicans were defeated at Philippi (42 B.C.), the struggle for power continued between the victors, Antony and Octavian. Finally, at the Battle of Actium (31 B.C.), Octavian routed the armies of Antony and Cleopatra, and emerged as the most powerful man in Rome. Four years later, when the name "Augustus" was confirmed on Octavian, the Roman imperial state (actually twenty years old already) was formally established.

The Emperor Augustus brought the hope of stability to eager Romans. However imperfect his system, his genuine devotion to Rome's welfare quickly gained him the support and devotion of the people. Continuing the work begun by Caesar, he rebuilt Rome and Italy—physically, politically, and morally. To further his purpose, he shrewdly fostered the Romans' yearning for a new Golden Age. And it was in part to promote the cause of Augustus that Vergil wrote the *Aeneid*—a great national epic exalting the Roman people and their new Empire.

Vergil's epic begins seven years after the end of the Trojan War and ends with the establishment of the Trojans in Italy. To

Dido, queen of Carthage, Aeneas recounts the incident of the treacherous Wooden Horse, the apparitions on the night of Troy's fall, and the flight which became a quest for the real homeland of the Trojans. (Old legends made Dardanus, founder of Troy, an Italian.) Many obstacles block Aeneas: the wrath of Juno, the passion of Dido, the weariness of his followers, his own feelings of exile and rootlessness. When he reaches the lowest point of despair, he is taken to Hades for advice from his father and for a vision of his descendants—virtually a roll call of Roman history. Strengthened, he returns to lead his thinning band of followers to Italy, where the hotheaded Turnus, in defiance of the oracles and against the better judgment of the King, provokes war. But the new Aeneas does not falter; he has now a clear view of his mission and an unshakeable will to accomplish it.

In characters like Dido and Turnus, Vergil represents the irrational and disordered world which the Romans must remake. In the prophecies which resound through the poem—prophecies about the descendants of Aeneas, the glory of Rome, the illustrious Augustus, and the "habit of peace" Romans were to bring to the whole world—Vergil welds the survivors of Priam's city into a union both with the twins suckled by the she-wolf and with the new men of his own time. In his youth, Vergil had aspired to write an epic account of Rome's history; ultimately he achieved a mythic version of her history—not an objective narrative, but one shaped to an ideal. In the *Aeneid* he embodied his concept of her tradition and his vision of her destiny; in it Romans found the expression of their aspirations for unity, honor, and dignity.

Vergil's success in giving shape to the Augustan dream made him the pride of Augustus' Rome and a legend to subsequent generations. And even before pagan civilization died, Christians saw in Vergil a Gentile prophet. They perceived—and perhaps exaggerated—the messianic overtones in the *Fourth Bucolic;* they allegorized the *Aeneid;* their exegetes, apologists, and poets adopted (and almost baptized) Vergil. Tertullian's view that Vergil's was a "soul naturally Christian" was widely adopted. By the Middle Ages, the legend of Vergil took a new form, developed and altered substantially: Dante's guide through *Inferno* and *Purgatorio* was more attuned to theology than to political art.

This Christianizing of Vergil led to a fuller understanding of his work. His "second voice" is that of the universal poet giving lyrical shape to the dreams of *all* men. Though the Augustan planners drew what they liked from the *Aeneid* and the other works, Vergil's full vision of the future was, more than they knew, essentially spiritual, presaging Christianity. Indeed, much of the poem contains warnings to the Romans, warnings which they ignored. Vergil was reappraising rather than discarding the old heroism; he was examining as well as advertising the political program of Augustus. The manner in which he used his material shows this. Whether his source was the harsh, annalistic epic of Ennius or the vibrant philosophical poetry of Lucretius, the idealistic dialogues of Plato or the lyrical tragedies of Sophocles, Vergil fused his material into a meaningful whole, to serve his larger intent. From Homer, his major model, he drew not only the framework of his poem but also innumerable incidents; but consistently he adapted Homer to his own purpose. Aeneas' journeys, for instance, have far more unity and meaning than do those of Odysseus; his descent into Hades has historical and religious significance; the duel between Aeneas and Turnus, though resembling that between Achilles and Hector, has richer implications.

If pious Aeneas is less attractive than furious Achilles and shrewd Odysseus, it is because Vergil was designing a different kind of hero. Almost a symbol, Aeneas incorporated Vergil's full response to the exigencies of the new world. One of Aeneas' greatest problems is his relationship to the gods—the reader must never forget how different the gods of the *Aeneid* are from any conceived in previous Greek or Roman literature. The solution of that problem traces a pattern that runs through the poem. The bond between Trojans and gods is far stronger and more significant; what Aeneas expresses best is the spiritual self-realization demanded by the world Vergil imaged. On all of these points, Vergil went beyond the Augustan program. True, Augustus sought to make religion a stabilizing force in the social and political order; he had three hundred chapels built to "Rome and Augustus." But he did not genuinely love the religion he advocated. Vergil did. Looking beyond the leveling process fostered by the Augustan social planners, he sought values more abiding than expedient political ones. Essentially, the task Vergil envisaged for Romans was that of bringing order to their world from within themselves. Rome was not equal to the task, nor was it fully ready for the fundamental virtues—humility, temperance, and justice.

The advent of Christianity, which Vergil foreshadowed (wittingly or not), provided a fitter audience. Far too honest to produce an easy idealization of Augustus, Vergil looked beyond the glory that was Rome. Humanity was more nearly his theme and the City of God more truly his home. In the interaction of narrative and theme, of prophecy and imagery, of war and the pity of war, of history being remade and myth being made, of light and fabulous darkness, Vergil dramatized in the *Aeneid* not just the hopes of his own times, but also the longings, the tensions, the possibilities of all human life —the longing for peace and order (though with an unflinching appraisal of the cost); the tensions of individualism and responsibility, strength and humility, grandeur and justice; the possibilities of human dignity, spiritual and religious greatness, and universal harmony. Troubled as it may be with his own sense of the "tears of things," his vision endures, majestic and compelling.

II. Questions for Study and Discussion

1. What is the theme of the *Aeneid?*
2. Describe the structure of the poem. Compare the structure of the first half to the *Odyssey*, of the second half to the *Iliad*.
3. In what sense is Aeneas an exile? In what sense a man returning home?
4. Why is Juno so hostile to the Trojans? Trace the development and expression of this hostility throughout the epic. What is its effect on Aeneas and on his quest? To what lengths does it lead Juno? What finally does she achieve?
5. What traits do the female characters of the *Aeneid* share?
6. Discuss Book II as a five-act tragedy. Compare it with a Greek tragedy. What was ultimately the cause of the Fall of Troy?
7. Discuss the conflict in Book II between Aeneas' personal motives and the decrees of Destiny.

8. Compare Vergil's use of similes with Homer's. Compare the travels of Odysseus with Aeneas' wanderings in Book III.
9. Characterize Dido and Anna. What is Anna's function in Aeneas' affair with Dido?
10. Why does Aeneas desert Dido? Why does Dido commit suicide? What is the significance of the sacrificial aspects of her death?
11. Characterize Anchises, Acestes, Achates. How does Achates compare with Achilles' Patroclus as a "comrade"?
12. Compare the Aeneas-Venus relationship with that of Odysseus and Athena.
13. Why must Aeneas go to Hades? How does he react to what he sees there?
14. Compare the procession of Roman heroes in Book VI with the prophecy of Jupiter in Book I and the Shield of Aeneas in Book VIII. What purpose do these and other prophecies, oracles, omens, and dreams serve in terms of Aeneas himself, Destiny, Rome, and the theme of the *Aeneid*?
15. Characterize Vergil's gods. Discuss Aeneas' relationship to the gods, especially to Jupiter, Juno, and Venus. What relation do these gods bear to Destiny (Fate)? Compare Vergil's views with Homer's.
16. What are the ultimate causes of the war in Italy? What does the immediate occasion of that war tell about civilization and society at the time of the poem's events?
17. What significance does Aeneas' alliance with Evander and the Arcadians have in terms of Vergil's attitude toward the Greeks throughout the epic?
18. The poem does not have a "happy" ending. Why not?
19. Explain Vergil's attitude toward heroism. Discuss this in connection with Sinon, Pyrrhus, Dido, Turnus, Pallas, Mezentius, Lausus, and Aeneas. Compare Vergil's view with Homer's.
20. Compare the Aeneas-Turnus duel with that between Achilles and Hector. What "richer implications" has the former?
21. Compare Vergil's attitude toward war with Homer's. Discuss this in terms of audience and theme.

22. In what ways does this national epic transcend propaganda?
23. What, according to Vergil, is the mission of the Roman people?
24. Trace the development of Aeneas' character throughout the epic. In what way has he grown? By what means? Is he a totally satisfying hero? Discuss.
25. Discuss Vergil's use of symbolism and imagery.
26. How does Vergil bridge the gap between paganism and Christianity?
27. What aspects of the *Aeneid* appeal most to a contemporary reader?

III. Readings in Background and Criticism

Bowra, C. M., *From Vergil to Milton* (Macmillan, 1945). A compact study of four epic poems, including the *Aeneid* and *Paradise Lost.* The chapter on Vergil and the ideal of Rome is the best brief treatment of the purpose, method, and significance of the *Aeneid.*

Duff, J. Wight, *A Literary History of Rome from the Origins to the Close of the Golden Age* (Barnes & Noble, 1953). The standard English history of Latin literature. The chapter on Roman character and religion provides valuable peripheral matter; the chapter on Vergil gives a useful account of the poet and his times.

Fowler, W. Warde, *Rome* (Home University Library, 1947). Covers the history and development of Rome and especially of the age of Augustus. Brief, perceptive, and graceful, the book presents a helpful survey of Roman character.

Glover, T. R., *Virgil** (Methuen, 1923). A sound account of the man, his times, and his work. Individual chapters can be read as independent units; especially recommended are those on Italy, Rome, Augustus, and Hades.

Hadas, Moses, *A History of Latin Literature* (Columbia University Press, 1952). Aimed at the non-Latinist reader. An introductory chapter cuts through many problems and points the intelligent approach to Latin literature. The treatment of Vergil in the context of his literary tradition is illuminating.

———, *A History of Rome* (Doubleday Anchor Books, 1956). A history of Rome from the beginnings to Justinian, drawn mainly from the

* Alternate spelling.

Roman historians themselves. The first four chapters summarize most of the history relevant to the *Aeneid*.

Highet, Gilbert, *Poets In a Landscape* (Knopf, 1957). Essays on Rome and on Vergil and six other Roman poets. The author limns the climate and terrain of Vergil's Italy and offers many insights into reading Vergil.

Knight, W. F. Jackson, *Roman Vergil* (Faber and Faber, 1944). Stimulating, occasionally eccentric. The chapter "Form, and Reality" offers brilliant, provocative insights to the advanced student.

Mackail, J. W., *Virgil and His Meaning to the World of Today* (Marshall Jones, 1922). A short but eloquent survey of Vergil's life and times, the sociological, political, and literary background of his work, and his significance for our century.

Prescott, H. W., *The Development of Vergil's Art* (University of Chicago Press, 1927). The best and fullest introduction to Vergil—lucid, analytic, provocative. Chapters on social and political setting, legend, and life after death offer a wide background. "Epic Tradition" compares the *Aeneid* with Homeric and Hellenistic epic. Five interrelated chapters consider large sections of the poem in detail.

IV. Translations and Editions

The lyric genius of Vergil defies translation as much as his superb poetry invites it. This note can refer only to some better attempts. Recent prose translations by W. F. Jackson Knight (Penguin) and John Jackson (Oxford University Press), though faithful and accurate, lack excitement. Kevin Guinagh (Rinehart) improves a readable translation with very useful headings and appendices. J. W. Mackail's version (Modern Library), though dated in style, is full, often sonorous, usually distinguished. Handling story well, Mackail also conveys much of the complexity of Vergil's theme and feeling. For those with some Latin, H. R. Fairclough's close translation (Loeb Classical Library) is useful.

Among the verse translations, John Dryden's, the first in modern English (1697), is great as an individual poem: spacious, resonant, generally forceful, frequently brilliant. William Morris' version (1876) is too romantic; E. Fairfax Taylor (Everyman's) and Rolfe Humphries (Scribner) set forth the story but lose much of the poetry. C. Day Lewis, if sometimes eccentric in interpretation, has produced a splendidly readable modern poetic version (Doubleday Anchor Books). Lewis' "stress-meter" lines often achieve the various metrical effects of the Vergilian hexameters. Without pruning or padding, Lewis conveys story, tone, and rhythm, and keeps intact Vergil's mood and pace.

10

Dante:

THE DIVINE COMEDY

I. Background of Dante (1265 - 1321)

Among its many strong claims on our attention today, the *Divine Comedy* stands as the consummate expression in literature of the Medieval Mind. By this vast, rather imprecise, though useful abstraction, we mean basically a manner of thinking quite different from that dominant today, one fundamental to everything Dante wrote. For, broadly speaking, the Medieval Mind was a priori, not a posteriori in method—that is, unlike modern science, which works from observation of irreducible facts to theories confirmed by experiment, it worked from theory to fact. What the medieval thinker was disposed to take as unquestionably primary and real was doctrine—the theology and philosophy that supported scripture. Any facts inconsistent with doctrine were—at least until Galileo's historic discoveries—ignored, suppressed, or rationalized away.

For centuries after the time of St. Augustine (A.D. 354 - 430) theological and philosophical doctrine was chiefly Platonic. It was Plato's conception of an illusory world of sense and a spiritual realm of real, eternal Ideas that supplied the rationale for Christian other-worldliness through the long, troubled "Dark Ages." By the close of this period, in the monastic islands of learning scattered about Europe, a synthesis had been achieved which gave intellectual stability to the faith; theology ruled the seven liberal arts, and theology meant Augustinian Platonism.

The man largely responsible for shattering this synthesis was Peter Abelard (1079 - 1142). A teacher of magnetic personality and commanding intellect, he won many converts to his position that the disinterested reason need not be subject to the strictures of theology. Feared, attacked, and persecuted by the Platonists, Abelard nevertheless cleared the way for a battle of philosophies that lasted over a hundred years, riddling Christendom with charges of heresy and filling the newly founded universities with students eager to gain true instruction from the brilliant and often bitter debates of the scholastic masters.

With doctrinal civil war raging, the medieval Church was in effect without a unifying philosophy. Its appeal to the faithful shifted from the rationalism identified with God the Father and Christ the Judge to the more intuitive and compelling cult of the Virgin. Thus it was that at a time of logical controversy and confusion, a time of apparent disintegration, the great 13th-century cathedrals soared heavenward by the score from the European plain, monuments of passionate aspiration, prayers in stone to *Notre Dame*. This unique, discordant, yet creative era reached its climax in the immense intellectual labor of Thomas Aquinas (1225 - 1274). His *Summa Theologica* finally resolved the ideological crisis by rebuilding Church doctrine on a new stabilizing foundation, one which combined the insights of Christian revelation with the complex, encyclopedic philosophy of Aristotle.

It is difficult for us today to imagine the effect of this fresh synthesis on the most aware minds of that age, and not least on those in the fine arts. For centuries Platonic orthodoxy had disdained the sense world as illusory. Now Aquinas, following Aristotle, recognized reality as consisting of two ultimately real constituents: form *and* matter. Thus the senses at last were vindicated as the bearers of valid knowledge, and art received a powerful impetus to treat the reasoned and revealed Thomist doctrines of the Church. Dante Alighieri, born the year Aquinas began his commentaries on Aristotle, became one of the first and without doubt the greatest of writers to benefit from this revolution in Western thought. His mind, equally as sensitive to philosophic concepts as to the moral history of his age, assimilated all these diverse developments and embodied them in his *Divine Comedy*—a poem which is both a cathedral in words, raised in Platonic adoration of a heavenly lady, and a magnificently organized edifice of rational thought, based squarely on Aristotle and Aquinas.

If Dante was born the lucky heir of a period of vast creative energy, if "ten silent centuries" found voice in him, we still know all too little about his life. The two events most deeply affecting the *Commedia* were his meeting in 1274 with his future inspiration, Beatrice, and his exile in mid-career from the prosperous, strife-torn city-state of Florence. Yet even in such vital data, the exact family name of Beatrice—traditionally Portinari—seems curiously to have gone unknown until Boccaccio's biography, the first written of Dante, fifty years after his death. However shadowy the historic identity of the lady, the transforming effect of Dante's great love on his life is made clear in his *Vita Nuova.* In this brief, cryptic account of the "new life" which Beatrice revealed to him, Dante adopted and sought to expand the only developed poetic convention of his age, the courtly song wherein the troubadours and later the Tuscan aristocratic poets poured out their love-yearning for highborn ladies, usually married and heartlessly indifferent. In the *Vita* he relates with compelling emotion how in his ninth year he first glimpsed the girl who seemed in her perfect beauty the image of divinity on earth; of her greeting him once when he was eighteen; of the shock of her early death; of her appearance to him when he was twenty-seven in a mystical vision, and his determination to write of her what had never been written of any woman before.

Following Beatrice's death in 1290 Dante plunged into a life of study, and his grief-stricken quest for the meaning of a personal loss became the preparation for his immense creative task. Reading frequently all night long, taxing his eyesight until, as he tells us, "the stars seemed blurred in a kind of mist," he gradually absorbed the whole of learning available to his time. Cicero, Ovid, Statius, Lucan, Horace; the authors of Latin antiquity; the contemporary Provençal, Italian, and medieval Latin poets; as well as Augustine, the Church Fathers, and the medieval philosophers and mystics—all found place in his passionate yet systematic mind. From Vergil particularly he derived a sense of Rome as the central, life-giving root of Western civilization, its imperial unity an ideal contrasting with the political chaos of the Italy he knew. And from Aquinas and Aristotle, of course, came the indispensable scaffolding of a total moral and metaphysical system.

In 1302 the second event that sealed the character of Dante's poem occurred: a government opposed to the poet's party, after seizing power through a conspiracy, condemned him to exile under penalty of being burned alive. For one of Dante's pride, independence of mind, and moral fiber, such treatment could not go unanswered. As a soldier he had fought for Florence at Campaldino and Caprona; he had spoken in her Council, acted as her ambassador abroad, served as one of the six supreme magistrates of the city. Now from 1302 until his death he was destined to wander Italy, dependent on the charity of patrons. This stroke of ill fortune sharpened his awareness of human ingratitude and depravity, but it gave him as well a compensating appreciation of the blessedness of right conduct. His answer to Florence—the *Divine Comedy*—became a celebration of what Dante never lost faith in: God's just plan for his creation, revealed in this world to the saints and poet-prophets through inspiration and made awesomely manifest to all men after death. (For Dante, members of the clergy, even certain popes, had betrayed that plan; the corruption and self-seeking prevalent in the holy orders of the time drew some of the poet's most scathing denunciation.) Against this eternal, panoramic order, he opposed the sinful, obstinate, fallen nature of man, which must be disciplined through the purgatorial climb of this life until man learns to recognize the true source of all his good in God.

That part of the poem wherein Dante is most medieval, a

priori, and scholastic—namely, the demonstration of God's order, the Unity in Trinity behind all things—is likely to be most remote and require most effort from the modern reader. Earlier, in the *Vita*, Dante had experimented with numerical symbolism (the trio of 9, 18, 27). The *Commedia* now expanded this symbolism on a cosmic scale: the unified poem consists of three main books, or *cantica*, each of 33 cantos, 99 in all, which with one introductory canto total 100, or 10 squared (9 plus 1—the square of the Trinity, plus its ineffable Unity). Nothing in this arithmetical conjuring would have struck the poet's contemporaries as artificial or forced; on the contrary, here the ultimate spiritual reality, God, pure form, would be seen bounding the entire complex matter of the poem.

Within this framework Dante chose to tell a story reflecting the oldest of mythical patterns: a physical journey which corresponds to a profound inward development. In the first book, the *Inferno*, Dante (like all the characters of the poem, both himself and the symbol of some permanent human attribute or condition: here the Pilgrim Soul) wanders lost in the Dark Wood of worldliness until he meets Vergil (Active Reason), who conducts him into the terraced pit of Hell. Here he witnesses the awesome fates of the eternally damned. who have set themselves unrepentantly and thus (in Aristotelian terms) formally against God. In the *Purgatorio*, Dante and Vergil, having passed through the earth's center, climb the seven-story Mount of Purgatory, one ledge allotted to each of the seven deadly sins. The contrite sinners here are guilty of preferring some earthly good to God; this material stain must be purged away in penance appropriate to the fault. Lastly, in the *Paradiso*, Beatrice (Divine Revelation) guides Dante into realms which Vergil cannot enter, up through the planetary spheres where the souls of the blessed *manifest* themselves, to the Mystical Rose of Paradise where the blessed *abide*, and finally to the climactic vision of God with which the poem ends.

The literal narrative of a work so vast and timeless in theme would in itself be enough to occupy a reader; it is a tribute to Dante's genius that he makes it attract and hold the reader fast. The brilliant images that exactly fix a scene, a gesture, an expression; the rapid pace that never falters; the fantastic imagination that bodies forth monsters, angels, and the harsh landscape of Hell; the ingenious punishments of the penitent and damned, so aptly congruent with their sins; the unforgettable vignettes of those who stop Dante in his journey and pour out their passion, malice, violence, remorse, or joy in dialogue as taut and sharp as any modern novel's—all these triumphs of the concrete and concise make their immediate appeal to us today.

But no reader who begins with the surface attractions of the *Divine Comedy*—as T. S. Eliot, a prime mover in the present Dante revival, rightly insists he should begin—will want to remain there. Indeed, Dante prevents his doing so. In the famous letter to his patron, Can Grande, he states that the literal action of the otherworldly journey is but one of four levels of meaning on which the poem was conceived and written. Thus every event in the *literal* plot also has significance symbolically on, first, a *moral* plane, giving man insight into the conduct of his personal life; then on an *allegorical* plane, describing the dissensions and potential remedy of man's life-in-community; and finally on what Dante calls the *anagogical* plane, wherein the soul is shown, apart from all earthly concerns, moving toward God, its eternal destination.

This fourfold method, while setting up the rich, multidimensional symbolism of the *Commedia*, does not in itself explain the magnitude of Dante's achievement. In the last analysis our interest must concentrate on exploring the powerful mind that included and used and transcended the technique of presentation, on the imagination that envisioned names and shapes for the entire range of man's responses to the dilemmas and temptations of his mortal pilgrimage. Even for those readers unable to share the articles of Dante's faith, or those who find his scholastic thought supplanted by the empirical methods of science, there remain these penetrating, endlessly suggestive images of the human situation, which disclose new profundities of idea and interrelationship with each rereading. Here, ultimately, Dante's greatness rests: in the grandeur of scale and depth of understanding with which he brings a universe of forms and meanings within the focus of one sustained and ordered vision.

II. Questions for Study and Discussion

"Inferno"

1. What does the character Dante symbolize? Vergil? Beatrice? What does the presence of both Beatrice and Vergil, not one or the other, show about Dante's view of life?
2. Why, symbolically, does Dante have to make the trip through the Inferno?
3. How, in the face of his obvious respect for them, can Dante put the great Greeks and Romans where he does?
4. Does Dante faint at the end of Francesca's story just from pity?
5. What is intended, symbolically, by having the walled city of Dis where it is?
6. Explain Vergil's repulse at the gates of Dis.
7. What is the criterion by which Dante organizes the moral topography of the Inferno?
8. Why are blasphemers, sodomites, and usurers classed together?
9. What did usury mean for Dante? Has the meaning changed? Why did Dante condemn usury so severely?
10. How is our conception of the moral nature of theft different from Dante's? How is his belief reflected in the punishment?
11. What is the significance of Ulysses' tale (Canto 26)?
12. What is the significance of Ugolino's story (Canto 33)?
13. Can you justify Dante's actions to the ice-blinded soul at the end of Canto 33? If so, how?
14. Why are traitors the most despicable sinners for Dante?
15. What is the symbolism in Dante's climbing down Satan's flank?

"Purgatory"

1. Why, symbolically, does Dante have to make his trip up the Mountain of Purgatory?
2. Why is Vergil instructed to gird Dante with the rushes that grow about the base of the mountain?
3. What is Antepurgatory? Who inhabits it?
4. What mode of awareness does Dante have in Antepurgatory? Why?

5. Why can the two pilgrims ascend only in the daytime?
6. What do the seven *P*'s inscribed on Dante's forehead signify?
7. What moral scheme underlies Dante's arrangement of the terraces of Purgatory (Canto 17)? What is the source of this scheme? Do you agree with the gradation of importance he gives the various sins?
8. How does the penance fit the crime in each class of souls? How do these sins differ from those in the Inferno?
9. What is the nature and structural function of each of Dante's dreams?
10. How does Dante explain the existence of evil in the world (Canto 16)?
11. Does he find human nature basically good or evil (Cantos 16-17)?
12. What does Dante learn of free will (Canto 16)?
13. What does he learn about the nature of love (Canto 18)?
14. What is Dante's attitude toward the church (Canto 16) and the relationship of church and state (Canto 32)?
15. What are the conditions of life in the Earthly Paradise?
16. One critic has written of the "Purgatory" as "Dante's drama of the mind." What justification do you see for calling the poem dramatic, rather than epic?

"*Paradise*"

1. What particular difficulties did Dante face in composing this book that were not present in those preceding?
2. What dominant image expresses the realm of the blessed? What devices does Dante use to give this image (*a*) variety, (*b*) progressive intensity?
3. If man's intellect and love instinctively move toward God, why do some turn aside from this natural direction (Canto 1)?
4. In what way are the souls in the lower, subsolar spheres defective? How do they regard their inferior status (Canto 3)?
5. What is Dante's defense of the artist's right and obligation to tell often painful truth in his work (Canto 17)?
6. What importance does Dante attach to the contemplative as against the active life (Canto 22)?

7. How do the four cardinal virtues and the three theological virtues figure in Dante's vision of heaven?

General Questions

1. How is Dante's view of what is important in life different from that of the Homeric Greeks? From that of Plato? From that of Lucretius? From that of Vergil?
2. Can the moral universe which Dante created be reconciled with the doctrine that "God is love"? If so, how?
3. Can Dante's forthright gradation of his contemporaries, living and dead, be reconciled with "Judge not, lest ye be judged"? How, or how not?
4. What qualities in Dante's literary art justify T. S. Eliot's claim that "the poetry of Dante is the one universal school of style for the writing of poetry in any language"?
5. How does Dante's rhyme scheme, *terza rima*, implement the grand design of his poem?
6. What elements has Dante taken over from the pagan epics, particularly Vergil? What new elements are present?
7. What idea of the man-woman relationship emerges out of the treatment of Beatrice in the poem? What social and psychological consequences are suggested?
8. How has Dante's religion shaped the form and content of the *Commedia?* Is he always orthodox?
9. To what extent was Dante's world-view bounded by the limited scientific knowledge of his time? Does this modify the greatness of his achievement for us today? If so, how?

III. Readings in Background and Criticism

Adams, Henry, *Mont-Saint-Michel and Chartres* (Anchor Books, 1959). Limited by Adams' late-19th-century romantic medievalism, this study still remains an eloquent and profound analysis of the period just before Dante wrote and of the forces and ideals—chiefly the cult of the Virgin—which made it great.

Curtius, Ernst Robert, *European Literature and the Latin Middle Ages* (Pantheon Books, 1953). With deeply informed scholarship, the author illuminates the medieval Latin tradition from which Dante derived much of his universality of mind and idiom; see particularly Chapter 12, "Poetry and Theology," and Chapter 17, "Dante."

Dinsmore, C. H., *Aids to the Study of Dante* (Houghton Mifflin, 1903). Invaluable anthology of articles on varied aspects of Dante's learning and art by leading scholars, many (such as Scartazzini, Witte, Comparetti) hard to locate elsewhere in English translation.

Eliot, T. S., "Dante," *Selected Essays* (Harcourt, Brace, 1950). Primarily an appreciation by a noted poet-critic, this short, lucidly phrased, perceptive essay is the best general guide for the reader approaching Dante for the first time.

Fergusson, Francis, *Dante's Drama of the Mind: A Modern Reading of the Purgatorio* (Princeton University Press, 1953). A close, canto-by-canto study of the central poem of the *Commedia:* in the author's view, a drama of the universal purgatorial journey of the moral life, from childhood and primitive awareness through the stages of spiritual struggle to mature understanding.

Moore, Edward, *Studies in Dante, Second Series* (Oxford University Press, 1899). One of several series of miscellaneous, specialized, but scrupulously researched articles by a particularly thorough Dante authority. "Dante as a Religious Teacher," pages 1-78, is helpful in relating the poet to Roman Catholic doctrine.

Sayers, Dorothy, *Introductory Papers on Dante* (Harper, 1954). Exceptionally clear, if at times overzealous, discussions of such basic and problematic subjects as the meaning of Hell, Purgatory, and Paradise; the fourfold interpretation of the *Comedy;* Dante's symbolic and pictorial imagery; and the City of Dis. (Much of this material can be found in the introductions and notes to Miss Sayers' Penguin Classics translations.)

Toynbee, Paget, *Concise Dictionary of Proper Names & Notable Matters in the Works of Dante* (Oxford University Press, 1914). Dependable factual reference for all persons, places, literary or philosophical works, mythological figues, etc. mentioned or alluded to in the *Comedy;* less useful with respect to general ideas. Arranged for use with bilingual text.

Vossler, Karl, *Medieval Culture: An Introduction to Dante and His Time,* 2 vols. (Harcourt, Brace, 1929). Part I treats the whole history of culture—religious, philosophic, ethical, political, and literary—brought together in the *Divine Comedy;* Part II offers interpretation of the poem itself. Included is a copious bibliography of works covering all phases of Dante's cultural background, usefully evaluated and complete to 1929.

Wicksteed, Philip, *Dante and Aquinas* (Dutton, 1913). Clearest and most complete exposition of the philosophical tradition behind Dante's writings, traced from the pre-Socratics, Plato, and Aristotle through Plotinus and the Arabian commentators to Aquinas and his considerable influence on the *Commedia*.

IV. Translations and Editions

For various reasons—archaic diction, muddy rendering of meaning, failure to indicate Dante's significantly chosen poetic form—the pioneer 19th-century translations of the *Divine Comedy* (made by Cary, Longfellow, Norton, and others) are generally inadequate for the modern reader. An exception is the Carlyle-Wicksteed prose translation (Modern Library), a version literally accurate, on the whole direct in diction, and well provided with notes and diagrams; the Temple Classics edition (Dutton) with facing Italian text permits fuller understanding of Dante's art.

The best translation for American readers, when completed, may well be John Ciardi's; his *Inferno* (New American Library) is vivid, idiomatic, and poetically resourceful. Dorothy Sayers' poetic talent, on the other hand, is weak and given to Victorian phrasings, but her three-volume translation (Penguin) can be recommended for its firm grasp and detailed exposition of Dante's theology. Another complete verse translation, Lawrence Binyon's (Viking), is smoother in execution than Sayers', but tends to blur Dantesque precision and, unlike the two just-noted versions, is inadequately annotated. The somewhat flat translation by Thomas Bergin (Crofts Classics) is further disadvantaged by abridgement; superior in format and style is H. R. Huse's rendering (Rinehart), although the frequent interruption of the text by explanatory matter will strike some as more irritating than helpful.

Numerous other contemporary translations of parts or the whole of the *Commedia* exist, many couched in flowery, decorative phrases far from the *bello stile* of the original. Those recommended above combine ready accessibility with at least the minimum standards of competence required of all who respond to the impossible, yet imperative, challenge of re-creating Dante's great poem in English.

11

Boccaccio: DECAMERON

I. Background of Boccaccio (1313 - 1375)

Giovanni Boccaccio's name is as widely recognized as his literary and intellectual stature is underestimated. Generally considered a mere raconteur of light and somewhat salacious though brilliantly fashioned short stories, he was actually one of the formative geniuses of the Renaissance and of modern literature. His *Decameron,* popular for centuries as a random collection of droll tales, is in fact a unified artistic and intellectual achievement ranking high among the masterpieces of world literature.

The son of a Florentine money broker, Boccaccio was trained for a commercial-legal career despite his preference for literature and classical studies. Assigned while still in his teens to a commercial post at Naples, he spent a number of years in the cultivated, aristocratic circle of King Robert and completed a course of studies in canon law at the University of Naples. The effects of this combination of middle-class and courtly experience are apparent even in so distinctly bourgeois a book as the *Decameron.*

Having begun to write seriously in the late 1330's, Boccaccio gave himself wholly to letters and scholarship thereafter—a commitment that brought him moderate fame and little money. His temperament remained so equable in the face of misfortune, however, that he was known to his friends as *Giovanni della Tranquillità.* A modest man himself, although generous in praise of others, Boccaccio seems never to have appreciated the magnitude of his own talent. In late life he regretted having written the *Decameron* and died without premonition of the honor in which he would one day be held.

Boccaccio's contributions to literature and learning were outstanding even in an age of greatness. Prolific in both poetry and prose, he worked in almost every literary form available and invented others. The most striking illustrations of his influence appear in Chaucer's liberal borrowings and in several of Shakespeare's plots. But even apart from these, Boccaccio exerted a vast influence upon the subsequent development of literature. It has been said that few post-Renaissance literary forms do not stem ultimately from him.

During the latter half of his creative life, following the completion of the *Decameron*, Boccaccio devoted himself increasingly to humanistic studies and the search for classical manuscripts. The first western European of modern times to sponsor the study of Greek, he was also the author of the first biography of Dante. But the work which contributed most to subsequent scholarship was his *Genealogy of the Gentile Gods*, an encyclopedic compilation and interpretation of classical mythology, which served for several centuries as the definitive text in its field. The last two books of the *Genealogy* embody the first systematic defense of classical literature, of liberal studies, and of poetry. In the face of clerical hostility to secular letters, Dante and Petrarch had propounded similar ideas, but it remained for Boccaccio to produce a comprehensive essay on the subject. This essay, together with Aristotle's *Poetics* (rediscovered in the 15th century), established the substance of Renaissance literary theory.

Thus Boccaccio was by no means either a one-book author or a purveyor of superficial tales. His importance in the history of literature and thought goes far beyond the *Decameron*, even if that book is the only basis of his contemporary reputation.

In form, the *Decameron* (1348-1353) is a spoof of the Christian hexaemeric literature of the Middle Ages—pious and edifying variations on the theme of the six days of Creation, for which Boccaccio substituted ten days of unvarnished worldliness. This fact alone suggests the satirical tone of the work and bids us beware of reading it naively. In structure, the *Decameron* combines the form of the medieval anthology with a slight but meaningful dramatic framework provided by a group of narrators. Its motivating mechanism is the Black Death of 1348, an epidemic of bubonic plague that killed from one-quarter to three-quarters of the population of Europe. The introductory essay—a brilliant report of the ravages of the plague in Florence, reconstructed from hearsay—was terrifyingly meaningful to Boccaccio's contemporaries. But beyond its topical relevancy, and beyond such other dramatic and philosophical implications as the reader may explore, the introduction projects a fact of crucial importance to our understanding of Boccaccio. Whereas Dante had employed death to coerce the living, Boccaccio used it to set off and justify their vitality. This shift from the Dantesque focus is more than a matter of technique; it reveals the essential secularity of Boccaccio's thought and is a measure of his achievement.

The dominant intellectual doctrines of the Middle Ages, rooted in a theological-ethical conception of life, had long obscured or anathematized the realities of human behavior. In the *Decameron*, at the very dawn of the Renaissance, those realities for the first time in centuries were laid bare to dispassionate scrutiny. Boccaccio may thus be said to have turned from the literary manipulation of men as they should be to a frank examination of men as they are—although this is by no means the limit of his achievement in the *Decameron*. A milestone in literary history—the work is the first great triumph of modern literary realism—the *Decameron* is also a high point in the development of man's awareness and acceptance of himself.

Boccaccio invented few of the stories assembled in the *Decameron*. His genius lay rather in selecting, adapting, and retelling available stories in meaningful fashion. The hundred tales, considered as a whole, constitute a panorama of the life and foibles of Italians in the first half of the 14th century—from cutthroats to clerics and from laborers to lords. Composed in the vernacular prose of Tuscany, the work established Boccaccio as the creator of a literature of the people as opposed to that of the aristocracy of the Middle Ages.

By the 14th century, Italian urban life was preponderantly bourgeois—dominated by the interests of the commercial classes which had been advancing toward economic and political power in the course of the preceding two or more centuries. Apart from the random and almost anonymous body of genre materials (those treating subjects of everyday life) that had been accumulating throughout the Middle Ages, there existed before Boccaccio no secular literature consciously adapted to the needs of this large audience. Chivalric romance was neither relevant nor congenial to men whose lives were immersed in practical affairs and whose interests were hostile to those of the old aristocracy. The literature of the humanists, on the other hand, although in some respects more pertinent to middle-class preoccupations, was unavailable to people who could not read Latin. Urban readers required a secular literature at once related to their lives, suited to their tastes, and written in their own tongue. This is what Boccaccio provided in the *Decameron.*

As the drama was to become the major literary form of Renaissance England, the short story, or *novella,* as developed by Boccaccio, became the distinctive literary form of Renaissance Italy. Characterized by realism, brevity, wit, and moral point, and drawn from the escapades of daily life, the short story was ideally suited to the needs of ordinary people. Because of its emphasis on brevity and moral, however, the Renaissance tale never aimed at the allusiveness, thematic subtlety, richness of characterization, or emotional force of the modern short story. The reader today, therefore, must suspend certain contemporary principles of judgment if he wishes to fully appreciate the *Decameron.*

The *Decameron* is vibrant with life; every reader will find many stories to his taste. A completely rewarding reading, however, requires that one look beyond individual stories to the effect of the whole. The work may be approached, in a sense, as a literary mosaic. Whatever the brilliance of individual tiles, it is the interrelationship of all the elements of design that creates the portrait of an age and the pattern of a great artist's philosophy of life.

II. Questions for Study and Discussion

1. Discuss the social and philosophical implications of Boccaccio's introduction.

2. Is the framework of the *Decameron* thematically related to the rest of the work or merely a convenient unifying device? Explain.
3. Why do you suppose Boccaccio was less interested in his story-tellers as individuals than in their stories? Do you consider this a weakness or a strength in the work? Compare Boccaccio with Chaucer in this respect.
4. Discuss the typical form and technique of the tales in the *Decameron* and characterize Boccaccio's art as a story teller.
5. Illustrate and discuss Boccaccio's satirical technique.
6. Summarize Boccaccio's attitudes toward women, love, and marriage. To what extent are his views medieval, to what extent modern? Compare them with the views of Plato, Paul, Dante, Chaucer, Rabelais, Montaigne.
7. Where does Boccaccio put the blame for sexual immorality and marital infidelity? What bases does he suggest for happiness in love and marriage?
8. Does he exploit sex merely for fun, or with thematic and symbolic meaning? Explain.
9. Do you consider his attitudes toward sex immoral? Why, or why not?
10. Define and illustrate Boccaccio's social views. How is his attitude toward love related to his social philosophy?
11. What is the social point of the several stories that end happily only because of the accidental discovery of the aristocratic lineage of one of the protagonists?
12. Define and illustrate Boccaccio's religious views. Explain whether his emphasis on the sexual adventures of the clergy is merely a matter of anticlericalism or something more.
13. What is Boccaccio's view of the relationship between man-made law and natural law?
14. What does Boccaccio consider the good life? How may it be achieved?
15. What is his estimate of the role of Chance (Fortune) in life?
16. What does Boccaccio consider the source of evil?
17. To what degree may Boccaccio be characterized as an environmentalist?
18. What is Boccaccio's opinion of human nature?

19. Is the *Decameron* the work of a cynic, a realist, or an idealist? Upon what do you base your answer?
20. To what extent is the *Decameron* a work of negation or of affirmation? What does it negate? What does it affirm?
21. Summarize Boccaccio's total philosophy of life. Compare his life view with that of Plato, Aristotle, Dante, Machiavelli, and Montaigne.
22. Defend or attack the thesis that the *Decameron* is a unified work of art.
23. Apart from his desire to present a comprehensive panorama of society, what is the significance of Boccaccio's selection of stories encompassing all social strata?
24. Which of Boccaccio's preoccupations in the *Decameron* are still relevant today?

III. Readings in Background and Criticism

Auerbach, Erich, *Mimesis* (Doubleday Anchor Books, 1957). Through detailed stylistic analysis of passages from the *Decameron* and contrasting works of an earlier period, Chapter 9 presents a sociological theory of the significance and limitations of Boccaccio's achievement.

Cioffari, Vincenzo, "The Function of Fortune in Dante, Boccaccio, and Machiavelli," *Italica*, XXIV (March 1947, 1-13). A valuable contribution, comparing and contrasting the meaning of "Fortune," as well as the function of the concept, in the works of the three men.

De Sanctis, Francesco, *History of Italian Literature*, 2 vols. (Harcourt, Brace, 1931). The discussion of Boccaccio in Volume I, Chapter 9, includes a useful comparison of medieval and Renaissance attitudes toward life. De Sanctis' interpretation of the *Decameron* as nothing more than a comedy of humanity, however, is superficial.

Hutton, Edward, *Giovanni Boccaccio* (John Lane, 1910). Still regarded as a basic biography, and still generally useful, this work should be approached with caution. Its scholarship is dated and its interpretation of the *Decameron* (Chapter 18) unsatisfactory.

Krutch, Joseph Wood, *Five Masters* (Jonathan Cape and Harrison Smith, 1930). With the chapter in the Symonds biography (see below), Chapter 1 provides the best approach to an understanding of the philosophy and social import of the *Decameron*.

Lee, A. C., *The Decameron: its Sources and Analogues* (D. Nutt, 1909). Still the standard work in its field, tracing the provenance of the stories in the *Decameron*.

Lipari, Angelo, "The Structure and Real Significance of the *Decameron*," *Essays in Honor of Albert Feuillerat, Yale Romanic Studies* XXII, (1943, 43-83). An interesting example of allegorical interpretation pushed to extremes. Lipari argues that the framework of the *Decameron* is an allegorical veil for a new poetic doctrine.

McManus, Francis J., *Boccaccio* (Sheed and Ward, 1947). The best contemporary biography.

Owen, John, *The Skeptics of the Italian Renaissance* (Macmillan, 1893). Chapter 2, a perceptive treatment of Boccaccio's skepticism and naturalism by a Protestant clergyman, is least objective in discussing Boccaccio's morals and religious attitudes.

Symonds, John Addington, *Giovanni Boccaccio as Man and Author* (John C. Nimmo, 1895). Chapter 5 ranks with the Krutch essay referred to above as the most sensible and perceptive approach to the *Decameron*.

———, *Renaissance in Italy*, 7 vols. (Scribner, new ed., 1900). Despite a tendency to Victorian moralizing, Symonds provides (Vol. IV, Chapter 2) a useful summary of Boccaccio's life and works, with emphasis on the *Decameron*. Vol. V, Chapter 10, includes a brief but incisive sociological analysis of the popularity of the *novella* in Renaissance Italy.

Wilkins, Ernest H., *A History of Italian Literature* (Harvard University Press, 1954). Chapter 11 contains the most up-to-date compendious summary of Boccaccio's life and works, by one of the foremost modern students of the Italian Renaissance.

IV. Translations and Editions

Several inexpensive translations of the complete *Decameron* are in print. The version by John Payne (Black and Gold, Living Library), done in the late 19th century and frequently reprinted since, is the most widely known although not the most accurate or authentic. It has an archaic style foreign to Boccaccio but favored by some readers. Of 20th-century translations, that by James M. Rigg (Everyman's, 2 vols.) is stilted and rather prudish, while that by Frances Winwar (Modern Library)—the best available—is straightforward, clear, and contemporary, although scarcely up to Boccaccio's stylistic art. Abridgements such as *Tales from the Decameron* (Pocket Books) are not recommended.

12

Chaucer: THE CANTERBURY TALES

I. Background of Chaucer (*c.* 1340 - 1400)

Because transition breeds turmoil, Chaucer's England, moving toward the threshold of modern history, knew little tranquillity. Its greatest literary artist could hardly blink at change and the human imperfections most apparent during times of change, but he could not find it in himself to weep over either. Joy in living, balance in judging, wit in recording—these are Chaucer's essential qualities. They abound in *The Canterbury Tales*, the masterpiece of his later years, enabling it to capture the pulsing life of the mid-14th century.

Chaucer's background and training helped to equip him for his task. Born about 1340 of a middle-class family that long since had earned wealth as wine-importers and civic reputation as customs officers, Chaucer was trained for public rather than literary life. From his youth, when his father's connections at court won him a place as a page, Chaucer served his king at home and abroad. During three reigns his civil career occupied him variously—as soldier, director of customs, commissioner of buildings and public works, foreign emissary, and member of Parliament. Barring his late years when he suffered occasional financial reverses (a year before his death in 1400 he wrote Henry IV *A Complaint to His Empty Purse*), nothing in Chaucer's public life hampered his avocation as a literary man. Rather, his duties helped to broaden his experience and to sharpen his perception.

His work in England pressed him against men and women of all classes. At court, in the streets, and along the wharves of London, he studied Englishmen: the proud remnants of a waning feudal class; the confident burghers of a rising *bourgeoisie*; bustling guildsmen; the venal and the virtuous among the clergy; impoverished students; and lusty housewives. Nothing about them escaped him—manner, speech, or thought. Abroad, he observed the most significant cultural activities on the Continent: in Italy, where he twice ventured on diplomatic missions, Petrarch and Boccaccio were still alive (though there is no sure evidence that he met either of them). Already versed in French and Latin literature, he had before he was thirty translated from the French *The Romance of the Rose*, a long allegorical poem. From the Italian writings of Petrarch and Dante, however, and especially from those of Boccaccio, he drew fresh insights into problems of structure, characterization, and tone invaluable for his literary practice. For a dozen years during his so-called "Italian period" (1373 - 1385) his numerous experiments in narrative poetry increasingly ranged beyond the limits set by the literary conventions of his time—allegory, rhetoric, stock characterization. Inspired by his Italian masters, Chaucer informed his writing with realism and humor even while he worked within the boundaries of tradition. Richly colloquial language, controlled but vivid imagery, and astonishingly skillful metrical variety (he introduced to English poetry both the heroic couplet and rime royal) characterized these years of literary apprenticeship. *Troilus and Cressida*, completed about 1385, happily measures Chaucer's achievement during the Italian period, for had he not written *The Canterbury Tales*, his fame might securely rest on *Troilus and Cressida*. Only loosely indebted to his source, Boccaccio's *Il Filostrato*, Chaucer here foreshadows the consummate artistry of *The Canterbury Tales* with his shrewd characterization, ironic wit, and poetic eloquence.

When Chaucer read at court from his manuscript of *The Canterbury Tales*, his audience already knew many of the stories the Canterbury pilgrims relate. Possibly they recognized also the narrative "frame" described in the "General Prologue" to the tales. But though neither the frame nor the stories were original, Chaucer, transmuting what he borrowed, rendered the old stunningly new. The frame, for example, Boccaccio had used at least thirty-five years earlier in *The Decameron;* similarly patterned, Ovid's *Metamorphoses* and *The Arabian Nights* long antedate Boccaccio. At first sight, as sketched in the "General Prologue," Chaucer's plan seems closely to resemble his predecessors'. About thirty pilgrims, including Chaucer, set out from Southwark, across the Thames from London, on a three- or four-day pilgrimage to St. Thomas à Becket's shrine at Canterbury. Traveling together for safety and companionship, the pilgrims (though their essential purpose is prayer) accept the suggestion of their innkeeper-host that they enliven their journey by telling stories —four by each pilgrim, two on the way to Canterbury, two returning. But even within the formal arrangement that methodizes the "General Prologue" lie indications of the dramatic and comic possibilities of Chaucer's plan. Holiness prompts the pilgrims to their journey, but how much sanctity can one expect when a bawdy miller, a leprous cook, and a tippling sailor are scheduled to tell stories, even in the presence of a knight and a prioress? This mildly ironic coupling of impropriety with piety hints at the liveliness to come. Furthermore, Chaucer's brief but graphic sketches of the widely assorted pilgrims whet the desire to hear them speak and see them in action.

Once the journey begins, the reader becomes a spectator at what has been aptly called a "moving stage." Chaucer's frame, now animated, enables him to dramatize and add dimension to the static portraiture of the "General Prologue." The Host, acting as toastmaster and mediator, permits the pilgrims as well as himself abundant opportunity to banter, to insult, and to interrupt. Occasionally these delightful and natural interludes occur during a tale (Chaucer, for example, makes himself a butt by reciting, until the Host halts him, a dull romance in hopeless doggerel); more frequently they appear as "head and tail links," or prologues and epilogues to each poem. The interplay of personality often incites the tellers to tales about related subjects, and these narrative clusters, apart from their literary merit, epitomize medieval social thought.

Chaucer's plan gives form and unity to *The Canterbury Tales* so perfectly that no part—"General Prologue," "links," or tales—ought to be separated from the others. The narratives are so expertly wrought, however, that frequently they are isolated and anthologized. Although he relies on stock literary types for his tales, Chaucer's feeling for character precludes any perfunctory recitation of plot. As diverse as his tales are the voices which relate them. Whether the tale is a bawdy *fabliau,* a moralizing *exemplum,* a beast fable, or a chivalric romance, its narrator's accent and personality are unique. But though characterization often controls plot in *The Canterbury Tales,* the plot, cleanly shaped and effectively directed, moves swiftly and economically to its denouement.

However delightful, Chaucer's stories do lose some of their savor when read apart from their context. One reason, perhaps, is that his pilgrims represent the essential genius of Chaucer's creativity. Most memorable among the portraits are those of pilgrims who contain and enact their personal drama: originally sketched in the "General Prologue," these characters develop more fully through the tale they narrate and, by means of the "links," even further in encounters with their fellows. Scholars debate how many of his characters Chaucer drew from life; we can only say that they achieve a life of their own—far beyond the requirements of plot. They may begin as medieval types; they emerge always as real people. To achieve his extraordinary fidelity, Chaucer often limns a conspicuous physical characteristic or mannerism, an idiosyncratic cast of mind, or—as in the finest characterizations—he adroitly blends the physical and the psychological.

But whether one prefers tellers or tales, together they display the poet's pervasive warmth and mature humaneness. Always incisively critical, occasionally capable of real indignation, Chaucer nevertheless accepts most of man's foibles without anger or even regret. Chaucer, like Dante, was deeply impressed by Boethius' doctrine of the limits of free will (he translated *The Consolations of*

Philosophy). But he restricted himself to studying the impact of determinism on external reality rather than on the soul. Chaucer's comedy, therefore, is social, not divine. What his people think about marriage, the functions and malpractices of the clergy, the virtues and follies of law and medicine, or the value of learning—such is the matter Chaucer works with to illustrate and to measure human behavior. Partly because he never finally resolves the dilemma of fate or freedom, he paradoxically couples an ironic detachment with a strong sense of social responsibility. Combined, they enable a comic sense that avoids bitterness, yet escapes sentimentality. Though one searches vainly in his work for the sublime, Chaucer does not, as Matthew Arnold complained, lack "high seriousness." A mind that accepts the wholeness of human experience must be serious, but it need not therefore be tragic. Chaucer's genius is comic: realism and satire invigorate his comedy; gentleness and tolerance mellow it. Upon finishing *The Canterbury Tales*, one's deepest regret is that its author completed but twenty-three of the projected one hundred-twenty tales. Perhaps he tired of his creation; few readers since have.

II. Questions for Study and Discussion

1. What is the theme of *The Canterbury Tales?*
2. Compare or contrast Chaucer's use of the frame device with Boccaccio's.
3. To what extent does Chaucer use imagery derived from nature? From what other sources does his imagery flow? What is *rime royal?* What other metrical and rhyming devices does Chaucer use?
4. How representative a cross-section of society does Chaucer give? Why is neither royalty nor serfdom represented?
5. Which characters are physically most striking? How, besides physical description, does Chaucer vitalize his characters?
6. Which of Chaucer's characters are stock types? Which realistic? To what extent are his characters merely exemplars of the medieval period? To what extent timeless and universal?

7. Which pilgrims engage in controversy during the journey? What does each altercation reveal about their personalities? How well does Harry Bailly function as moderator on these occasions?
8. After reading the tales in the "Marriage Group," what do you think is Chaucer's attitude toward marriage? Toward women?
9. How just is Chaucer's criticism of the Church? Would you consider him heterodox? Why? Does his view of the clergy agree with or differ from Dante's in *The Divine Comedy*?
10. Which pilgrims does Chaucer satirize? Which does he praise most highly? How does his treatment of these people indicate his own ideals about man?
11. Read sample passages of *The Canterbury Tales* in the original and in some modernized version. Which do you prefer? Why?

Note: The following questions apply to a selected few of *The Canterbury Tales*. They suggest a pattern usable for other tales as well.

"The Knight's Tale"

1. Characterize the Knight. What unexpected contradiction appears in his psychic make-up? Does it render him more or less attractive? Why?
2. To what extent does his tale grow out of his personality?
3. What literary category would this tale fall into? Where does Chaucer elsewhere in *The Canterbury Tales* treat this genre satirically?
4. Compare the portrait of Emily in the Knight's story with that of Alison in the Miller's. Which is the more convincing portrait? Why?
5. What are the chief merits and weaknesses of this story?

"The Miller's Tale"

1. How does Chaucer combine descriptive and psychological detail to characterize the Miller?
2. Does he tell his tale for any particular reason? How does this reason help to elucidate its structure?
3. What kind of tale is this? Some critics have deplored Chaucer's use of such material; they consider it smutty. How justifiable is their charge?

"The Pardoner's Tale"

1. Characterize the Pardoner.
2. Why might the Pardoner be called "the one completely lost soul among the pilgrims"? How clearly does Chaucer indicate his personal feelings toward the Pardoner?
3. After confessing what he is, why does the Pardoner attempt to fleece the pilgrims and the Host?
4. What is the literary type of this poem? Where else has Chaucer used the same type? The Pardoner's tale has been called the most brilliantly executed of all. Why?

"The Wife of Bath's Tale"

1. Characterize the Wife of Bath? Why is her tale appropriate to her?
2. What is her opinion about the relative merits of virginity and the married state? Compare her attitude with those of the Clerk and the Franklin. Which do you regard as the most balanced view? Why?
3. Is Chaucer feminist or antifeminist in this prologue and tale? Justify your answer.
4. Which among the Canterbury pilgrims would be most suitable as the Wife of Bath's sixth husband? Which would be least suitable? Why?

"The Nun's Priest's Tale"

1. No description of the Nun's Priest appears in the "General Prologue"; Harry Bailly describes him briefly at the end of the tale. How, nevertheless, does his narrative enable you to characterize him?
2. How does the tale merge boudoir and barnyard? Characterize Chaunticleer and Pertelote.
3. What is a mock-epic? How does this tale illustrate that genre? To what extent is it also an exemplum? How seriously does Chaucer intend the moral at the end of the poem? What has Chaucer tried to accomplish in this tale?
4. How serviceable is the metrical and rhyming pattern?

III. Readings in Background and Criticism

Bennett, H. S., *Chaucer and the Fifteenth Century* (Oxford University Press, 1947). One of the best volumes in the *Oxford History of English Literature*, it includes essays on Chaucer, his contemporaries, and medieval religion as well as detailed bibliographies and chronological tables.

Bowden, Muriel, *A Commentary on the General Prologue to The Canterbury Tales* (Macmillan, 1954). An exhaustive study of each of the pilgrims, presented against a broad background of political, social, and literary history.

Chute, Marchette, *Geoffrey Chaucer of England* (Dutton, 1946). A gracefully written introduction to Chaucer's life, work, and time, popular but reliable.

Coghill, Nevill, *The Poet Chaucer* (Oxford University Press, 1949). A brief but warm and intelligent appraisal of Chaucer's life and work, stressing his wit and compassion, particularly as manifest in *The Canterbury Tales.*

Coulton, G. G., *Chaucer and his England* (Dutton, rev. ed., 1930). The first half of this useful and readable work examines Chaucer's life and the environmental forces molding his work. Chapters 11-13 assemble the pilgrims and analyze the social and literary problems they represent. The second part of the book studies various social forces of the period, notably clerical objections to those Church practices that may have undermined Chaucer's orthodox Catholicism.

French, Robert D., *A Chaucer Handbook* (Crofts, 1927). A standard reference work, the handbook sketches Chaucers' life, language, and literary output. Chapter 5, "The Canterbury Tales," offers an excellent introduction to Chaucer's methods and sources in each of the tales.

Kittredge, George L., *Chaucer and His Poetry* (Harvard University Press, 1927). A brief, witty appraisal of Chaucer as a *modern* writer whose human comedy, *The Canterbury Tales,* is a dramatic representation of people and situations as vital today as they were 500 years ago.

Lawrence, William W., *Chaucer and The Canterbury Tales* (Columbia University Press, 1950). A distinguished collection of short, well-written essays about significant problems in *The Canterbury Tales:* their order and arrangement; the alleged tastelessness or immorality of the *fabliaux;* the "marriage sequence"; the over-all tone of *The Canterbury Tales.*

Lumiansky, Robert M., *Of Sondry Folk: The Dramatic Principle in The Canterbury Tales* (University of Texas Press, 1955). Lumiansky cogently argues his arguable thesis: that each of the tales exists not only for itself but also to illumine the personality of the teller. He suggests that Chaucer consciously applied this principle, employing his several techniques to achieve clearly motivated dramatic effects.

Power, Eileen, *Medieval People* (Doubleday Anchor Books, 1954). Chapter 3, "Mme. Eglentyne, Chaucer's Prioresse in Real Life," paints a vivid, amusing portrait of a nun's life in medieval England. From contemporary church records, Miss Power gives a graphic account of the confusion of psalms and simperings prevalent inside the Prioress' convent wall.

Rickert, Edith, compiler, *Chaucer's World*, edited by Clair C. Olson and Martin C. Crow (Columbia University Press, 1948). An anthology of contemporary—and rather grim—accounts of life in the 14th century. Most effectively used with Eileen Power's and G. G. Coulton's books to sketch a backdrop against which Chaucer's pilgrims lived, worked, and prayed.

Tatlock, J. S. P., *The Mind and Art of Chaucer* (Syracuse University Press, 1950). The final work of an eminent Chaucerian, its section on *The Canterbury Tales* was shortened by illness, but the book is nevertheless valuable for the opening chapter detailing the influence upon Chaucer's art of English and French social and literary traditions.

IV. Editions

Among the several available editions of *The Canterbury Tales*, the best for general use is F. N. Robinson's *Complete Works of Geoffrey Chaucer* (Cambridge edition, Houghton Mifflin). W. W. Skeat's inexpensively reprinted Oxford text (Modern Library) lacks the notes, line numbering, and section divisions of the Robinson edition, but has less bulk and more readable typography. For those desiring a more scholarly edition, there are the eight volumes edited by J. M. Manly and Edith Rickert; Volumes 3 and 4 contain the actual text of *The Centerbury Tales*.

Chaucer "readers," often used in college classes and discussion groups, serve those who wish first to sample a few tales. J. M. Manly's selection (Henry Holt), furnished with excellent introduction and notes, is good despite irritating expurgations. Even better is Charles W. Dunn's inexpensive paperback, *A Chaucer Reader* (Harcout, Brace), which contains the "General Prologue," six tales, and summaries of several others. Dunn provides a useful introductory essay and marginal glosses to help the beginning reader understand Chaucer's frequently obscure language.

Chaucerians vigorously differ about the need for "translations" or modernizations of *The Canterbury Tales.* Most hold that Chaucer's language should not long deter any reader from enjoying the poems; some, however, insist that reading the tales in modern English increases one's pleasure. Certainly, readers should first try Chaucer in his own words. If they find the going too difficult, they may fall back upon "translation" in either prose or verse. Probably the best prose translation is that by R. M. Lumiansky (Rinehart), a brisk, readable version which appends the "General Prologue" and the "Nun's Priest's Tale" in Middle English as well as in modern. Nevill Coghill's verse translation (Penguin), originally prepared for BBC presentation, is lively and less often than its competitors unfaithful to Chaucer's manner and meaning. Theodore Morrison's verse translation for *The Portable Chaucer* (Viking Press) is almost as successful a version of the original. Whether verse or prose is preferable remains a matter of personal taste, though it may be noted that verse more readily than prose captures Chaucer's grace and ease.

13

Machiavelli: THE PRINCE

I. Background of Machiavelli (1469 - 1527)

Niccolò Machiavelli's *The Prince*, a book slim enough to be read in two hours, is one of the most stimulating and controversial political treatises of all time. Moralists and patriots have variously execrated and eulogized it, dictators have learned their craft from it, scholars have hailed it as a liberating force in the evolution of modern thought. Whatever degree of political sophistication the reader may credit himself with, his first reading of *The Prince* is likely to produce the effect of ice water dashed in the face. In the four-and-a-half centuries since the book first outraged Machiavelli's contemporaries, it has gained rather than lost relevance and potency.

In genre, *The Prince* follows the tradition of the "mirror-of-princes" literature of the Middle Ages, an often tedious body of unsolicited advice to various sovereigns. In substance, it is a handbook of power politics and political psychology for the instruction of a despot. In spirit, it marks the nadir of the moral optimism of the Italian Renaissance. The impact of this work has tended to obscure its author's stature as a brilliant historian *(History of Florence)*, a first-rate comic dramatist *(Clizia* and *Mandragola)*, and a lively biographer *(Castruccio Castracane)*. More important, in certain respects, it has all but eclipsed the reputation of Machiavelli's major political treatise, the *Discourses*, and has thus perpetuated a distorted impression of his political views.

The historical key to *The Prince* is the two hundred years of political and social chaos in Italy preceding its appearance, and the simultaneous rise of powerful national monarchies in western Europe. From the end of the 13th century, when most of the Italic cities freed themselves from imperial and ecclesiastical rule, until the end of the 15th, when nearly all the cities had long since succumbed to the dominion of Milan, Naples, Venice, Florence, or the Papal State, the peninsula was an arena for internecine strife and a battleground for predatory neighbors. Torn by intracity struggles of class and faction, exhausted by interminable warfare, afflicted by repeated incursions of French, Spanish, and imperial arms, Italy lay prostrate by Machiavelli's time. Two years before he died, Spain's victory over France at Pavia (in nothern Italy near Milan) in 1525 heralded Spanish domination of the Italian peninsula. Rome was sacked in the year of his death, and the last Florentine republic fell three years later.

The end of Italian independence was imminent when Machiavelli wrote *The Prince*. It seems clear that the book was at least in part a patriot's last-ditch attempt to stave off the inevitable. If it had succeeded, Machiavelli would surely have won instant recognition as the theoretician of Italian nationhood and as one of the world's great political prophets. Because it failed, such recognition was delayed for more than three centuries and his reputation suffered unparalleled opprobrium. The remedy that Machiavelli prescribed for his country's sickness was as pernicious as the disease itself. He was doomed to be as helpless before the moral judgments of mankind as he was before the facts of contemporary history.

Despite the process of revaluation and rehabilitation that Machiavelli's reputation has been undergoing for the past century, his name still connotes craftiness and duplicity. Yet there are those who believe that Machiavelli was a thinker of singularly pure motives as well as of that bold and uncompromising originality with which he is now widely credited. It is a mistake to judge *The Prince* in reference to recent history alone, for then one can scarcely avoid connecting Machiavelli with modern proponents of totalitarianism.

Even if the reader bears in mind the peculiarities of 16th-century politics, he will still judge unfairly if he takes *The Prince* to be Machiavelli's total profession of political faith. That faith is most fully embodied in the *Discourses*, a political treatise based upon its author's observations as citizen and servant of the Florentine Republic.

The history of Florence, like that of the rest of Renaissance Italy, was characterized by turmoil and violence—by class conflict and revolution, by factional strife, by almost innumerable wars of offense and defense, by frequent and tumultuous changes of government, by political cynicism and gangsterism. During eighteen years of Machiavelli's adult life, control of the city changed hands three times—from the Medici dictatorship to a theocratic republic under the Dominican monk Savonarola (1494), then to a secular republic dominated by the great guilds (1498), and finally back to the Medici (1512). During those years Machiavelli rose from an obscure clerkship in Savonarola's government to a Secretaryship in the Foreign Office of the regime that hanged and burned the friar. As administrator and diplomat Machiavelli acquired the intimate knowledge of high-level political and military affairs which he incisively demonstrated in his treatises on those subjects. With more time, he might have become a leading figure among the men who made Florentine foreign policy. But Spanish troops restored the Medici in 1512, and Machiavelli was ousted from his job and exiled from Florence. He retired to his small farm at San Casciano, where he died, poor and frustrated, fourteen years later.

To these unhappy circumstances of unemployment and exile we owe Machiavelli's greatest writings, for he wrote no work of lasting importance until he had nothing else to do. His major political works are *The Prince*, the *Discourses*, *The Art of War*, and the *History of Florence*. It is apparent from the *Discourses*, as from the *History*, that Machiavelli was a convinced republican. Devoted to government based upon the free consent of the enfranchised, and to political liberty under a regime of law, he opposed all forms of arbitrary rule. His political ideal was a commonwealth patterned after the ancient Roman Republic. The astonishing contrast between these convictions and the doctrine set forth in *The Prince* will probably never cease to fascinate, challenge, and distress the serious student. It is unlikely that any attempt to reconcile the antagonism will satisfy everyone, if only because Machiavelli wrote *The Prince* with the confessed purpose of wooing employment from the Medici. For the whole of his mature life he had been immersed in political activity, and he found enforced idleness a spiritual death as well as an economic hardship. "I wish these Signori Medici would begin to make some use of me," he confided to a friend, "if it were only to the work of rolling a stone."

To reconcile his ideal with the doctrines presented in *The Prince*, various scholars have periodically suggested that *The Prince* is actually a masterly *jeu d'esprit*—a tongue-in-cheek exposé of tyranny masquerading as a defense. If this could be established as fact, it would provide one of the most comical denouements in the history of scholarship and establish Machiavelli as the unintentional father of one of the most successful literary hoaxes of all time.

Unfortunately, *The Prince* did not recover Machiavelli's job for him, but it did earn him the hatred of his Florentine compatriots, who considered the book a death blow to republican freedom. It may be observed in passing that the oligarchic republic which tortured and hanged Savonarola and strove by every means to extinguish the liberty of its neighbors offered little more in the way of freedom than the tyranny of the Medici. At all events, it was apparent to Machiavelli that although a republic may be the ideal form of government in theory, it is not always ideal in practice. Two hundred years of Italian history had demonstrated the incapacity of republics like Florence to maintain either popular liberty or stable government, much less to sacrifice parochial interests to the welfare of the whole nation. The central and consistent political aim of Machiavelli's works was the unification and liberation of Italy; from this point of view republicanism, however attractive in the abstract, was bankrupt. The ever-present and threatening examples of France and Spain provided the pattern for survival: national unification and independence through absolute monarchy. To this necessity Machiavelli bowed without sentimental breast-beating.

Studied in its historical context, *The Prince* is neither a personal commitment to despotism nor a theoretical exaltation of perfidy, but a practical handbook for accomplishing the salvation of Italy by the most effective means available. With a Medici ruling Florence and another (Giovanni de' Medici, Pope Leo X) at the head of the Papal State, Italy might yet be saved from foreign subjugation. *The Prince* showed how. If its rejection of traditional morality offends us, we must remember that Machiavelli did not invent political cynicism. His misfortune is that having recognized force and fraud as the techniques of successful rulers of corrupt states, he was honest enough to advocate them in his own corrupt time and place. Seldom has a great thinker followed the logic of unpleasant convictions to their conclusions with such intellectual audacity and integrity. The most brilliant analysis of *Realpolitik* ever written, set forth in a style so lucid, pithy, and concise as to remain a marvel after nearly five hundred years, *The Prince* is one of the toughest fibers in the fabric of modern thought.

II. Questions for Study and Discussion

1. What is the subject of *The Prince*? What is its apparent purpose at the outset?
2. What does Machiavelli consider the basic instrument of political power? Why?
3. What personal quality does he consider basic for success as a prince? Why?
4. Explain Machiavelli's attitude toward the use of cruelty as a political tool.
5. Explain the symbolism of the lion and the fox.
6. What is Machiavelli's attitude toward traditional morality in private life? In political life?
7. Explain what Machiavelli means when he asserts that in political affairs "the end justifies the means."
8. What does Machiavelli consider the basic criterion of political actions?
9. Do you consider his theories moral, immoral, amoral, or nonmoral? Why?

10. Explain Machiavelli's view of human nature. How is it related to his political philosophy?
11. What is his attitude toward war? Toward the duties of the prince as a military leader?
12. How does Machiavelli regard religion? Compare his concept of sin with Dante's.
13. What is his evaluation of the effects of the temporal power of the Church in Italy? Compare or contrast his view with Dante's.
14. How does Machiavelli explain the relationship of Fortune and Free Will in human affairs? Compare his view with those of Homer, Dante, and Montaigne.
15. Evaluate Machiavelli's grasp of the importance of economics in the life of the state.
16. Compare Machiavelli's views with Plato's on: (*a*) political ethics; (*b*) the political use of force and fraud; (*c*) the relationship between the state and the people; (*d*) the common people; (*e*) the role of religion in the state. Which of the two men do you consider the more moral political philosopher? Why?
17. List the qualities embodied in Machiavelli's ideal prince. Compare his ideal with Rabelais'. How would Machiavelli criticize the Rabelaisian ideal? The major characters in Shakespeare's *Hamlet* and *King Lear*?
18. How does the last chapter of *The Prince* require you to revise your initial impressions of:
    a. Machiavelli's purpose in writing the book
    b. The frame of reference of his ethics and politics
    c. His preoccupation with monarchical government
    d. His emphasis on military matters
    e. His lack of interest in popular rights and duties

    In general, does this chapter complicate your reactions to its author, and if it does, how?
19. How is Machiavelli's style related to his approach to politics?
20. To what extent is his method of reasoning inductive? To what extent deductive? If his argument rests on any prior assumptions, what are they?
21. Evaluate Machiavelli's understanding of the historical process and his use of historical examples in argumentation.

22. In what respects did Machiavelli's doctrines reflect and/or anticipate important political developments in Europe?
23. What other Renaissance authors whom you have read shared Machiavelli's approach to life in a significant degree?
24. What do you consider Machiavelli's most important contributions to political theory? To modern thought?
25. If it were proved that Machiavelli wrote *The Prince* as a sly joke, how would that knowledge affect your evaluation of the man? Of his work?
26. What influences of Machiavellianism can you detect in 20th-century world politics?

III. Readings in Background and Criticism

Allen, J. W., *A History of Political Thought in the Sixteenth Century* (Barnes & Noble, 3rd ed., 1957). Chapter 2, Part IV contains a first-rate study of Machiavelli's political theories, explaining the relationship between *The Prince* and the *Discourses* and clarifying the problem of Machiavelli's ethics.

Burd, L. Arthur, "Florence: Machiavelli," *Cambridge Modern History* (Macmillan, 1903), Vol. I, pages 190-218. A fine essay relating *The Prince* and the *Discourses* to the political background in Florence and the rest of Italy, and evaluating Machiavelli as a thinker.

Burnham, James, *The Machiavellians, Defenders of Freedom* (John Day, 1943). Part II includes a stimulating analysis of Machiavelli as a political scientist in his historical setting and argues that his political ethics were superior to Dante's.

Burns, Edward McN., "The Liberalism of Machiavelli," *Antioch Review*, VIII (Fall 1948, 321-330). A brief but challenging critique of Machiavelli's alleged liberalism, suggesting that the author of *The Prince* would have approved many of the crimes of Hitler and Mussolini.

Cassirer, Ernst, *The Myth of the State* (Doubleday Anchor Books, 1955). Chapters 2-10 of Part II survey Machiavelli's changing reputation and evaluate his importance as a thinker who broke with the medieval outlook. "With Machiavelli," Cassirer wrote, "we stand at the gateway of the modern world."

Cioffari, Vincenzo (see Boccaccio readings, page 97).

De Sanctis, Francesco, *History of Italian Literature*, 2 vols., trans. by Joan Redfern (Harcourt, Brace, 1931). A cogent essay (Volume II, Chapter 15) views Machiavelli's work as a negation of medievalism and emphasizes his affirmation of new political, religious, ethical, and methodological outlooks.

Dunning, William A., *A History of Political Theories: Ancient and Medieval* (Macmillan, 1902). Chapter 11 of this standard work is devoted to an effective exploration of Machiavelli's political ideas, stressing his break with tradition, his expansionist views, his interpretation of history, and his rationalism.

Gilbert, Felix, "Nationalism in Machiavelli's *Prince*," *Studies in the Renaissance I* (1954, 38-48). Gilbert outlines nationalistic tendencies in Italian thought from Petrarch's time to Machiavelli's, and finds the peculiarities of Machiavelli's nationalistic ideas explained on the basis of his position outside the political parties of Florence.

Hexter, J. H., "*Il principe* and *lo stato*," *Studies in the Renaissance IV* (1957, 113-135). After a detailed study of Machiavelli's use of the terms *il principe* and *lo stato*, Hexter concludes that *The Prince* is not concerned with the welfare of the body politic, but only with the technique of acquiring and retaining political power.

Sabine, George, *A History of Political Theory* (Henry Holt, rev. ed., 1950). Chapter 17 offers an excellent summary and evaluation of Machiavelli's political assumptions and position, and relates his thought to the growth of absolute monarchy in western Europe.

Symonds, John Addington, *Renaissance in Italy*, 7 vols. (Scribner, new ed., 1900). Despite a tendency to Victorian moralizing, Symonds (in Volume I, pages 243-290) presents a useful summary of Machiavelli's life and prose works, with an analysis of *The Prince* in its historical context. Chapter 16, Volume V, elucidates concisely Machiavelli's philosophy of history and politics.

Wilkins, Ernest H., *A History of Italian Literature* (Harvard University Press, 1954). Pages 208-222, Chapter 23, provide a succinct authoritative summary of Machiavelli's life and works.

IV. Translations and Editions

Inexpensive editions of *The Prince* are published in satisfactory translations by W. K. Marriott (Everyman's), Thomas G. Bergin (Crofts Classics), Burton A. Milligan (Scribner), and Luigi Ricci, revised by E. R. P. Vincent (World's Classics; Modern Library—paper and cloth-cover editions; New American Library). The World's Classics edition also contains the *Utopia* of Thomas More and *The Courtier* of Castiglione, in a volume titled *Three Renaissance Classics*. The Modern Library edition, with a lively and illuminating introduction by Max Lerner, includes a translation of the *Discourses*, and therefore will be preferred by some students of Machiavelli. The volume of *The Prince* edited by Christian Gauss (New American Library) is recommended for its low cost, attractive format, and trenchant introduction.

14

Rabelais: GARGANTUA AND PANTAGRUEL

I. Background of Rabelais (*c.* 1494 - 1553)

Francois Rabelais's *Gargantua and Pantagruel* is a literary phenomenon without parallel in western experience, a work of such mental riches, comic genius, and exuberant fancy that it all but overwhelms critical analysis. Perhaps for this reason there has not been a wholly satisfying interpretation of the book. But another weighty reason is the fact that *Gargantua and Pantagruel* is not, except in the broadest sense, a unified work. Its five books, only the first four of which are definitely from Rabelais's hand, were composed and published separately over a period of more than twenty years. Like the *Essays* of Montaigne, they reflect their author's changing experiences, interests, and attitudes as well as the unstable intellectual and political climate of Renaissance France.

Although the date of Rabelais's birth, like that of his death, is uncertain, it was close enough to 1494 for us to accept that year for its symbolic value. In 1494 the armies of France crossed the Alps into Italy, inaugurating a thirty-year contest with Spain for control of the peninsula. The effort ended ignominiously for France; Spain triumphed decisively at Pavia (near Milan) in 1525. But from the standpoint of cultural history France won an unexpected moral victory: a generation of contact with Italian art and letters inspired and helped to fashion the French Renaissance. Thus the French Renaissance and one of its greatest and most authentic voices were born at about the same time. A child in the old French world, Rabelais grew to manhood with the new; and the peak of his artistic power coincided with—indeed *was*—the high point of the Renaissance in France.

Little is known of Rabelais's life until he was almost thirty. The son of a prosperous middle-class lawyer, Rabelais was born at the family's small farm near Chinon, in the valley of the Loire. His early education was probably monastic, the kind of training he later caricatured so wonderfully in the twenty-first and twenty-second chapters of Book I of *Gargantua and Pantagruel.* Next, he served a novitiate in the Order of St. Francis, supplementing his theological studies with so enthusiastic an immersion in the classics that he nearly foundered in the first wave of antihumanist repression to sweep France.

Until the early 1520's, French humanism developed fruitfully without antagonizing the zealous guardians of Catholic orthodoxy on the theological faculty of the Sorbonne. But the publication of Erasmus' critical *Commentaries* on the Greek text of Luke in 1524, following Luther's open break with the Papacy in 1521, stung the ecclesiastical authorities into action. The Greek language was banned in France; Rabelais was deprived of his classical library and put under restraint by his superiors. This minor episode, concluded by his transfer to a more enlightened order, the Benedictine, was Rabelais's first experience with the bigotry that was to shadow his later years and bring less elusive humanists to the stake.

Abandoning monastic life in 1526, Rabelais apparently made just such a tour of the universities of France as he lampooned in the second book of *Gargantua and Pantagruel.* His considerable legal knowledge suggests that he studied law during this period. In September 1530, enrolling as a medical student at the University of Montpellier, he entered at last upon his life work. Coincidentally, the disciplines that run riot through *Gargantua and Pantagruel*—

theology, letters, law, and medicine—had now been brought together in Rabelais's own life.

From 1532 until almost the end of his life, two decades later, Rabelais was a practicing physician, achieving prominence as the foremost doctor, anatomist, and botanist of France. But he was already a writer as well. In 1532, under the pseudonym "Alcofribas Nasier," he published his first original work—*Pantagruel*—which was to become the second book of *Gargantua and Pantagruel.* Like *Gargantua,* issued under the same pseudonym two years later, *Pantagruel* is in form a burlesque of classical epic and chivalric romance. In both books the form serves as a vehicle for a many-sided satire on medievalism as well as for Rabelais's constructive social and philosophical views. Central narrative features of *Pantagruel* are a thirst theme suggested by the great drought of 1532, a tour of Paris and French universities, an adventurous journey revealing the influence of the contemporary voyages of discovery, and a fantastic war reflecting his awareness of some military and political problems of the age.

The satirical thrusts of *Pantagruel* are fairly obvious, especially the attacks on religious dogma. Like many other humanists, Rabelais was stimulated by the liberalizing intellectual currents set in motion by early Protestant propagandists. The Protestant rejection of monkery and of the authority of a worldly Church, coupled with appeals to the principles of early Christianity, was powerfully attractive to a mind already disaffected by personal experience and classical thought. In 1533 *Pantagruel* was suppressed by the censors of the Sorbonne as sacrilegious and obscene. Thereafter, Rabelais was attacked repeatedly by the theologians, escaping prosecution only through the protection of powerful friends or by judiciously timed disappearances. On this occasion he joined his patron, Cardinal Jean du Bellay, on the first of several trips to Italy.

The publication of *Gargantua* in the fall of 1534 was particularly untimely, coming at the height of a violent anti-Protestant campaign. As tinged with unorthodoxy as its predecessor, the book was suppressed immediately, and Rabelais disappeared again until the spring of 1535, when the persecutions had subsided. *Gargantua* repeats the biographical form and satirical method of *Pantagruel.*

Its main episodes involve the birth, childhood, and education of its gigantic hero; the famous Pichrocoline War; and the great discourse on humanistic education in the chapters on the Abbey of Thélème.

For most of the dozen years that intervened between the publication of *Gargantua* and Book III of the expanding *Gargantua and Pantagruel* (1546), Rabelais was busy practicing and teaching medicine. During the same period he became a secular priest (1536) —unattached to a monastic order and therefore legitimately free of the monk's robe and the vows he had previously abandoned without permission. Book III, which was issued under a royal privilege which Rabelais secured in the fall of 1545, was the first to appear under the name of "M. Francois Rabelais, Doctor of Medicine." Almost devoid of the gigantesque elements and extravagant fancy of the first two books, Book III is also less effervescent, less daring, more erudite, and more sophisticated. The changed circumstances of the author's life help explain this alteration of spirit, which was matched by a radical shift of form and content. Past fifty when he completed Book III, Rabelais was the leading physician of France, a renowned if harassed writer, and the protégé of some of the most influential figures in the land. One may therefore assume that his youthful contentiousness and flamboyance had been tempered and that his wit had matured.

Rabelais would also seem to have passed, by this time, the height of the transitory interest in Protestantism evident in Books I and II. Protestant orthodoxy had as little attraction for most humanists as Roman orthodoxy. Both threatened intellectual freedom, and John Calvin's gloomy French Protestantism was even less compatible than was Catholicism with humanistic doctrines of man's goodness and perfectibility. Rabelais was, therefore, among those who recoiled from Calvin as Erasmus had recoiled from Luther.

One cannot tell how much this change of heart may have been encouraged by a rapidly deteriorating political situation. Rabelais had previously declined the opportunity to martyrdom as often as it was offered, and there is no reason to suppose that he found it more attractive now. But whether it was mature sobriety, altered opinion, or mere caution that had dulled the satiric edge of Book

III, the work nevertheless was banned soon after publication—despite the royal privilege—and Rabelais "did a duck" again.

Book III substitutes for biographical narrative an intellectual tour-de-force comprising a set of variations on the theme of woman and marriage, embellished with lively digressions on a number of Rabelais's favorite butts—including law, philosophy, and superstition. The central discussion was a contribution to the famous "*Querelle des femmes*," a literary debate on the "woman question," which had been raging for about a century with increasing heat. Born out of a reaction against the idealized, sentimental tradition of courtly love, the *Querelle* produced a spate of feminist and antifeminist tracts in the first half of the 16th century. Critics have differed almost as sharply about Rabelais's position in the controversy as they have about his religious convictions.

Book IV, published in fragmentary form in 1548, appeared in its entirety in 1552 and was suppressed the same year, its nationalistic religious orientation at odds with a temporary relaxation of Franco-Papal hostility. Based on Lucian's *True History*, this book is both a parody of popular stories of exploration and discovery and a satire of medieval quest stories, most pointedly the legend of the Holy Grail. The only consistently political section of *Gargantua and Pantagruel*, its patriotic posture did not save Rabelais from further obloquy; it was rumored, in the autumn of 1552, that he was in prison. Book V, which appeared nine years after Rabelais's death (usually dated April, 1553), is not generally accepted as his writing, though it was apparently worked up from his notes. An extension of the fantastic travels begun in Book IV, it is markedly inferior to the first four books and often rather tedious.

Mainly because of the earthiness and ribald humor of *Gargantua and Pantagruel*, its author's reputation remained unsavory until the early 19th century, when the modern revaluation of his work began. Scholarly debate continues on Rabelais's philosophy of life; on his religious, political, and social orientation; and on his attitude toward women and marriage. But no thoughtful person today denies his stature as a serious and important Renaissance thinker and one of the few comic geniuses of all time. A joyous paean to the modern world—to mankind emerging eagerly and lustily from the shadows of the Middle Ages—*Gargantua and Pantagruel* is a great doctor's antidote to the melancholy "humours" of the human spirit.

II. Questions for Study and Discussion

1. In what respects is *Gargantua and Pantagruel* a unified work of art?
2. What are the main targets of Rabelais's humor? What is the historical significance of his choice of targets?
3. What are the main sources and techniques of Rabelais's humor?
4. In what respects is *Gargantua and Pantagruel* a satire? What satirical techniques does Rabelais use?
5. What symbolic meaning may be found in Gargantua's gigantic proportions and powers?
6. What philosophical significance may be found in Rabelais's interest in the human body and its functions?
7. How is his interest in the human body related to the intellectual and artistic tendencies of the Renaissance? In what other Renaissance authors have you found such interests?
8. What is the symbolic meaning of the thirst theme in Book II?
9. Trace and interpret Panurge's development in Books II through IV.
10. Do you consider the diminution of gigantesque elements, as the work progresses, a gain or a loss for the work as a whole? Explain why.
11. "Rabelais's humor is obscene." Attack or defend this assertion.
12. Explain Rabelais's view of human nature. His view of the source of good and evil in individual men, and of evil in the world at large. To what other author you have studied are his views closest? Explain.
13. Summarize Rabelais's educational doctrines. What is their historical and social significance?

14. Outline Rabelais's social orientation. How is it related to the style and subject-matter of his work? Compare his social views with those of Boccaccio, Chaucer, and Montaigne.
15. Define Rabelais's political orientation.
16. Describe Rabelais's concept of the ideal prince. Compare his views with Machiavelli's and Shakespeare's.
17. Explain Rabelais's views of religion and the Church. What does his portrayal of Friar John, in Book I, suggest about his attitude toward the clergy? Compare his views on these subjects with Dante's.
18. What is Rabelais's attitude toward women and marriage? Compare his views with those of Plato, Paul, Dante, Chaucer, Boccaccio, Montaigne.
19. What is Rabelais's attitude toward war? Compare it with Machiavelli's.
20. What is Rabelais's view of the role of Fortune, Fate, and Free Will in human life? Compare his view with the opinions of other Renaissance writers you have read.
21. To Rabelais, what is the good life? How can it be achieved?
22. Summarize Rabelais's philosophy of life.
23. What does Rabelais mean by "Pantagruelism"?
24. In what sense may Rabelais be characterized as a rationalist? An empiricist? A sceptic? An epicurean?
25. What stature would you accord Rabelais as a serious thinker in comparison with other great authors you have read? Explain whether, in your opinion, his humorous treatment of serious subjects weakens or enhances the impact of his writing.
26. What, besides entertainment, does Rabelais offer the modern reader?

III. Readings in Background and Criticism

Auerbach, Erich, *Mimesis* (Doubleday Anchor Books, 1957). Chapter 11 provides a close analysis of the relationship between style and substance in *Gargantua* and *Pantagruel*, illuminating the manner in which

Rabelais put medieval stylistic devices to antimedieval and anti-Christian uses.

Keller, Abraham C., "The Idea of Progress in Rabelais," *PMLA* LXVI (March 1951, 235-243). In an interesting article, Keller argues that Rabelais expressed the modern idea of progress, especially in Book III of *Gargantua and Pantagruel.*

Lewis, D. B. Wyndham, *Dr. Rabelais* (Sheed and Ward, 1957). The most recent biography, interesting if sometimes opinionated and stylistically turgid.

Mallam, Duncan, "Joyce and Rabelais," *University of Kansas City Review* XXIII (Winter 1956, 99-110). An excellent discussion of the similarities between James Joyce and Rabelais in comic spirit and style.

Putnam, Samuel, *Francois Rabelais, Man of the Renaissance* (Jonathan Cape and Harrison Smith, 1930). A fluent and absorbing biography, embodying wide scholarship and creative imagination.

———, "Introduction," *The Portable Rabelais* (Viking Press, 1946). The best brief introduction to Rabelais's life, character, reputation, work, and thought. In a controversial judgment, Putnam sees Rabelais as a pantheist and characterizes him as "unmistakably progressive" in all his attitudes.

Rascoe, Burton, *Titans of Literature* (Putnam's, 1932). A popular evaluation of Rabelais and his book, written with gusto. Rascoe sees Rabelais as anti-Christian, appreciates him as a satirist, underestimates him as a creative thinker.

Saintsbury, George, *French Literature and Its Masters*, edited by J. H. Cairns (Knopf, 1946, Chapter 2; reprinted from the *Encyclopaedia Britannica*, 11th ed., Vol. XII, 769-773). A brief summary of Rabelais's life, works, and thought. Saintsbury interprets Rabelais's religious views as generally compatible with Christian orthodoxy.

Tilley, Arthur, *Francois Rabelais* (Lippincott, 1907). Chapters 5-9 interpret *Gargantua and Pantagruel;* Chapter 10 treats its sources, characters, and art; Chapter 11 provides a thoughtful and dispassionate—if debatable—analysis of Rabelais's religious views, which Tilley regards as essentially Catholic.

———, *Literature of the French Renaissance*, 2 vols. (Cambridge University Press, 1904). Although more recent scholarship has advanced beyond some of Tilley's facts and interpretations, Chapter 10 of Volume I is still an interesting analytical survey of Rabelais's life and work.

———, *Studies in the French Renaissance* (Cambridge University Press, 1922). Chapter 9 is as illuminating for its analysis of the meaning of "Nature" in Rabelais and Montaigne as it is for the comparisons and contrasts it draws between the views of both men.

IV. Translations and Editions

Excellent translations of *Gargantua and Pantagruel* are available at low cost. The most famous and frequently reprinted version—the 17th-century masterpiece by Urquhart and Motteux (Everyman's, 2 vols.; World's Classics, 3 vols.)—is something of a travesty of Rabelais's style and quite inaccurate too, although hilarious in its own right. Contemporary translations by Jacques Le Clercq (Modern Library Giant), Benjamin Cohen (Penguin), and Samuel Putnam (Viking Portable) are improvements on the older rendering in fidelity if not in charm. Although the Putnam version is abridged (omitting all of Book 5 and several inessential portions of the other books), it is recommended because of its fine introduction and generous notes.

15

Montaigne: ESSAYS

I. Background of Montaigne (1533 - 1592)

Michel de Montaigne—like his older contemporary and compatriot Francois Rabelais—left his claim to immortality in the form of a single book. But that book, the *Essays*, is enough to secure his reputation. Written during the last two decades of Montaigne's life, the *Essays* embodies a spiritual autobiography, a testament of the author's view of life, and a critical analysis of the nature, faculties, beliefs, mores, and behavior of man. It bears the weight of this formidable burden with unfailing ease and wit. Moral philosophy can be arduous and tedious as well as instructive, but in Montaigne's hands it is always engaging.

That Montaigne was able to accomplish so genial a work in late-16th-century France is certainly remarkable. The first half of the century found France, like England, in the throes of Renaissance, Reformation, and national consolidation simultaneously. Rabelais's *Gargantua and Pantagruel* reflects the turbulence of those developments, as its author's life reflects the predicament of liberal intellectuals in the period. Yet within a decade after Rabelais's death in 1553, France plunged into convulsions that made the previous half century seem uneventful. For it was then that the accumulated tensions in the religious and political life of the nation exploded into a quarter century of civil war—the religious wars of 1562-1593.

Goaded by decades of persecution under the Catholic monarchy of the Valois, French Protestants (Huguenots) took up arms in 1562 in a determined struggle for religious freedom, a struggle exacerbated and prolonged by factional conflict for control of the throne, by an intricate complex of shifting political alliances, and by the rival interventions of Protestant England and Catholic Spain. The political results of the civil wars were the establishment of the Bourbon monarchy and a century of toleration for French Protestants. The price was a generation of bigotry, slaughter, and devastation. Yet it was during this chaotic period that Montaigne, living in comfortable retirement within earshot of the alarums of battle, penned the leisurely, reflective, and incomparably sophisticated *Essays*. Genius apart, the happy combination of endowments that went into the making of the *Essays* included: the author's birth into a most unusual family, a phenomenal education, an independent fortune, and the urbanity of a gentleman of leisure.

Born in 1533 at the ancestral Chateau of Montaigne, Michel Eyquem (who later styled himself "*seigneur de Montaigne*") was one of eight children of a wealthy Catholic father and a Jewish mother who had been converted to Protestantism. The children were raised as nominal Catholics, but one of Montaigne's brothers and two of his sisters later became Protestants. Familial tolerance in matters of faith undoubtedly cultivated the freedom from dogmatism that characterizes Montaigne's writings on religion as well as his generally independent mind.

The effortless classical scholarship that graces the *Essays* was also the product of a unique domestic atmosphere. Under the supervision of a father inspired by humanistic educational theories, Montaigne was reared with Latin as his mother tongue, Greek as his second language, and the classics as his ordinary literary fare. Not until the age of six, when he entered the College of Guienne, did he acquire French, the vernacular language in which he was to write the *Essays*. Seven years later, well schooled in humanism under such renowned masters as Marc-Antoine Muret and George Buchanan, he left Guienne to study law, probably at Toulouse. After graduation from law school he engaged in a brief but instructive—if not particularly congenial—career as counsellor in the Parlement of Bordeaux. This experience was later to figure significantly in both the theme and substance of the *Essays*.

When he was thirty-five (three years after the outbreak of civil war), Montaigne dutifully married a girl selected for him by his father. At thirty-eight, disenchanted with a legal career, unwilling to be drawn into the holocaust that was sweeping France, and under no financial compulsion to continue working, he retired to the family chateau to devote the rest of his life to reading, writing, and managing the estate that had fallen to him upon his father's death.

For the next quarter of a century, amid the crises and agonies of a nation at war with itself, Montaigne contrived a life in which occasional public service was but a spice to comfortable privacy and unhurried creative work on the *Essays*. Elected mayor of Bordeaux without his solicitation in 1581, he administered the post conscientiously for four years and then retired again. A nominal Catholic, he rendered services to both sides in the civil war without offending either, was honored by five successive kings of France, and suffered none of the disabilities that would have resulted from partisan commitment. In a country devastated by fire and pillage he remained secure in his unfortified estate, peacefully expanding and polishing his literary legacy to mankind.

In the *Essays* Montaigne created and perhaps named a new literary form. For him the informal essay—consistent with the meanning of the French term *essai*—was an attempt, an exploration, a weighing of ideas, by which he might test opinion on any subject that struck his fancy and arrive at reasoned independent conclusions. But although the form he developed has no precise equivalent among the several classical and postclassical genres to which its ancestry may be traced—the moral treatise in particular—it involves, in some respects, the application of the Socratic dialectical method (see page 40) to the reflective monologue.

Like Socrates, whom he admired above all other men, Montaigne assumed the role of intellectual gadfly to society, attempting to sting his fellows out of their complacent acceptance of traditional opinion and equally complacent violations of humanity in the name of piety. Convinced that tormented mankind needed not more fetishes to kill and die for, but saner values to live by, he subjected the whole spectrum of contemporary dogmas to searching though good-humored scrutiny. Religion, politics, war, education, folkways, domestic relations—every significant human conviction or activity invited his inspection in the *Essays*, and many seemingly insignificant ones attained new dimensions. For Montaigne was determined to reveal man as he really is, and to that end the kitchen, the bedroom, and the lavatory were perhaps more relevant than churches and chambers of state.

Although objective examination of the validity of traditional belief is rarely received with favor by guardians of the status quo, particularly in times of social upheaval, Montaigne escaped censure. If he had been as outspoken as Socrates, he would probably not have lived to finish his book. But unlike his hero, Montaigne was ill-disposed to martyrdom; his *Essays*, like his life, observed a prudence that disarmed criticism. Iconoclastic and often downright revolutionary in implication, they are carefully oblique in method, and Montaigne re-edited them frequently to mask or eliminate passages that might offend the hostile reader. Scholars have interpreted this caution variously and inconclusively. Each reader, therefore, has the opportunity to decide for himself whether Montaigne's detached approach to the issues that divided France was the product of spinelessness, opportunism, or a philosophy of such fundamental humanity that it precluded partisanship in the quarrels of his time. Certainly the *Essays*, because of their objectivity, are as devoid of overt passion as they are rich in intellectual substance. Montaigne added no fuel to the fires consuming France, but the flame of rationality that he kindled still burns wherever men struggle to be human and humane.

The *Essays* comprehends twenty years of its author's intellectual growth and change. The line of that development is unfortunately blurred by Montaigne's several revisions, but its central tendency is not difficult to discern. In general, Montaigne moved from criticism to creation—from the subversion of threadbare values and beliefs to the construction of a new design for living. The style of the *Essays*, at once lucid and complex, discursive and concentrated, deftly ironical and deadly serious, is both a source of delight and a measure of the man whose seemingly casual prose often contains more high explosive than the most passionate dramatic poetry.

Montaigne's generation was schooled by experience to uncertainty and doubt. The lusty dream of the Renaissance acclaimed by Rabelais was over; the bitter awakening—and with it the need for sober reappraisal—had come. Montaigne's *Essays* are a searching revaluation of human life and thought, based upon unsparing self-examination. But if they begin in scepticism they end in affirmation, in a new and clear-eyed vision of the human condition and the dignity of man.

II. Questions for Study and Discussion

1. To what extent does Montaigne's foreword adequately state his purpose in writing the *Essays*?
2. What recurrent themes run through the *Essays*?
3. Describe the style and intellectual method of the *Essays*, and show how they are related to the content of the work.
4. Illustrate and discuss Montaigne's use of irony as an intellectual tool.
5. What does Montaigne mean by "Nature"?
6. What sociological and philosophical views lie at the root of Montaigne's interest in primitive peoples?
7. What is Montaigne's opinion of man? What basic assumption about men underlies the *Essays*?
8. Explain Montaigne's views on the role of Chance (Fortune), Fate, and Free Will in human life. Compare and contrast his views with those of other Renaissance authors you have studied.
9. What ironical paradox is involved in Montaigne's insistence on the fallibility of human reason?
10. What does Montaigne regard as the good life? As the highest good in life? What guides does he recommend for attaining the good life? In what order of importance?

11. What is Montaigne's attitude toward the Platonic and Christian tradition of the relationship of body and soul?
12. Summarize Montaigne's attitudes toward women, love, and marriage. Compare his views with those of Dante, Boccaccio, Chaucer, and Rabelais.
13. Explain Montaigne's philosophical justification for his preoccupation with himself.
14. What philosophical significance may be found in Montaigne's frank discussions of old age, sickness, and man's physical functions and appetites?
15. Summarize Montaigne's social, political, and religious convictions.
16. Compare Montaigne's ethical principles with those of Plato, Aristotle, Dante, and Machiavelli.
17. How can you reconcile Montaigne's espousal of both conformity and nonconformity, of conservatism and liberalism?
18. What are the cardinal doctrines in Montaigne's total philosophy of life?
19. Does Montaigne's philosophy suggest any justification of his neutrality in the crises of his time? Explain.
20. Discuss the social implications of Montaigne's philosophy.
21. What were Montaigne's attitudes toward the traditional institutions, authorities, values, and mores of his epoch? Explain and illustrate.
22. In what respect was Montaigne's choice of subject matter for the *Essays* unique in literary history? Discuss the historical significance of that choice.
23. In what respects does Montaigne exemplify major tendencies in Renaissance thought? In what respects do his ideas run counter to such tendencies?
24. Summarize Montaigne's educational principles. Evaluate his achievement in the *Essays* in light of those principles.
25. What do you consider Montaigne's most important contributions to modern thought? For what characteristics or ideas do you find him least congenial?

III. Readings in Background and Criticism

Auerbach, Erich, *Mimesis* (Doubleday Anchor Books, 1957). Chapter 12 analyzes in detail the style and structure of the opening paragraphs of Book III, Chapter 2 of the *Essays* in order to illuminate Montaigne's attitude toward man and life.

Frame, Donald M., *Montaigne's Discovery of Man* (Columbia University Press, 1955). A lucid survey of the development of Montaigne's thought through stoical, skeptical, and epicurean phases, relating each to the biographical, historical, and literary background.

Green, William, "Montaigne: Sceptic or Apologist?" *Sewanee Review*, XLVI (January 1938, 70-73). Four pages of scathing denunciation of Montaigne, the wealthy landowner, as a pious apologist for the status quo. His skepticism is dismissed as an instrument for the defense of conservatism.

Keller, Abraham C., "Montaigne on the Dignity of Man," *PMLA*, LXXII (March 1957, 43-54). An excellent article which distinguishes Montaigne's grounds for believing in the worth of man from traditional grounds and relates them to his philosophical optimism.

———, "Optimism in the Essays of Montaigne," *Studies in Philology*, LIV (July 1957, 408-428). A rewarding discussion that locates the source of Montaigne's contradictory liberalism and conservatism in his philosophical optimism.

Lowndes, M. E., *Michel de Montaigne* (Cambridge University Press, 1898). Because of a dearth of sound biographies in English, this scholarly and substantial life is the best available although superseded in matters of detail by more recent scholarship.

Mauzey, Jesse V., *Montaigne's Philosophy of Human Nature* (St. Stephen's College, 1933). A useful if occasionally overfacile study of Montaigne's view of man, nature, human knowledge, and the good life.

Menut, Albert D., "Montaigne and the *Nicomachean Ethics*," *Modern Philology*, XXXI (February 1934, 225-242). A competent examination of the direct and indirect influence of Aristotle's *Ethics* on Montaigne's *Essays*.

Murry, John Middleton, *Heroes of Thought* (Julian Messner, 1938). In Chapter 4, an enthusiastic appreciation of the matter and manner of the *Essays*, Murry credits Montaigne with "the creation of the first conscious Individual man."

Owen, John, *The Skeptics of the French Renaissance* (Macmillan, 1893). Chapter 5 presents, in rather quaint style, an intelligent and well-informed estimate of Montaigne, characterizing him as a skeptic without closing the door to other interpretations.

Spencer, Theodore, "Montaigne in America," *Atlantic Monthly*, CLXXVII (March 1946, 91-97). Presented in popular and amusing form, this imaginary colloquy between Montaigne and an investigating committee of American college professors is one of the finest elucidations of Montaigne's philosophy available.

Tilley, Arthur, *Literature of the French Renaissance*, 2 vols. (Cambridge University Press, 1904). Volume II, Chapter 21, is still a useful analytical survey of Montaigne's life, character, and work, although its interpretations—like all interpretations of Montaigne—are open to question.

IV. Translations and Editions

The best modern translation of Montaigne's *Essays* is Donald M. Frame's recent and expert rendering in his rather expensive edition of *Montaigne, The Complete Works* (Oxford University Press), which is provided with notes and a brief, up-to-date introduction to the author's life and thought. Among low-priced editions, the justly popular Elizabethan translation by John Florio is wonderful, racy Florio but neither accurate nor authentic Montaigne. Blanchard Bates' revision of the old Cotton-Hazlitt version (Modern Library), and translations by Donald M. Frame (Crofts Classics) and Benjamin Cohen (Penguin) offer only selected essays. The Bates edition is the most generous in scope and format, but none of the three is suitable for serious study. The best choice, therefore, is the translation by E. J. Trechmann (Oxford University Press), which, although neither as accurate, as contemporary, nor as fluent as Frame's expensive edition, is modern and complete.

16

Shakespeare: HAMLET and KING LEAR

I. Background of Shakespeare (1564 - 1616)

Although William Shakespeare was not a political dramatist in a narrow, systematic sense, he was profoundly concerned with the social, psychological, and philosophical implications of political affairs. The historical plays preceding his great tragedies testify to his preoccupation with problems of state power and with the effects of unbridled political ambition. This interest, broadened and enriched by mature reflection, persisted in the famous tragedies including *Julius Caesar*, *Macbeth*, *Hamlet*, and *King Lear*. Throughout these plays one cannot fail to perceive Shakespeare's abiding concern with the status, character, and conduct of the Prince, and with their influence upon the life of the state.

It is not surprising that Shakespeare was thus preoccupied in an era that witnessed the brutal consolidation and turbulent career of the first national monarchies in western Europe. On the Continent, society was everywhere in unprecedented political motion. In England, a glittering facade of Elizabethan propaganda could not conceal the defects of a social structure that would collapse in revolution and civil war within a quarter century of Shakespeare's death.

The stuff of tragedy abounded in the daily life of nations, and the ambiguous but pivotal figure of the Prince bestrode the stage of history while Shakespeare took its measure for the stage of the Globe Theatre. But if Shakespeare's political interests and anxieties were those of all thoughtful people of the late Renaissance, his power of expressing them was unrivalled. Not even Machiavelli produced a more trenchant or memorable analysis of power politics than Shakespeare did in a dozen plays.

Yet it is equally, and more significantly, true that the particular life, whether of individual or of nation, was for Shakespeare a veiled exemplum of the larger life of man. The essence of his art, as of all great art, is the lifting of the veil—the revelation of truth transcending persons and events. In this respect his literal subjects, many of which now retain only historical interest, are as irrelevant as the literal subjects of Greek tragedy, and we properly acclaim him a timeless and universal artist. Scarcely any aspect of the human condition escaped Shakespeare's attention. The great tragedies, in particular, explore the largest philosophical questions confronting humanity—questions of the meaning, value, and responsibilities of life. No one doubts that the man who wrote these plays had experienced, if only imaginatively, a tremendous range of personal drama. But so little is known about his life that attempts to interpret the plays with the aid of biographical data are fruitless, and we must turn to history for help.

Shakespeare was born in 1564, in the midst of a century of social and intellectual revolution. Six years earlier, Elizabeth I had ascended the throne of an England in which feudalism was dead, modern capitalism not yet born, and absolute monarchy the arbiter of national destiny in a period transitional between the two. The Protestant Reformation, touched off by Martin Luther in 1517, had but recently triumphed in England under Elizabeth's father, Henry VIII. Abroad, the voyages of discovery that opened the western hemisphere, inaugurating a new historical epoch, were in full career. Natural science had just been revolutionized by the work of Copernicus (astronomy), Paracelsus (chemistry and medicine), Vesalius (anatomy), and Agricola (mineralogy), while Gilbert's studies in magnetism opened yet another highroad to the future. The practical arts of navigation, metallurgy, ship-building, handicrafts, and manufacture also had made decisive advances, with far-reaching effects on commerce and politics. When we add to these explosive developments the intellectual impact of the revival of classical learning effected by the Renaissance, it becomes apparent that every major aspect of medieval life had been radically transformed by the time of Shakespeare's birth.

One cannot hope to apprehend fully the mental and emotional ferment induced by these changes or to grasp the number and magnitude of the problems they created. But it is important to remember that in an incredibly brief time a host of traditional beliefs and values had been overturned—in religion, science, politics, economics, and social relations—and that the men of western Europe suddenly had to adjust to a bewildering variety of new worlds. Moreover, the optimism initially inspired by material and intellectual progress was in short order counterbalanced by anxiety at the cost in social dislocation and spiritual stress. For the decline of medieval ways of life was accompanied by the rise of new forms of injustice and oppression.

In theory, at least, the medieval world was a corporate society of caste and community with universally recognized ethical standards. The Renaissance and Reformation, bursting the confines of that world, weakened the traditional ties among men and unleashed a flood of competitive individualism. Machiavelli's *The Prince* (see Chapter 13), which elevated cynicism to the dignity of a political virtue, underscores the antagonism between Renaissance man and his community. But the old values were too deeply rooted to be excised; the public wars of princes and peoples were endlessly mirrored by the unremarked but more decisive battles raging in the lives and consciences of private men. In this respect too the characters who grapple in mortal struggle in Shakespeare's plays were drawn from life, and again, that life was but the symbol of greater struggles and larger mysteries. Certain fundamental philosophical problems are always with us—problems involving the relationship of man to the universe, to his fellows, and to himself. But since every age poses them in new contexts, men must constantly redefine and reassess them. The violent dislocations of the Renaissance and Reformation urgently demanded fresh solutions, and Shakespeare rose to the challenge. Though the topical referent of his tragedies is the hurly-burly of Elizabethan England, their inner light illuminates the timeless groping of humanity for self-realization. In anarchic individualism, ethical disorientation, and alienation from the community at large, Prince Hamlet and King Lear bear the unmistakable stigmata of the Renaissance hero. In human fallibility, suffering, and aspiration they are brothers to all men.

Because of its thematic elusiveness and the complexity of its protagonist, *Hamlet* has attracted far more critical attention than *King Lear*. Its central problem, for many critics, is the source (and consequently the significance) of Hamlet's delay in accomplishing his revenge. The major interpretive hypotheses have variously located that source in a defect of character, in revulsion from murder, in psychic disturbance, in the paralysis of will resulting from misanthropy, and in the difficulty of the task itself. A few critics deny that Hamlet procrastinates at all. Still others, despairing of a solution, adjudge *Hamlet* an artistic failure, but this opinion has neither discouraged further analysis nor diminished the play's popularity. Perhaps the most edifying approach is that which, without minimizing the importance of Hamlet's dilemma, concentrates on a study of the interplay of human agents and motives in the tragedy. Hamlet is the hero of the drama, but his fate, like that of any human being, is inseparable from the fate of those whose lives are interwoven with his own. If we cannot interpret his problem to everyone's satisfaction, we can, through study of the form and content of the play, arrive at a deepened awareness of his creator's vision of life. Such an approach requires detailed analysis of *all* the characters; of the attitudes toward life that meet in conflict; of the functions of will, reason, and chance in the total destiny; of symbolism and imagery; of the structure of the play by act and scene—and sometimes even by line.

Like some painters, Shakespeare returned often to the same subject, examining it afresh from new angles and in different lights. *King Lear*, like *Julius Caesar*, *Macbeth*, and *Hamlet*, focuses on a struggle for political power. Scrutinizing the effects of that struggle on individuals, families, and states, *King Lear* also widens Shakespeare's bold exploration of the interpenetration of ephemeral human actions and the forces of the universe itself. Although its literal meanings are less ambiguous than those of *Hamlet*, its human texture is perhaps richer, its implications more difficult to exhaust. Critics argue not only about the nature and meaning of the tragedy but even about the qualities and culpability of the central characters. And as with *Hamlet*, much investigation of *Lear* has centered on Shakespeare's imagery, the verbal devices that project and advance the tragic theme. But such analysis need not be left to scholars. Each reader's independent interpretation, whatever its depth, strengthens that act of imaginative re-creation which is the richest reward of reading. Again, the most fruitful analysis is that which comes to grips with the play as a whole rather than with the unique problems of its central figure.

One can read and understand Shakespeare's plays quite satisfactorily without technical aids other than a simple glossary to clarify occasional difficulties of vocabulary. But the reader unfamiliar with the conditions of the Elizabethan theater may be puzzled by certain peculiarities of form and dramatic method. Elizabethan plays were written without thought to publication, for repertory companies performing on three-sided stages before an audience drawn from every section of English society. Playwrights supplied no stage directions other than entrances, exits, and minimal indications of scene, a situation less trying for their producers and actors than for ours, since the men who wrote the plays were often among those who acted and staged them. A theater that made almost no use of scenery, moreover, had little need for detailed scenic instructions. Descriptive passages in the dramatic poetry and imagination in the audience sufficed to create theatrical illusion, just as they occasionally do on the modern stage. The absence of cumbersome scenic machinery permitted a flexibility of production that accounts in large measure for the kaleidoscopic movement and fantastic effects of plays like *King Lear*, which cannot be reproduced convincingly by the realistic methods of today. Finally, the heterogeneous character of an audience at once boisterous and keenly critical demanded brilliant, varied, unflagging, and yet searching entertainment. More fully than any playwright before or after him, Shakespeare provided this.

Although only about half a dozen of the hundreds of plays written and acted in England between 1560 and 1590 survive, it is known that the five-act verse drama was a firmly established form before Shakespeare took it in hand. The surviving plays, together with those written by his contemporaries, reveal beyond question that Shakespeare was unrivalled in his art. But he worked with the tested tools of the trade. Such devices as blank verse, violence of theme and action, double plots, stock characters, soliloquies and asides, repetition of motifs, alternation of comic and tragic scenes, and discontinuity and mobility of scene and action were common resources of Elizabethan dramatists. Shakespeare borrowed these as freely as he appropriated plots from a variety of sources, including Boccaccio, Chaucer, classical drama, and contemporary plays. In *Hamlet* and *King Lear* the narrative framework is provided by tales already centuries old when he adopted them, but first endowed with significant life and meaning by his genius. Shakespeare's dramatic and emotional power, his unsurpassed poetry, his psychological insight, his matchless ability to touch imaginary characters with the flame of life, his unsentimental compassion for suffering humanity—these are the original ingredients that make his plays works of high art and endear *Hamlet* and *King Lear* to the millions.

II. Questions for Study and Discussion

General questions:

1. What is the main theme of each play? What other themes are explored?
2. What are the major conflicts in each play? How are they related to the themes? What basic human conflicts do the specific conflicts in each play symbolize?

3. Explain the dramatic and thematic function of each scene and act. How does each scene advance, retard, heighten, clarify, or resolve the conflicts?
4. Where do the turning point and climax of each play occur? Justify your choices.
5. Explain the dramatic and thematic relationships between the main plot and the subplot.
6. Indicate the occurrence of parallel and contrasting scenes, incidents, characters, and speeches, and of repetition of motifs in the play. What purposes do they serve?
7. What are the functions of setting in each play? How is setting indicated? Where and to what extent does Shakespeare use setting symbolically?
8. Where and why does Shakespeare employ prose instead of poetry in the play?
9. Where and why does he use humor? What kinds of humor?
10. Where and why does Shakespeare employ dramatic irony? How large a role does irony play in each drama? Discuss the major ironies involved. Compare Shakespeare's use of irony with Sophocles'.
11. What are the functions of the soliloquies? How would each play suffer if soliloquies had not been used?
12. Identify the ritual and/or mythic aspects of each play.
13. What is the prevailing mood of each tragedy? How is it established? What is the relationship of mood to theme? Of mood to the intellectual and emotional crises of Shakespeare's age?
14. Identify the dominant images and metaphors in each play. How does the imagery reinforce and clarify the themes? How is it related to the intellectual and emotional problems of the English Renaissance and Reformation?
15. Characterize the protagonist of each play and analyze the elements of his personality that contribute to the tragedy. If he has a tragic flaw, what is it? Why does he behave as he does? Trace his development throughout the play.
16. Characterize the other main persons in the play. What is the

dramatic and thematic function of each? How does each clarify the personality, problems, and actions of the protagonist?

17. What relationship does Shakespeare establish or imply in each play among the individual, the family, the state, and the cosmos? What is the importance of that relationship to the total meaning of the play?
18. What is the nature of the tragedy developed in each play? To what extent is each major character responsible for the tragedy? To what extent is it occasioned by deliberate evil intention, by good intentions, by circumstances beyond the characters' control? What is the role of Chance in the drama? What do your answers to these questions suggest about Shakespeare's view of the relationship of Fate, Fortune, and Free Will? Compare and contrast each play with at least one Greek tragedy.
19. What seem to be Shakespeare's social, political, ethical, and religious views in each play? Where does he locate the sources of evil, and how does he suggest that man cope with evil? How does he treat the problem of idealism?
20. What positive elements does Shakespeare project out of each tragedy? For example, what is the significance of the survival of Horatio and Fortinbras in *Hamlet*, and of Kent and Edgar in *King Lear?*
21. What significance do you find in Shakespeare's use of madness as a dramatic device? How is madness related to the themes of each play?
22. How and where does Shakespeare treat the problem of illusion and reality in each play?
23. In what respects may each play be considered a critique of rationalism?
24. How does your knowledge of Machiavelli and Montaigne clarify the issues in each play?
25. Summarize the total philosophy of life projected by each play.
26. How are the problems explored in each tragedy related to Renaissance life and thought in general?
27. How does each play transcend its plot and age—that is, what universality do its themes, problems, characters, and revelations have?

Hamlet:

1. Defend or attack the view that "*Hamlet* is the tragedy of a man who cannot make up his mind" and the thesis that Hamlet procrastinates in taking his revenge. If you believe that he delays, explain why he does so.
2. How does Act I establish the main themes, motifs, conflicts, mood, and philosophical import of the play?
3. What are the functions of the Ghost?
4. What is Hamlet's attitude toward life and people? How does it affect his actions? What is the basic problem that confronts him?
5. Is Hamlet mad or only pretending madness? Defend your answer.
6. Why is Hamlet's wild appearance to Ophelia reported instead of staged (II, i)?
7. Why does Shakespeare eliminate the original threat of war from the play? Why does he introduce the subject of a rebellious populace?
8. Analyze the results of the "Mousetrap."
9. What is Hamlet's frame of mind when he returns from his experience at sea? What are the philosophical implications of the graveyard scene? Why does Hamlet agree to fence with Laertes?
10. The dying Hamlet says, "Had I but time . . . O, I could tell you—" What could he tell us?
11. Why does Fortinbras give Hamlet a soldier's funeral?
12. Explain whether Hamlet is a constructive or a destructive figure. Why do most people identify with him?
13. What does Hamlet have in common with Achilles, Don Quixote, Gulliver, Faust, Pierre Bezuhov, Ahab, Raskilnikov, Emma Bovary?
14. Compare Hamlet and Claudius. How does the personality of Claudius help to illuminate Hamlet's character and actions?
15. Why did not Shakespeare provide a positive female character in the play?
16. What would have happened to the focus and meaning of the play if Shakespeare had developed Horatio more fully?

King Lear:

1. Analyze the methods by which Shakespeare establishes characters, themes, and conflicts in Act I.
2. What is the significance of the question of Lear's retainers in the play?
3. What are the functions of the Kent-Oswald scene (II, ii)?
4. What is the significance of the storm and Lear's speeches in the storm in Act III?
5. What is the dramatic and thematic value of bringing Lear, Edgar, and the Fool together in the hovel (III, iv)?
6. Compare the mad trial in III, vi with the trials in I, i and III, vii.
7. What is the significance of the servant's revolt against Cornwall in III, vii?
8. What is the significance of Gloucester's being blinded instead of abused in some other way? How are Gloucester's blindness and Lear's madness related? Compare the two men.
9. Why is Cordelia's attitude toward Lear reported before it is staged, in IV, iii and iv?
10. In IV, i, what enlightenment does Gloucester experience besides that about Edgar?
11. Analyze Edmund's conduct at the end of the play. How consistent is it with his earlier principles? What significance do you attach to his change?
12. How is Lear's scene with the dead Cordelia saved from melodrama?
13. Compare and contrast the ending of *King Lear* with that of *Oedipus Rex* in terms of the effect of the tragic experience on the protagonist.
14. What are the functions of the Fool in the play?
15. Why are Kent and Cordelia seen only in relation to Lear?
16. What values and principles do Goneril, Regan, Cornwall, and Edmund live by? What are their weaknesses? What values and principles motivate Lear, Cordelia, Gloucester, Edgar, and Kent? What are their weaknesses?

III. Readings in Background and Criticism

Bradley, A. C., *Shakespearean Tragedy* (Meridian Books, 1955). The culmination of the 19th-century Romantic approach to Shakespeare, this classic study interprets *Hamlet* (Lectures 3 and 4) and *King Lear* (Lectures 7 and 8) primarily in terms of the psychological problems of the protagonists.

Chute, Marchette, *Shakespeare of London* (Dutton, 1949). A most enjoyable and knowledgeable introduction to Shakespeare and his time, vividly portraying the men, the life, and the theater of Elizabethan England.

Conklin, Paul S., *A History of Hamlet Criticism, 1601-1821* (Kings Crown Press, 1947). A valuable and readable survey of critical attitudes in England, France, and Germany, with discussion of the histrionic tradition and excerpts from the critics.

Fergusson, Francis, *The Idea of a Theater* (Doubleday Anchor Books, 1953). Chapter 4 of this penetrating book on the art of the drama interprets *Hamlet* in terms of its total social complex; the close relationship of Elizabethan drama, audience, and state; and the ritual quality of the play.

Granville-Barker, Harley, *Prefaces to Shakespeare, First Series:* "King Lear"; *Prefaces to Shakespeare, Third Series:* "Hamlet" (Sidgwick and Jackson, 1927, 1937). Classic analyses of the plays and the problems of production, in terms of the dramatic effect intended by the playwright.

Heilman, Robert B., *This Great Stage* (Louisiana State University, 1948). A new critic's full-scale study of *King Lear*, supporting earlier religious interpretations of the play by a detailed analysis of its imagery and structure.

Jones, Ernest, *Hamlet and Oedipus* (Doubleday Anchor Books, 1955). A fascinating if rather tortured Freudian interpretation of *Hamlet*, more valuable for its critique of earlier non-Freudian analyses than for its insistence on the centrality of the Oedipus complex in the play.

Kitto, H. D. F., *Form and Meaning in Drama* (Barnes and Noble, 1956). Chapter 9 is a rewarding venture into *Hamlet* criticism by a brilliant interpreter of Greek tragedy. Analyzes the play by analogy to the Greek pattern of religious drama and points up its similarities to Sophocles' *Oedipus Rex*.

Lewis, C. S., "Hamlet: the Prince or the Poem?" *Proceedings of the British Academy* XXVIII (1942, 139-154). A penetrating demonstration of the inadequacy of analyses centered on the character of Hamlet. Argues that the greatness of the play is its revelation of the human condition.

Mack, Maynard, "The World of Hamlet," *Shakespeare: Modern Essays in Criticism* (Oxford University Press, 1957). Perhaps the most brilliant analysis of our time, this essay (pages 237-257) interprets the play in terms of the psychological atmosphere of Shakespeare's age.

Murray, Gilbert, *The Classical Tradition in Poetry* (Harvard University Press, 1927). Chapter 8 explores the similarities between *Hamlet* and Aeschylus' *Oresteia*, and argues that Shakespeare's play is rooted in the persistent folk tradition of fertility ritual.

Spencer, Theodore, *Shakespeare and the Nature of Man* (Macmillan, 1942). One of the most fruitful and illuminating modern studies. Chapter 4 interprets *Hamlet* as a conflict between illusion and reality; Chapter 5 analyzes *King Lear* in terms of the Elizabethan world view.

Stoll, E. E., *Art and Artifice in Shakespeare* (Barnes and Noble, 1952). Arguing (in Chapter 5) that Hamlet is neither a procrastinator, a weakling, nor a mental case, Stoll attributes the structure of *Hamlet* to Shakespeare's artful manipulation of an old plot.

IV. Translations and Editions

Among the best editions of Shakespeare's plays complete in one volume are those by George Lyman Kittredge (Ginn and Company) and Hardin Craig (Scott, Foresman). Inexpensive editions of plays published separately or in varying combination are legion. Apart from differences in price and format, the most important distinguishing features are the scope and quality of introduction and annotation. Especially recommended are the individual paperback volumes of the Arden Shakespeare (D. C. Heath), the Pelican Shakespeare (Penguin), and the Kittredge edition reprints (Ginn and Company).

17

Cervantes: DON QUIXOTE

I. Background of Cervantes (1547 - 1616)

A great novel—only the Bible and Shakespeare have attracted more readers—*Don Quixote* transcends while it expresses its age. Universal in its appeal, it is nevertheless the product of Renaissance traditions and aspirations, of sixteenth-century Spain, and of Cervantes' life experiences.

Paradoxically, the Renaissance man of learning was often both an optimist and a skeptic, both an idealist and a realist. As a result of material advances and the humanist revival of classical learning, he was slowly abandoning his medieval preoccupation with the hereafter and shifting his aspirations to the here and now. For many Renaissance men of culture, concern with the here and now was the starting point for a code of conduct emphasizing the earthly, amoral, and esthetic. No longer evaluated solely in terms of right or wrong, good or bad, human action became (as it had been in the time of Homer) its own reward—"good" when appropriate, zestful, well-rounded, and successful. If man exercised his God-given will and intellect (his *virtù*), his reward was fame and glory in his own day and—if he was fortunate—thereafter. Hence, Renaissance man placed faith in intense, uninhibited, egocentric living.

But while Renaissance man bravely held that life's meaning

lay in positive achievement, he suspected that doing might not be enough, that the purpose of life might reside in something other than activity. He often questioned whether his humanism was an adequate substitute for the grand cosmic unity of design envisioned by medieval man and so consummately projected by Dante. Sometimes his loss of faith in the final intelligibility of the universe led to melancholy—to a sense of loss and void such as we find in *Hamlet*. Thus, while glorifying man's intellect and rational knowledge of the universe, Renaissance thought and literature ultimately mistrusted man's sufficiency; while advocating a world shaped by practical considerations, it admired Christian ideals; while apparently satisfied with the world as perceived by the senses, it really doubted that sense experience was all-in-all; and while often finding life good, it was intrigued by the problem of evil and how to cope with it. This ambivalence gave much Renaissance literature distinctiveness and vitality.

The typical Renaissance hero, therefore, simultaneously prides himself in his human capacities and fears that he is misusing them. Having lost a universal frame of reference, he substitutes an individual code of behavior. It is such a system, determined by his notion of an ideal, that Don Quixote attempts to impose on himself—and on the world. In his vaulting affirmation of man's potential, in his faith that he can realize his vision, in his melancholy that *what is* denies *what seems*, Don Quixote is a Renaissance hero—however fantastic.

But *Don Quixote* was created specifically in the *Spanish* Renaissance. It is difficult for us today to remember Spain's preeminence in western Europe during the first half of her Golden Age (roughly 1550-1625), when her rule extended over most of Italy and what we know today as Germany and the Netherlands, as well as over the richest part of the Americas. Champion of the Catholic faith, she spearheaded the Counter Reformation and the Inquisition. Proud, regal, passionately religious, she was also grotesque and fanatical. Economically backward, she exploited her colonies and the European countries she dominated rather than developing their resources or her own. Riddled with intrigue and incompetence, her massive empire was crumbling at its foundations. Late in the sixteenth century Spain lost important wars to the Dutch and the English, both of whom nibbled away at her New World holdings. Cervantes saw Spain's magnificence becoming as hollow as a tinsel ball. The analogies between Spain and the world of *Don Quixote* force themselves on the reader. Just how consciously Cervantes drew his historical parallels is for scholars to debate, but they are clearly implicit in his conception of the Don. From his sense, however undefined, of this national struggle between the illusion of a glorious past and the reality of a disintegrating present springs part of the book's symbolic vitality.

Much of the life of Miguel de Cervantes Saavedra seems in retrospect to have been calculated as preparation for *Don Quixote*. Believing, like his hero, that only two roads lead to wealth and fame —that of letters and that of arms—Cervantes walked both; and he emerged poor and bereft. From the time he scribbled schoolboy verses until he died at sixty-nine, he tried to win glory by writing poetry, pastoral novels, and plays; but only in his last years did he succeed with *Don Quixote* (and even then not in the fashionable critical circles he most respected). During his twenties, he served in the Spanish army. In the best Quixotic tradition he rose from a sickbed to fight in the victory over the Turks at Lepanto (1571), winning his red badge of courage—a permanently crippled left hand. Yet distinguished service and five harrowing years in Turkish captivity did not secure for him military preferment commensurate with his apparent ability. Crushed by poverty and frustrated by petty government jobs and hack writing, he never ceased aspiring to success. In the process of serving in the army, following the government from capital to capital, and acting as a government collector of provisions, he came to know all of Spain—highways and mountain paths, city slums and remote hamlets, monasteries and gypsy camps. Much of this experience, literally and symbolically, entered into his masterpiece.

Cervantes wrote *Don Quixote* (Part I, 1605; Part II, 1615) as a potboiler. In other writings he had aimed at critical recognition; from this he desired popular success and a modest income. His original plan was to burlesque chivalric ballads and romances, to ridicule the endless yarns of noble knights aiding damsels in distress by conquering giants and enchanters—stories distantly related to our "westerns." To do this he created a contemporary man who acted in his real world as if he were a knight of old. On this level Cervantes achieved clever burlesque and parody, effective low comedy and farce.

But Cervantes did not continue for long on this level. Progressively discarding his original plan, he molded *Don Quixote* into something different from a burlesque—and vastly more profound. As he lived with the Don and Sancho, they developed in depth and complexity until they symbolized his own life problem. Scholars cannot say firmly when Cervantes came to realize the scope and meaning of his creation, though they agree that he did not envision its possibilities from the first. But once he had perceived the new dimension of his creation, he peopled it with scores of vivid characters and authentic settings, the product of a mind stored with an intimate knowledge of his homeland. And when the vicissitudes and hardships of Don Quixote were filtered through Cervantes' personality, they yielded an approach to life that was courageous and manly, sweetened by rich humor and a deep faith in God.

Several aspects of the literary tradition that Cervantes inherited are also operative in his masterpiece. The romances he satirized and the chivalric ideal that motivates the Don were popular enough in Cervantes' Spain to make them worthy objects of ridicule. Both church and state had already opposed them for the pernicious falsity of their conception of life, and they had been satirized by writers before Cervantes. But, portraying life in brilliant colors and glorifying the military ideal, they still appealed to the impoverished hidalgos of a semifeudal Spain. Second, the framework of the novel is that of the picaresque tale (a story chronicling in loose, episodic fashion the adventures of a rogue on the road). Like the picaro, the Don roams the countryside, his misadventures unconnected by cause and effect. But unlike the picaresque novel, *Don Quixote* derives unity from a coherently developed theme as well as from its double focus, its centering on two main characters. Finally, Cervantes, taking his cue from the mixture of tragedy and comedy in much Renaissance literature, especially in the drama, incorporated into *Don Quixote* a blend of comic and tragic elements. After the first few chapters of unadulterated farce—that is, after Sancho becomes the Don's squire—the comic and serious are blended. From the incongruity between the real situation and the imagined one arise both the playful and the thoughtful aspects of the novel. *Don Quixote* is one of the rare masterworks that use comic elements more than occasionally or incidentally, but its comedy widens and deepens to embrace the tragic as well as the comic implications of man's plight.

In creating living characters Cervantes wrote what many scholars consider the world's first novel—and one of the best. Though the Don and Sancho begin as types, they soon ascend to reality. Like living people, they are complex and dynamic, complementing and reacting on each other. Their fascinating discussions as well as their experiences make them live, filling out the bare bones of action and symbol. Moreover, all Spain inhabits the novel's pages: illiterate peasants and educated churchmen, frivolous nobles and village sluts, staid gentlemen and amoral mountebanks, country innkeepers and humanitarian highwaymen. And where the translator is skillful enough to reproduce the effect of the Spanish, each character speaks with a distinguishable voice and idiom. Cervantes thus advanced the realistic tradition of Boccaccio, Chaucer, and Rabelais while broadening the scope of the *novella* to that of the novel.

Few great books are at once so charming and so searching, so filled with delightful incident and with meaningful situation as is *Don Quixote*. And few offer greater opportunity for individual interpretation.

II. Questions for Study and Discussion

1. What, according to Cervantes, is the theme of his novel? What does the theme or central problem develop to be?
2. How does the Renaissance preoccupation with the illusion-reality theme have relevancy to *Don Quixote*?
3. How is the Renaissance blend of optimism and melancholy manifested in *Don Quixote*?

4. How does the Renaissance concern with the problem of evil appear in *Don Quixote?*
5. What is the basic setting of Book I? Of Book II? How representative a picture of Spanish life does Cervantes seem to give?
6. Describe the structure of the novel. What are the sources of its unity?
7. The rescue of Andrew and the windmills episode set the pattern followed in most of the Don's adventures. What is that pattern? How does each adventure dramatize the theme of the novel?
8. How "good" are the Don's motives for action? How "good" is the usual outcome?
9. Assuming that Dulcinea is the heroine, how is she different from Odysseus' Penelope? From Dante's Beatrice? What does she symbolize to Don Quixote? To Cervantes? What is her significance in the romantic tradition?
10. In what ways do the Don and Sancho develop and change? Aside from his madness, what flaws in character does the Don develop? Considering the work as a whole, what do the Don, Sancho, and their relationship symbolize?
11. Where are the enchanters introduced? Who are they—here and elsewhere? What is their symbolic relationship to the illusion-reality theme?
12. What significance do you attach to Mambrino's Helmet? Does the Don know what the Helmet "really" is? Who Dulcinea "really" is?
13. How does Sancho complicate his own life, the whole question of Dulcinea, and the problem of the enchanters in Chapter 31?
14. How mad is the Don? What is the significance of his madness in light of the illusion-reality dilemma? How does your attitude toward him change?
15. How does Samson's discussion of Part I complicate the whole situation of the novel?
16. Compare the Don's distinction between bravery and rashness (Part II, Chapter 17) with that of Aristotle in the *Ethics*. Is the Don's nobility brightened or tarnished in light of his attitude?

17. Characterize the Duke and the Duchess. How do they affect the theme? How do they compare with other "enchanters"?
18. Why does Sancho renounce the governorship? How does this show evidence of his growth? What is the thematic significance of his renunciation?
19. What developing interrelations, personal as well as philosophical, can be seen between the Don and Sancho?
20. What do the Don and Sancho learn? What does Cervantes want the reader to learn?
21. Why must the Don die? Explain how his deathbed statement about his soul can form the basis for a religious interpretation of the novel.
22. What is the process by which the Don regains his sanity? How is this related to the theme?
23. What ambivalence do you find in Cervantes' attitude toward his hero?
24. Identify the types of humor employed by Cervantes. How does his humor affect the serious aspects of the book? Compare his use of humor with that of Dante, Chaucer, Rabelais, Mark Twain.
25. In what sense is Don Quixote tragic? In what sense comic? In what sense is he negative in his orientation toward life? In what sense positive?
26. Explain Cervantes' position on free will and human responsibility.
27. Describe Cervantes' social views.
28. "Cervantes maintains that idealism is folly." Defend your agreement or disagreement with this judgment.
29. For what other novels has the form and structure of *Don Quixote* provided a model?
30. Compare Cervantes' and Montaigne's views of man and the human intellect.
31. Compare and contrast Don Quixote and Hamlet as Renaissance heroes and as men.
32. Trace the development of the appearance-reality theme through Homer, Plato, the Bible, Dante, Chaucer, Machiavelli, Montaigne, Shakespeare, and Cervantes.

III. Readings in Background and Criticism

Auden, W. H., "Ironic Hero: Some Reflections on Don Quixote," *Horizon*, XX (August 1949, 86-94). Argues that Don Quixote is neither an epic, tragic, nor comic hero in the traditional senses, but an ironic portrait of a Christian saint, "innocent of all sins except that of being always interesting."

Bell, A. F. G., *Cervantes* (University of Oklahoma Press, 1947). One of the best of recent studies, a full portrait of Cervantes the man and a sound analysis of *Don Quixote* his masterpiece.

Brenan, Gerald, "Novelists-Philosophers: Cervantes," *Horizon*, XVIII (July 1948, 25-46). A short, thoughtful interpretation of *Don Quixote* as a projection of Cervantes' life, as an expression of the classic Spanish theme of disillusion, and as a mirror of Spanish life.

Cervantes Across the Centuries, edited by Angel Flores and M. J. Benardete (Dryden Press, 1947). Fifteen essays by outstanding scholars and critics on a wide variety of single topics: theme, social background, structure, style, symbolism, influence on various literatures. Particularly recommended are Casalduero's "The Composition of Don Quixote," arguing that Cervantes' novel was carefully structured, an example of Baroque "disordered order"; and Castor's "Incarnation in *Don Quixote*," with its illuminating discussion of a theme of the novel: "self-creation and expression in contexture with all possible circumstances."

Crocker, L. G., "*Hamlet, Don Quixote, La Vida Es Sueño*: The Quest for Values," *PMLA*, LXIX:1 (March 1954, 278-313). A difficult but rewarding examination of three early-17th-century classics in each of which the hero's system of values is tragically affected by his new awareness of the evil in men.

Krutch, Joseph Wood, "Miguel de Cervantes," *Five Masters* (Jonathan Cape and Harrison Smith, 1930). Contends that Cervantes' contribution to the development of the art of the novel lies in his use of "dynamism"—of complex characters who constantly change, grow, expand. This gracefully written essay also discusses the novel as a statement of the chief intellectual problem of the Renaissance—illusion-reality.

Levin, Harry, "The Example of Cervantes," *Society and Self* (English Institute Essays, Columbia University Press, 1955). Defends the importance of *Don Quixote* as the prototype for all other novels in its presentation of the antithesis of art and life.

Lowenthal, Leo, *Literature and the Image of Man* (Beacon Press, 1957). A chapter on Cervantes identifies some of the social insights implicit in *Don Quixote*, arguing that the novel's themes reflect conflicts which arose from the replacement of an old way of life by a new one.

Parker, A. A., "Fielding and the Structure of *Don Quixote*," *Bulletin of Hispanic Studies*, XXXIII:1 (January 1956, 1-16). Demonstrates convincingly that this seemingly rambling novel has a carefully delineated structure. The bases of deception and "enchantment" lead logically to the final humility of both the Don and Sancho.

Putnam, Samuel, "Introduction," *Don Quixote* (Viking Press, 1949). Perhaps the best brief presentation of the literary and historical information needed by the beginner; comprehensive in scope and up-to-date in its scholarship.

Unamuno, Miguel de, *The Life of Don Quixote and Sancho Panza* (Knopf, 1927). A chapter-by-chapter exposition of Cervantes' classic, expanding on key sentences to demonstrate the Don's madness as the highest wisdom. Frequently illuminating; frequently vague, given to rhapsodic nationalism.

Van Doren, Mark, *Don Quixote's Profession* (Columbia University Press, 1958). Three closely integrated lectures, presented with beautiful lucidity and charm, arguing that Don Quixote is more actor than madman. Also contains searching comments on characterization, style, and the illusion-reality problem.

Van Ghent, Dorothy, "On *Don Quixote*," *The English Novel: Form and Function* (Rinehart, 1953). A brilliant short essay tracing the variety and artistic individuality of *Don Quixote* to Cervantes' elaborately systematic use of extreme contrasts of character, incident, motifs, images.

IV. Translations and Editions

The debates over the relative merits of the many translations of *Don Quixote* are of small interest to the general reader. It is important, however, that he read the world's first great novel in a translation that preserves our contemporary idiom while recreating the fluid, racy, proverbial style of Cervantes. Samuel Putnam's two-volume work (Viking Press) is unsurpassed; it is terse, vigorous, direct. Since the general reader will lose little if he omits large portions of this very long novel, Putnam has skillfully abridged his version for the *Portable Cervantes* (Viking), furnishing the edition with a helpful introduction and notes. The complete translation by J. M. Cohen (Penguin) is inexpensive, trustworthy, and readable, though its British idiom makes it somewhat less suitable for an American audience than the Putnam work. A useful and lively abridged version by Walter Starkie (New American Library) was issued in 1957. The Modern Library editions, most easily available, produce the revised 18th-century version by Motteux and are not recommended by most Cervantistas.

18

Molière:

TARTUFFE
THE MISER
THE MISANTHROPE

I. Background of Molière (1622 - 1673)

Jean Baptiste Poquelin—a young man with a prosperous father (official upholsterer to the king), a sound Jesuit education, and a promising future in business—exchanged security, respectability, and the family name for a career in the risky, often opprobrious demimonde of the theater. It was a lucky trade: as "Molière," he became an accomplished actor and, eventually, a great comic playwright. Like Shakespeare, he learned both acting and writing through extended experience in the theater—first as cofounder of an amateurish and soon bankrupt Paris acting company; then, for a dozen years, as manager, star, and occasional writer for a successful road troupe; and, finally, as managing director, leading comedian, and foremost playwright of the premier company of 17th-century France (a group that eventually provided the nucleus for the Comédie Française). Out of his practical theatrical training grew Molière's mastery of comic techniques. Because of his long intimacy with farce, the dominant comic form in the French theater, he knew its deficiencies quite as well as he realized its potentialities. From farce, Molière fashioned a new type of comedy, and he refined and polished his creation until it became the adequate vehicle of his genius.

Though the Elizabethan playwrights had set a glorious example and their Spanish contemporaries (particularly de Vega and Calderón) a distinguished one, French drama was imitative and unformed. Beset by religious and political wars throughout the 15th and 16th centuries, France was too poor and unsettled to develop and support a flourishing theater. Classical tragedies were revived in colleges (where Molière may have been introduced to the theater); farces and buffoonish skits delighted popular audiences at fairs and in town squares; Italian *commedia dell'arte* troupes touring the country were enormously popular with all classes; lavish spectacles staged at court diverted the aristocracy. But drama in France, officially condemned by the Church and therefore disapproved of by most of respectable society, did not come of age until Cardinal Richelieu and Louis XIV (the "Grand Monarch" and "Sun King") gave it their active encouragement and financial support. Then, with astonishing rapidity, France developed three of her greatest dramatists—Corneille, Racine, and Molière.

The theaters in which Molière performed and for which he wrote his best plays were crude and makeshift. The few permanent theaters in Paris, adapted from indoor tennis courts, were long, rectangular rooms with proscenium-framed stages at one end. The upper classes sat in balconies (and even on the stage itself), while the lower classes stood in the pit. Lighting—from candlelit footlights and chandeliers—was dim; scenic effects were simple, formal, and unvaried. Elaborately machined and costumed extravaganzas (operas, ballet-comedies, masques) were often commissioned for private castles, but the professional theaters could afford no scenic luxuries. The predominant theatrical fare—farces patterned on the *commedia dell'arte* style of improvisation—featured stereotyped characters in stock situations, low intrigue, and slapdash buffoonery.

Molière's provincial touring—his repertory included some French classical tragedies, several Spanish plays of intrigue and derring-do, and many Italian farces—taught him what audiences liked.

Particularly, it familiarized him with the standard comic ingredients: deception and disguise, misrepresentation and misunderstanding, discovery and reversal, coincidence and hoax. When he introduced his second company to Paris in 1658, he soon impressed the king and won his patronage.

The Paris to which Molière returned was dominated by an aristocracy for whom manners constituted a fine art, wit a profession. Supremely confident of the ultimate sanity and reasonableness of the universe, Parisian aristocracy thought its society, which exalted rationality, almost perfect. French literature, catering to the tastes of this civilized elite, was preoccupied with social man; its reiterated plea was for social harmony, for obeisance to the norm. Authority was its keynote; good sense and good taste were its verities. Respected writers championed reason over passion, moderation over excess, conformity over eccentricity. Molière, dedicating his talents to pleasing this mannered society—both in the professional playhouse and at private court "entertainments"—transformed the theater into an elegant salon. Starting from broadest farce (and not renouncing it) he developed a subtle, versatile art, urbane and sophisticated—the comedy of manners, or social comedy.

The source of social comedy resides in the disparity between the imperatives of social harmony and the impulses of individual eccentricity. Critically and aloofly surveying man in society, the social satirist sketches him with wit and dispenses justice through ridicule. Shrewdly observant of manners (of speech and of dress as well as of behavior) and respectful of prevailing social codes, he caricatures without rancor, criticizes without censoriousness. Minimizing plot, social comedy focuses on character and situation. It exposes eccentrics to circumstances that highlight their social aberrations and absurd incongruities. Cold and impersonal, it exhibits people as they are, ignoring how they got that way and what will become of them. Because plot need provide only occasions for social intercourse, a social comedy can, like *The Misanthrope*, be little more than extended conversations.

In the best of his satirical social comedies—some of which border on farce, all of which employ its techniques—Molière spotlighted many social phenomena typical of his times: the cultural affectations of women *(The Learned Ladies)*, masculine tyranny over women *(The School for Husbands* and *The School for Wives)*, religious hypocrisy *(Tartuffe)*, medical quackery *(The Physician in Spite of Himself)*, unreasonable reasonableness *(The Misanthrope)*, social climbing *(The Would-Be Gentleman)*, abusive parental authority *(The Miser)*. In these plays Molière ignores the political and economic bases of life: accepting the structure of society as valid and permanent, he castigates only individual excesses. Remarkably similar in comic method and moral philosophy, these "thoughtful comedies" are object lessons of how perverted natural instincts may become social hazards to the individual, the family, or the wider community. Thus Molière amused many people, not least of all the king; but because his attacks often infuriated many others, he was frequently personally maligned and sometimes officially censored.

The three comedies recommended here epitomize the range, comic genius, and moral orientation of Molière. *Tartuffe*—written and privately shown in 1664 but, because of Church objections, not produced publicly until revised in 1669—was the most popular play of the century. The Church—triumphant after a century of religious wars, but still sensitive to criticism, direct or implied—viewed *Tartuffe* as an attack on religion itself rather than on religious hypocrisy and abuse. Sociologically or psychologically, *Tartuffe* seems to be a triple study: of the influence of a false religious concept on group thought and behavior, of the possible consequences of a warped ideal on a middle-class family, and of the relationship between religious hypocrisy and the drive for power and sexual gratification. Church opposition to this play was so intense that Molière was denied Christian burial. To this day readers and viewers debate the play's exact meaning.

The Miser (1668), composed after censorship difficulties with *Tartuffe* and financial failure with *The Misanthrope* had apparently convinced Molière that controversial subjects and philosophical comedies reap more pains than profits, depends on absurd situation rather than on the play of ideas. Since it is packed with hilarious visual action, *The Miser* can be appreciated fully only in production. Yet even in print its comic virtues show through, although fitfully.

The Misanthrope (1666) is widely acclaimed as Molière's masterpiece. Less broad, more complex and subtle than his other comedies, it has the least action and the most inconclusive denouement. Molière's irony barbs not simply the eccentricity or *malade* of one man, but also the hypocrisies of all social intercourse. Alceste wages a triple campaign: against the prevailing social mores in general, against the particular vagaries of justice, and for the surrender of Célimène to his way of life. Perhaps because the reader can readily identify with Alceste's misanthropy, his reactions to the hero's unreasonable insistence on probity involve more than laughter. After audiences in his own day found the plot vapid and the situations painful, Molière never again wrote such a sober, slowly paced play.

A writer for the theater rather than for the study, Molière is as skillful in suggesting stage business as in fashioning a living line. Without penetrating deeply, he created a glittering panorama of a tinsel society, filling his canvas with psychologically realistic portraits of types of the age as well as of all humanity. At once fanciful, charming, witty, and cynical, Molière etched faithfully the fragile and fastidious Paris of the Sun King.

II. Questions for Study and Discussion

General questions

1. What is the theme of each play?
2. What foibles of society and of human nature are satirized in each play? Are they traits of 17th-century French society or of man in general?
3. What fundamental incongruity forms the comic basis of each play?
4. What is the importance of the physical setting in each play? To what extent does each depend on scenery and costumes for its effectiveness?
5. Describe the pattern of conflicts in each play. Does each new incident advance the plot, broaden and sharpen the characteriza-

tion, deepen the theme, or accomplish more than one of these things? How?

6. What human traits does Molière ridicule in each character? To what extent does the central character transcend the type he exemplifies to become an individual creation?
7. How important is plot in each Molière play? To what extent do the characters control and direct the plot? To what extent are they manipulated?
8. What comic techniques or devices does Molière employ to define or develop character and to give point to a scene?
9. What symbols (of action, setting, costume, or language) does Molière use to enforce the central idea of each play?
10. How does Molière establish a point of view for each play—that is, who provides the norm against which the eccentric can be measured? What are the social principles Molière apparently respects?
11. Summarize Molière's views on marriage, religion, social conformity. Where does he stand on issues such as illusion versus reality, individual responsibility and free will, progress, man's relationship to God? Does his thought add up to a world-view? Explain.
12. Compare and contrast Chaucer, Swift, Cervantes, Voltaire, Twain, Molière as social satirists.

Tartuffe

1. In *Tartuffe* is Molière attacking piety in general or a particular brand of religious hypocrisy?
2. Why are Orgon and Madame Perneille so easily duped by Tartuffe when everyone else sees him for what he is?
3. What seems to be Molière's view on love and marriage?
4. How credible is the denouement? Why does Molière conclude with a glowing tribute to a reasonable and just prince?

The Miser

1. Identify the technical devices of farce that Molière employs in *The Miser*.
2. To what extent is *The Miser* a social comedy? To what extent a farce? Explain.

3. In what ways does Molière use love and the objects of love to achieve comic effects?

The Misanthrope

1. In *The Misanthrope* why do you sympathize with Alceste as well as laugh at his excesses?
2. Since probıty is generally considered a moral virtue, why is Alceste's honesty comic?
3. How comic is this play? What are the sources of its comic effect? What tragic overtones can be heard?
4. Which social standards does Molière ridicule and which does he support in this play? How critical is he of the accepted norms?
5. How satisfactory is the ending? How adequately is the conflict resolved?

III. Readings in Background and Criticism

Auerbach, Erich, *Mimesis* (Doubleday Anchor Books, 1957). A short chapter, "The *Faux Devôt,*" contains an illuminating analysis of Molière as a psychological realist.

Chapman, Percy, *The Spirit of Molière* (Princeton University Press, 1941). Traces the evolution of Molière's art from farce to witty comedies of manners, arguing that his central clown-figure grew more human and his torturing situations more real as he developed.

Macgowan, Kenneth, and Melnitz, William, *The Living Stage* (Prentice-Hall, 1955). Chapter 7, "France in and out of the Renaissance," sketches the history of the theater in 17th-century France and assesses Molière's contributions.

Matthews, Brander, *Molière* (Scribner's, 1910). A standard but somewhat stodgy study of the dramatist's life, times, and art.

Moore, W. G., *Molière,* A Critical Study (Oxford University Press, 1949). A useful but uneven book, viewing Molière as a theatrical artisan rather than as a critical thinker. Best in examining Molière's art—his debt to the farcical tradition and his conception of the comic.

Palmer, John, *Molière* (Brewer and Warren, 1930). An objective and solid account of his life and times; unusually good in analyzing Molière's age. Credits Molière with introducing three qualities into French drama: realism, critical detachment, and the corrective comic spirit.

Turnell, Martin, *The Classical Moment* (New Directions, 1948). Perceptive, illuminating study of Corneille, Molière, and Racine against the backdrop of 17th-century France. Sees the key to Molière in his application of the critical spirit to a self-satisfied aristocratic society, most confident of its stability just as it was verging toward decline.

Walley, Harold, *The Book of the Play* (Scribner's, 1950). An essay on "Social Comedy (pages 217-222) describes and characterizes, acutely yet briefly, social comedy as a dramatic type and *The Misanthrope* as the epitome of the type.

Wood, John, *Molière: Five Plays* (Penguin, 1953). In a sprightly introduction to his new translations, Wood is especially helpful in describing Molière's achievement as a social critic.

IV. Translations and Editions

There is, unhappily, no wholly suitable text for the study of the Molière comedies here recommended. Very few distinguished translations, especially of his verse plays, have been made, and the best are not available in a one-volume edition. Older versions, which generally lack ease, grace, and wit (all indispensable ingredients), include those by Baker and Miller (Everyman's, 2 volumes), Lady Gregory (Kiltartan *Molière*), Curtis Hidden Page (Putnam's), Henri van Laun, Charles Heron Wall (Bohn's Select Library), and an anonymous translator in the old Modern Library editions.

A scant few excellent translations have been made recently, however. Richard Wilbur's superb adaptation, in verse, of *The Misanthrope* (Harcourt, Brace) captures much of the polish and brilliance of the original. John Wood has admirably translated five prose comedies (for Penguin), but of the plays recommended here only *The Miser* is included. A satisfactory verse translation of *Tartuffe* has not yet been made. A recent (1957) collection, *Eight Plays by Molière* (Modern Library), presents Morris Bishop's adequate though undistinguished new translations.

19

Milton: PARADISE LOST

I. Background of Milton (1608 - 1674)

In the life and work of John Milton, art and politics are inseparable. Milton's world was the troubled and bloody world of post-Armada England, his lifetime an era of social and religious conflict culminating in revolution and civil war. Until the last years of his life Milton was a spirited partisan in these struggles. His political pamphlets and treatises exceed his poetry in volume, and an overwhelming proportion of the verse is political as well, either overtly or in motivation and implication.

The defeat of the Spanish Armada in 1588 signalled the end of English national unity centered in the Tudor monarchy. With the elimination of the threat of Spanish aggression and Counter Reformation, long-restrained centrifugal forces in English political and religious life erupted violently. The two pivotal conflicts in Milton's time were simultaneous and interrelated struggles for control of Church and State. Culminating in the civil wars of 1642 to 1649, these struggles pitted the middle and lower classes against the Stuart monarchy and its allies among the secular and ecclesiastical nobility. Military victory went to the popular armies under Oliver Cromwell; Charles I was beheaded in 1649. But instead of ushering in the dawn of liberty, the victory was perverted into Cromwell's military dictatorship, followed within a decade by restoration of the monarchy and the Established Church. Thus the bright hopes of English republicans and religious liberals, so nearly realized after tremendous sacrifice, were ruthlessly extinguished.

An ardent champion of the revolution, Milton served it tirelessly as propagandist and public official through two decades of political tension, war, and reconstruction. In addition to composing a series of memorable tracts and exhortations in defense of civil and religious liberties, he served for eleven years (1649 - 1660) as Secretary in Foreign Tongues to the Council of State under the Cromwells. His last pamphlets were lonely, rear-guard actions to avert restoration of the monarchy, an event which resulted in his being expelled from office and forced into hiding by the government of Charles II in 1660.

Several years earlier, Milton had begun work on *Paradise Lost.* Now he concentrated all his energies on the poem. In part an attempt to rationalize on an artistic level the loss of the republican paradise that was to have emerged from the civil wars, *Paradise Lost* was as deeply rooted in political experience as Milton's explicitly political prose works. Although its immediate inspiration was partly topical, its epic form reached backward to the roots of literary history and its vision probed beyond time and place to the roots of the human condition.

In the 17th century, epic poetry modeled after Homer and Vergil was the ideal of serious poets. John Dryden had characterized epic as "the greatest work the soul of man is capable to perform," and a host of assenting poets labored to emulate the ancients. In this effort patriotism spurred ambition. English and French poets were determined to produce vernacular epics superior to Ariosto's *Orlando Furioso,* and so to glorify their own nations and languages. John Milton was especially well equipped to reach this goal. Possessed of superb poetic and intellectual powers, he also commanded the languages, literature, and thought of classical antiquity, of the Judaeo-Christian tradition, and of the Renaissance. Moreover, he had been deeply involved in the social upheavals of his time, emerging from the crucible, as *Paradise Lost* reveals, with all his fervor, compassion, and integrity unimpaired. Great poetry, Milton believed, is the work of great men, and he was himself a most convincing exemplar of his theory.

Selection of a suitably elevated subject for an epic masterwork had troubled Milton for nearly three decades. His final choice was made from a list of nearly one hundred tentative subjects. In the flush of optimism generated by Puritan victories in the civil wars, he had inclined toward an Arthurian epic glorifying England after the patriotic fashion of Vergil. But the failure of his political hopes had made mockery of such a theme. In addition, the chivalric vein was fairly well exhausted. Italian poets had satirized and burlesqued it; Edmund Spenser, in the allegory of *The Faerie Queene*, had pushed it about as far as one reasonably could along pseudohistorical lines; Cervantes had virtually ridiculed it out of countenance. But if chivalric epic had reached the end of the road, classical epic was still adaptable to new content. Dante had foreshadowed the way in *The Divine Comedy*, and Milton finally elected to follow his monumental precursor in the heroic treatment of a Christian subject.

Decisive factors in his decision included the ethical, spiritual, and emotional superiority of Christian doctrine to chivalric themes as well as the cosmic range of the Christian idea in comparison to the parochial perspective of English nationalism. Furthermore, England was long accustomed to the formulation of social philosophy in religious terms, a situation perfectly suited to Milton's view of poetry as a secular ministry. Finally, the story of the Fall of Man provided an ideal vehicle for exploration of the philosophical problems that challenged Milton after the collapse of the revolutionary regime. Why, he pondered, does man suffer in this life? How can the fact of suffering be reconciled with belief in divine love? To what extent is man responsible for his fate? What hope is there for the human race? These are some of the questions that Milton proposed to answer when, at the age of fifty-two, and totally blind, he went into enforced retirement and resumed work on *Paradise Lost*. His answers form the heart of the greatest narrative poem in our language.

Although its verse form is adapted from Elizabethan blank verse, *Paradise Lost* is patterned after the *Iliad* and the *Aeneid* and is copiously elaborated with classical and biblical lore. This enrichment of its texture with learned allusion and figurative device usually requires annotation for the modern reader. But since frequent reference to footnotes removes the difficulty at the expense of the poetry, many readers will prefer an initial reading that surrenders to the poetry and the story, leaving minor uncertainties to subsequent clarification.

Paradise Lost demands to be read aloud. Its style, conforming to its subject, is elevated, sonorous, and heroic—poetry in the grand manner, of Renaissance opulence and authentic epic power. Such difficulties as it presents in the form of long sentences, bookish vocabulary, and occasional syntactical complexity yield readily to attentive reading. Milton was as great a lyrical as an epic poet, and the work is figured with passages of utmost simplicity and sweetness. Eve's confession of devotion to Adam (IV, 641-656), for example, is surely one of the gentlest and most beautiful love poems ever written. Yet Milton's genius was so prodigal that this poem often passes almost unheard in the larger music of its setting. Only a poet of surpassing gifts could have afforded such a gesture.

Like Dante, Milton succeeded in encompassing within a simple narrative framework the all-embracing Christian view of life, which organizes the universe into an interrelated and uniformly meaningful system. But the precise religious implications of *Paradise Lost* are still debated. The son of a Puritan father, Milton championed the popular Presbyterian cause before and during the first years of the civil wars. When, after their early victories, the Presbyterians proved as intolerant as their predecessors of the Established Church, he shifted allegiance to the liberal Independents. Finally, when the Independents also compromised his hopes, he withdrew from institutional religion altogether. Yet *Paradise Lost* and its sequel, *Paradise Regained*, testify that the poet remained deeply religious to the last, whatever the heterodoxy of his final beliefs.

Despite the importance of theology in his poetry, Milton, like Dante, was primarily concerned with the earthly life of man. For all its cosmic sweep, *Paradise Lost* centers ultimately on the relationship of the prototypical couple—Adam and Eve. It would be unwise to interpret that relationship too literally in the light of Milton's marital experiences, but the biographical data are certainly illuminating. Of his three marriages, the first was so unhappy that we cannot doubt its importance in the genesis of his famous tracts on divorce; while the last, late in life, was apparently a matter of convenience. Only the second, movingly memorialized in a sonnet antedating *Paradise Lost*, was a fully satisfying union of love. The living portrait of Adam and Eve in *Paradise Lost* bears the lineaments of Milton's memories and yearnings as well as the objective features of his philosophy.

Like any genuine work of art, *Paradise Lost* is a symbolic response to the artist's experience of life. In studying it, therefore, the reader should also remember that its author was a political rebel chastened but unbowed by defeat. As a document, the work is a synthesis of formidable erudition in many fields, infused with the spirit of Renaissance humanism, and shaped by Milton's religious philosophy. As a poetic drama it owes its life to the fire of the poet's personality. Perhaps the most inspiring aspect of *Paradise Lost* is the fact that Milton's Adam, like Sophocles' Oedipus and Goethe's Faust, triumphs in defeat.

II. Questions for Study and Discussion

1. What are the themes of *Paradise Lost?*
2. What similarities do you find between *Paradise Lost* and classical epic? Greek tragedy? Shakespearean tragedy?
3. Compare Milton's epic manner with Dante's. Account for the differences in terms of subject and purpose.
4. Explain Milton's concept of the origin of the universe. What force or principle does Satan represent? What is his function in the Divine plan?
5. What qualities distinguish the Son of God from God the Father? How does this distinction relate to Old and New Testament concepts of deity?

6. What does Milton regard as the Son's greatest virtue? Is this a typical Christian attitude? How is this virtue related to the themes of *Paradise Lost?*
7. Compare Satan and the Son of God, taking note of ironic parallels.
8. What motives does Milton assign to God's creation of man? To His giving men and angels Free Will? How acceptable are these motives to you?
9. Explain Milton's view of the basic relationship between man and God. Is it nearer the Old or the New Testament concept? How?
10. How does Milton explain Free Will? Compare his doctrine with Dante's. How does Milton attempt to resolve the apparent contradiction between God's foreknowledge and man's Free Will? How satisfying is his explanation?
11. Explain Milton's doctrine of salvation. What powers or aids did God give man to enable him to qualify for salvation? Which of these does Milton consider decisive? Compare his view with Dante's. What are its implications for the forms of Christian worship?
12. Explain Milton's ethical theory of the soul. Where have you encountered similar ideas in your study of great books? How does Milton explain the fact that man falls into error despite the possession of "Right Reason"?
13. What does Milton regard as the ultimate defect of human character? Where have you encountered this idea before? How is this defect related to the themes of *Paradise Lost?*
14. How do the motives that lead Satan, Eve, and Adam to fall differ? What do these motives have in common?
15. Characterize Satan, Adam, and Eve. Which is the most impressive character? Why?
16. What does Milton's portrait of Eve reveal about his opinion of women? What other elements in the poem project this attitude?
17. Explain Milton's view of the essential differences between men and women. Of the proper consequent relationship between husband and wife. Of conjugal love. Compare his attitude to-

ward women, marriage, and sex with the views of other authors whose books you have read. Is Milton's the traditional attitude?

18. What literal moral projects from the consequences of Eve's sin? From Adam's decision to share her fate? What larger ethical concepts do these elements of the story symbolize?
19. What is Milton's general opinion of human nature? Compare his view with those of Homer, Vergil, Dante, Machiavelli, Montaigne, Shakespeare.
20. How are Milton's political preoccupations and experiences reflected in the themes, characters, and events of *Paradise Lost?* What inferences can you make about his political views? How does he explain man's loss of political liberty?
21. What is Milton's attitude toward the Church? Compare it with Dante's.
22. How does Milton's view of the significance of the Fall of Man change in the course of the epic? Of man's acquisition of the knowledge of good and evil? How do these attitudes compare with the point of view of *Genesis?* What contradiction may be found between Milton's attitude toward pride and disobedience and his final view of their results?
23. Several critics have argued that Satan is the hero of *Paradise Lost*. Evaluate this contention.
24. In what sense is *Paradise Lost* a justification of the ways of God to man? In what sense a justification of the ways of man?
25. Summarize the philosophy of life expressed by Milton.
26. Apart from its poetry, what values may *Paradise Lost* have for the modern reader—even for the reader who accepts neither Milton's religious convictions nor his philosophy of life?

III. Readings in Background and Criticism

Bowra, C. M., *From Virgil to Milton* (Macmillan, 1945). Chapter 5 provides a clear and sensible discussion of Milton as "the last great practitioner of literary epic," and of the central characters, actions, and meanings of *Paradise Lost*.

Bush, Douglas, *English Literature in the Earlier Seventeenth Century* (Oxford University Press, 1945). Chapter 12 contains an excellent survey of Milton's life, works, religious thought, and prosody. Other chapters provide valuable background material on the political, religious, and scientific thought of the period.

———, *Paradise Lost in Our Time* (Cornell University Press, 1945). A fine discussion of modern criticism of *Paradise Lost* as well as of the meaning and some of the central problems of the poem. Here, as elsewhere, Bush characterizes Milton as a Christian humanist.

Hanford, James H., *A Milton Handbook* (Appleton-Century-Crofts, 4th ed., 1946). The best compendium and summary analysis of the life, works, art, and influence of John Milton. Chapter 4 deals with *Paradise Lost*, Chapter 6 with Milton's prosody.

Lewis, C. S., *A Preface to Paradise Lost* (Oxford University Press, 1942). A brilliant and entertaining, if highly controversial analysis of the doctrine, characters, action, and structure of the poem; colored by Lewis' Anglo-Catholic orientation.

Samuel, Irene, *Plato and Milton* (Cornell University Press, 1947). An attempt to explain the poetic and ethical theories underlying *Paradise Lost*, *Paradise Regained*, and *Samson Agonistes*, on the basis of Milton's study of Plato and the Platonists.

Stein, Arnold, *Answerable Style; Essays on Paradise Lost* (University of Minnesota Press, 1953). Stimulating studies by a new critic who re-examines some central problems of the poem in the light of a close analysis of imagery, metaphor, structure, and dramatic situation.

Summers, Joseph H., "Milton and the Cult of Conformity," *Yale Review* (Summer 1957, 511-527). A good short essay on Milton as a nonconformist, illustrating his differences from all sectarians who would claim him today, outlining his attitude toward poetry, and suggesting his value for our time.

Thorpe, James, ed., *Milton Criticism, Selections From Four Centuries* (Rinehart, 1950). A handy but limited anthology of critical essays and comments from 1674 to our time, including important articles by T. S. Eliot, J. H. Hanford, C. S. Lewis, E. E. Stoll, and E. M. W. Tillyard.

Tillyard, E. M. W., "Milton," *Bibliographical Series of Supplements to British Book News*, No. 26 (Longmans, Green, 1952). An excellent analytical digest of the life and works, with emphasis on *Paradise Lost*.

Waldock, A. J. A., *Paradise Lost and Its Critics* (Cambridge University, 1947). Waldock's jousts with other interpreters of *Paradise Lost* provide a bibliographic introduction to modern criticism. His own view of the poem centers on an alleged tension between what Milton wants us to believe and what he makes us feel.

Willey, Basil, *The Seventeenth Century Background* (Chatto and Windus, 1949). In pages 219-263, Willey attempts to account for the appearance of *Paradise Lost* in a period increasingly uncongenial to the traditional imagery of poetry and religion. A brilliant portion of a brilliant book.

IV. Translations and Editions

William Vaughn Moody's one-volume collection of *Milton's Complete Poetical Works* (Houghton Mifflin), a standard edition, provides a good introduction and copious annotation. Among numerous low-priced Milton anthologies that include *Paradise Lost*, Maynard Mack's *Milton* (English Masterpieces, Vol. IV, Prentice-Hall) is similarly distinguished by excellence of introduction and notes, but its presentation of *Paradise Lost* is somewhat abridged. Only one of three recent paperbacks reproduces all the poems as well as selections from the prose works (Modern Library); it has a good introduction by Cleanth Brooks, but no notes. Another edition (Rinehart) offers useful notes and an interesting introduction by Northrop Frye. The third (Viking Portable) presents a splendid introduction by Douglas Bush, scanty notes, and the least taxing print of the three. The best inexpensive edition of *Paradise Lost* itself, prefaced by a fine scholarly essay and excellently annotated, is that by Merritt Y. Hughes (Odyssey).

20

Swift:

GULLIVER'S TRAVELS

I. Background of Swift (1667 - 1745)

Milton's *Paradise Lost* was published in 1667, the year of Jonathan Swift's birth. No sooner had archangel Michael led Man out of Eden than philosophers like John Locke and mathematicians like René Descartes endeavored to effect his return. Their angle of vision was hardly congruent with Milton's: seeing God's ways differently, they proposed a simple, practical thesis. Because reason and observation (rather than revelation) prove that God, man, and nature exist in absolute harmony, man need only observe the universe to discover its perfect design, exercise his reason to comprehend its divine origin. From the Stuart Restoration (1660) through the Hanoverian accession (1714)—and well beyond—this bright vision engendered a spirit of optimism, tolerance, and compromise. By the time Swift entered public life, the new Adam had been restored, if not to Paradise, at least to "a place of rest and refreshment." There, as Swift's friend, Alexander Pope, noted,

> Hope springs eternal in the human breast:
> Man never is, but always to be blest.

In such neat couplets the Age of Enlightenment and Reason packaged its faith.

Perhaps more than any of his contemporaries Swift was aware that the 18th-century Eden was imperfect. Reason and natural law guided him, too, but never led him to share Pope's benign view that "Whatever is, is right." For twenty-five years before writing *Gulliver's Travels* Swift had mocked the gullible for accepting appearance as reality. Unwilling to inhabit a fool's paradise, he chaffed and taunted those who did. Sometimes genially, more often angrily, he ridiculed man in the hope that he might prevent him from becoming ridiculous. In *Gulliver's Travels* Swift loosed the indignation of a lifetime. Shortly before its publication in 1726 he wrote to Pope: "The chief end I propose to myself in all my labors is to vex the world rather than divert it . . . I have ever hated all nations, professions, and communities . . . But principally I hate and detest that animal called man, although I heartily love John, Peter, Thomas. . . ."

A lifelong ferment of hatred and love, disgust and pity leavened *Gulliver's Travels*. Swift was fifty-nine when he wrote it—the same age at which Milton completed *Paradise Lost*. Like Milton, though less successfully, he was a man of affairs as well as of letters. Though spurred by fame, Swift attained neither the place nor the power he sought. As a young Anglican priest he served—reluctantly and unheralded—in Ireland, where he had been born (of English parents) and educated. Not until Queen Anne ascended the throne did Swift, already in his middle thirties, gain recognition among English politicians as a powerful ally and a savage foe. For almost fifteen years thereafter, first as a Whig, later as a Tory champion, Swift tilted peerlessly in the lists of political journalism. Although his victims were chiefly politicians, he occasionally ranged afield to satirize literary pedants, pseudoscientific quacks, and religious sectarians. The idea of progress in science or government upset him; "enthusiasm" (synonymous in the 18th century with "fanaticism") in literature or religion appalled him. Tory and Anglican, Swift abhorred all who threatened the reasonable, natural order. With wit, invective, and irony he goaded them into angry but futile retaliation.

By his own choice, Swift published anonymously (or pseudonymously), remained unsalaried, and held no official post. As immediate reward he demanded only the absolute respect and complete confidence of Harley and Bolingbroke, the leaders he served. As ultimate reward he aspired to a bishopric. During the four years the Tories held power, Swift exulted: he shared "political breakfasts" at court and helped map strategy; he condescended to nobility; and he enjoyed membership in the Scriblerus Club with England's keenest literary Tories. But his hopes for a career in England were doomed even before the Tories fell in 1714. Swift's fierce independence and inordinate pride irritated church as well as state officials. Although Deists, Papists, and Dissenters were his chief clerical targets, he derided Anglicans as well when their practice belied their faith. Because neither Queen Anne nor the Established Church admired outspoken criticism among those seeking preferment, Swift's reward was rebuke—"banishment" to the deanery of St. Patrick's, Dublin.

Among the Irish, whom he claimed to detest, Swift lived his remaining years, wrote his finest work, and, strangely, became a national hero. Ireland had long anguished beneath English economic exploitation and social oppression. Masked by a pseudonym—though most people knew his hand—Swift fiercely defended the rights of Irishmen against English tyranny. In the *Drapier's Letters* (1724-5), a succession of indignant and impassioned essays, he fought—and defeated—an English proposal to mint new Irish coinage at Ireland's expense; in the brilliant and mordant *A Modest Proposal* (1729) he ironically suggested that Ireland avoid starvation by raising its children for the English dinner table. Swift may have derived incidental satisfaction from his blows at old Whig enemies in England; the Irish—Papists and Protestants alike—ignored the minor motives and set Dublin's streets ablaze with bonfires honoring Dean Swift.

With *Gulliver's Travels*, published a year after the *Drapier's Letters*, Swift kindled a blaze of his own. "I have got materials toward a treatise," he wrote to Pope, "proving the falsity of the definition *animal rational*, and to show it would only be *rationis capax* (capable of reason). Upon this great foundation of misanthropy . . . the whole building of my *Travels* is erected; and I never will have peace of mind, till all honest men are of my opinion." Projected a dozen years earlier at the Scriblerus Club as a timely parody of travel literature, *Gulliver's Travels* became a timeless satiric novel savagely indicting irrationality.

Supremely average, Gulliver tries, with diminishing success, to guide his adventurous but innocent soul through four journeys to unknown lands in uncharted Pacific seas. Thoroughly convinced that "whatever is"—in England—"is right," Gulliver epitomizes at the outset of his travels man's prideful confidence in faith, patriotism, and reason. But the ceaseless spectacle of man's spiritual and moral degeneracy, ranging from pettiness to bestiality, disenchants even Gulliver. At first Gulliver fails, obtusely, to see obvious points of identity between his own kind and the "foreigners" he ridicules. In time, however, as he rehearses the horrors of war and poverty, the vicious intrigue of politics and business, the folly of educators, doctors, and scientists, Gulliver acknowledges that he is, after all, a Yahoo—the degraded, loathsome animal "man." Expelled from what he has come to consider Eden—the humane, rational world of horses —Gulliver finds refuge and solace in a stable.

If Swift seems a misanthrope because Gulliver is so absolutely misanthropic, then the *Travels* corrodes and crumbles human mettle. What, however, if Gulliver is not Swift? What if Gulliver is but the dramatic and ironic embodiment of man's inability to distinguish illusion from reality, reason from unreason? If Swift wants us to know that man, however brutish, has the potential of humaneness, then the reader must not accept Gulliver's conclusion as Swift's message. If man is *rationis capax*, not *animal rational*, Swift's satire, though pungent and penetrating, arraigns only "the animal called man"; it spares John, Peter, and Thomas.

Swift's ambivalence and irony induce ambiguity but not confusion. *Gulliver's Travels* is meaningful on each of its several and readable levels: as a social and moral satire, a political allegory, a utopian novel, a fictional narrative of travel, and even a child's fantasy or adventure story. And yet, like its author, *Gulliver's Travels* is considerably more than the sum of its parts. Contradiction textures Swift's life and work. In his life, he wanted recognition but masked his identity; he avoided marriage but indulged in the chaste adoration of two women; he dedicated himself to reason but died a madman. Similarly in his works, Swift diverts as he vexes, affects the comic as he implies the tragic, writes simply but means complexly. Whether his vision of man finally emerges as good, evil, or good-and-evil; whether Gulliver is Swift or just himself—these are questions scholars debate: the reader must determine for himself. Whatever his decision, the reader who discovered *Gulliver's Travels* in his childhood does well to rediscover it in his maturity. Losing the enjoyment of innocence he gains insight, for no satirist has more imaginatively tried man's complacency, tortured his sensibilities, or goaded his understanding.

II. Questions for Study and Discussion

1. What is the theme of the book?
2. To what extent does the structure of *Gulliver's Travels* help develop the theme? Could the four books effectively be arranged in any other order? Why?
3. Why did Swift put his ideas and philosophy in a form so fanciful and imaginative? What is the effect of the form on the content?
4. How does Swift create verisimilitude even though his settings and characters are obviously unrealistic?
5. Discuss Swift's satirical methods and techniques. What method does he use most effectively? What things does he satirize most successfully? Least successfully?
6. How would you characterize Swift's diction? His sentence style? To what extent would you term his style modern?
7. Characterize Gulliver. Are you sympathetic toward him or antagonistic? Why? To what extent does he possess qualities you expect in the hero of a novel? To what extent does Gulliver gain insight in the course of his travels?
8. What characteristics of man does Swift emphasize by putting

Gulliver in a country peopled by very small men? By giants? By horses?

9. In general, what does Swift satirize in *Gulliver's Travels?* Specifically, what characteristics of man and of his social, religious, and political institutions does Swift expose?
10. To what extent does Swift expose man's follies simply to provoke laughter? To what extent does he intend to stimulate re-examination and reform?
11. Describe Swift's position on each of the following: ritual, religion, immortality, education, pride, women, war, science, education, sex, politics, the human body and its functions.
12. To what extent does Swift intend his reader to accept man as a Yahoo?
13. To what extent does Swift idealize the Houyhnhnms? Does Swift share Gulliver's admiration for them? Do you? Why?
14. To what extent do you identify Gulliver with Swift? Would you label Swift a misanthrope from his attitudes towards man and society? Why? Would other labels seem more appropriate? Which and why?
15. How much of Swift's satire is still pertinent today? To what extent is he concerned with universal qualities in man, to what extent with conditions more or less exclusive to his own day?
16. To what extent is satiric literature limited? How does it compare with tragedy as an expression of human experience?
17. To what extent are Brobdingnag and Houyhnhnm Land utopian societies?
18. How do you account for Swift's inordinate preoccupation with filth?
19. How does the tone change from Books I and II to Books III and IV? Why does it change?
20. How do you account for *Gulliver's Travels*' long popularity as a children's classic?
21. Compare Swift's objects of satire and his artistic methods with those of Chaucer, Rabelais, Cervantes, Voltaire, and Mark Twain.
22. What is the significance of Swift's thought for us today? If you

have read George Orwell's *Animal Farm* and Aldous Huxley's *Brave New World,* evaluate Swift's influence upon these contemporary satirists.

III. Readings in Background and Criticism

Bullitt, John M., *Jonathan Swift and the Anatomy of Satire* (Harvard University Press, 1953). A close, scholarly account of Swift's techniques of satire. Bullitt insists that Swift's satiric devices are not imposed on his material but evolve out of his awareness of the conflict between illusion and reality.

Case, Arthur E., *Four Essays on Gulliver's Travels* (Princeton University Press, 1945). An excellent study of the various problems of text, geography, chronology, political references, and the like. The fourth essay deals meaningfully with the significance of *Gulliver's Travels:* Books 1 and 3 are topical satire on the evils of bad government; Books 2 and 4 are expositions of good government. In all, Case concludes, the novel is the work of a social and moral reformer, not of a misanthrope.

Ehrenpreis, Irvin, "Swift and Satire," *College English* (March 1953, 309-312). Ehrenpreis suggests that Swift uses invective, irony, and the mask of ingenuousness to seduce the reader into identifying with Gulliver. Once the identity is complete the reader will be doubly shocked when finally he dissociates from Gulliver.

Monk, Samuel, "The Pride of Lemuel Gulliver," *Sewanee Review* (Winter 1955, 48-71). Argues that Gulliver is *not* Swift, who was too honest to accept the optimism of the Enlightenment. Gulliver, a creature of pride, is the supreme example of the folly that brings man to tragic consequences.

Murry, John Middleton, *Jonathan Swift: A Critical Biography* (Noonday, 1955). An important critical and biographical study, temperate in judgment, clear in presentation. Chapters 21-22 discuss significant problems in *Gulliver's Travels.* Murry states that as Swift's "reasonableness" about sex thwarted his deepest impulses, so at length does Gulliver's rejection of his wife as a Yahoo frustrate the ultimate integrity of the novel.

Orwell, George, *Shooting an Elephant* (Harcourt, Brace, 1950). A latter-day disciple of Swiftian irony (see Orwell's *Animal Farm*), Orwell examines *Gulliver's Travels* in the essay "Politics versus Literature." Orwell designates Swift as a "Tory anarchist," opposed to both totalitarianism and to the common people. Nevertheless, Orwell admires the novel for its artistry and for its exposure of a part of experience man often refuses to acknowledge.

Price, Martin, *Swift's Rhetorical Art* (Yale University Press, 1953). A careful analysis of diction, syntax, and symbolism in Swift's writing. Chapter 5, "The Symbolic Works," contains a good account of the dramatization of symbolic patterns in *Gulliver's Travels:* of greatness and baseness, rationality and bestiality, order and disorder.

Quintana, Ricardo, *The Mind and Art of Jonathan Swift* (Oxford University Press, rev. ed., 1954). The best biography. Quintana estimates Swift's mind and art as they project the rational and antirational elements of his time. Swift's genius lay in his artistry, not in his originality. Book V (pages 289-330) contains historical and critical material valuable in interpreting *Gulliver's Travels.*

Roberts, Donald R., "A Freudian View of Jonathan Swift," *Literature and Psychology* (February 1956, 8-17). Contains a useful summary of Freudian theories about Swift. Roberts maintains that Swift knew his symptoms and tried to sublimate—by disengaging himself from normal instincts. Thus he laughed at man rather than loved him, satirized him rather than sentimentalized him.

Van Doren, Carl, *Swift* (Viking Press, 1930). A readable and popular life, but one to be used with caution. Van Doren selects only data supporting his thesis that Swift became a misanthrope because his ambitions for power were frustrated.

IV. Editions

The standard edition is that by Herbert Davis (Basil Blackwell) with a brief and valuable introduction by Harold Williams. The beginner will find useful also Arthur Case's edition (Ronald), which contains supplementary notes and a distinguished critical essay. Among the innumerable inexpensive editions (Rinehart, Signet Classic, World Classics, Modern Library, and the like), the best choice is the *Viking Portable Swift* (Viking Press), edited by Carl Van Doren. In addition to the complete text of *Gulliver's Travels,* this volume includes selections from Swift's other work: poems, letters, journals, and miscellaneous satires.

21

Voltaire:
CANDIDE

I. Background of Voltaire (1694 - 1778)

Till the French Revolution exploded in 1789, the sovereign reigned absolute over 18th-century France: Louis XIV had consolidated for the monarchy the powers that Richelieu had seized from the nobility. Even a great nobleman counted politically only to the extent that he could get power delegated to him. But if his feudal position had been undermined, he still retained an abundance of feudal privileges. He paid no direct taxes—very few of any kind, in fact. He could compel his peasants to labor without pay on his land. He could extort a multitude of feudal dues and tolls from them. And for these privileges he had no balancing duties to perform—neither to protect, to intercede, nor to administer.

Since the ruling ecclesiastics were generally men of noble birth, they exercised the same privileges, plus those belonging to their Estate—levying tithes, especially. Thus, the cost of government was borne, as de Toqueville observes, not by the people best able to pay but by those least able to escape paying. The manifold splendors of Versailles could hardly have gratified the peasant who, to keep the fountains flowing, had to surrender more than eighty percent of his income in taxes, tithes, and feudal dues.

Yet affairs were even worse in other continental countries,

the clergy and nobility more grasping, the feudal exactions more crippling. While characteristically the French nobility were absentee landlords and the dignitaries of the church preferred gathering tithes for themselves to gathering souls for Christ, still there were noblemen faithful to their tradition and priests devoted to their calling. Why, then, did France explode in 1789 and not Russia—where conditions were significantly worse?

Part of the explanation, of course, is that France had suffered a catastrophic series of wars, that Louis XV and Louis XVI were dedicated to political stupidity, that their mistresses cost a ruinous amount of money, that the plurality of tax exemptions deprived the government of revenue and hurtled it toward bankruptcy, that the emergent middle class could not maneuver freely in the anachronistic French state. But also, in France as in no other country, the philosophers, political economists, men of letters, even geologists and physicists, were energetically sapping the foundations of absolutism and blueprinting (though diversely) a new structure for society. Under the leadership of Diderot they wrought the great *Encyclopédie* (1751-1772), the manifesto, in twenty-eight volumes, of the Age of Reason.

While they masked their purpose, only purblind readers could fail to discern it. If one of the *philosophes* analyzed the English constitutional system or traced the progress of science, readers appreciated that he was criticizing unlimited monarchy or religious obscurantism. Thus, in the name of Nature, Reason, and Humanity, *philosophes* like Montesquieu, Diderot, D'Alembert, Rousseau, and Voltaire attacked most of the varieties of social privilege, economic error, political immorality, and clerical abuse.

Voltaire was the presiding intelligence of the Age of Reason. For sixty years, from the Regency (1715 - 1723) almost to the Revolution, he vitalized the thought of the 18th century: historians, in fact, often call the period "The Age of Voltaire." Convinced that every sort of evil from unfair taxation and corrupt administration to bigotry, fanaticism, war, and slavery was spawned by the failure of intelligence, and that wickedness and stupidity were ugly synonyms, he strove all his life to make reason prevail. The hundred volumes of Voltaire—political essays, philosophical treatises, scientific popularizations, historical surveys, as well as poems, plays, and tales—bear witness how prodigiously he labored.

His contemporaries esteemed him as an amalgam of Vergil and Corneille, Newton and Locke. Our generation sets his value distinctly lower. Even in France, readers today shun the poems and dramas, at most skim the *Philosophical Dictionary* and perhaps the *Letters on the English.* But they prize the short philosophical romances—*Micromegas, Zadig,* and, above all, *Candide.*

Voltaire was 64 when he wrote *Candide.* His fame had made him nearly untouchable by the authorities—nearly, he thought, but not quite: he had in 1755 taken the precaution of buying *Les Délices,* just inside the Swiss border, and in 1758 *Ferney,* within easy running distance of it. It was in flight from persecuting authority that he had spent three of the most important and productive periods in his life. From 1726 to 1729, an exile in England, he studied current fashions in English thought and observed the operation of English constitutional government. From 1734 to 1739, he lived and worked with Mme. du Châtelet, for whom his attachment was equally intellectual and amorous. And from 1750 to 1753, he resided at the Prussian court, having yielded to Frederick the Great's insistence that he come to Potsdam as friend and philosopher. During all these years he never ceased hurling books and pamphlets against the forces of absolutism, especially against the Church which had allied with it. Through reason, he believed, he would ultimately "*écraser l'infâme,*" "crush the infamous thing"—the unreason which had entrenched itself in a thousand places but most strongly in religious orthodoxy.

The "sufficient cause" of *Candide* was the Lisbon earthquake of 1755. If it was a divine visitation, as some pious men maintained, then certainly God had calculated diabolically; for the disaster occurred at 9:40 A.M. on November 1—All Saint's Day—when most people in Lisbon were on their knees in one or another of the city's many churches. At 9:45 Lisbon was in ruins; fifteen thousand men, women, and children were dead and as many dying. Fire, flood, and disease completed the work attributed to God.

Voltaire was appalled at the disaster, outraged by the justifications. The facile explanation of the religious, that Lisbon had been destroyed, like Sodom and Gomorrah, because of the manifold sins of its inhabitants, he countered with a sneer. Was Paris notably a more moral city than Lisbon? But the Optimist vindication of God's ways, a far subtler and more philosophically respectable defense, could not be dismissed quite so casually.

Though Optimism can boast a distinguished pedigree, its effective source was Gottfried Wilhelm Leibnitz (1646 - 1716), a man of great and diverse abilities. God, Leibnitz asserted, is all-wise, all-good, all-powerful. Being all-wise, God knew what kind of world was best for man; being all-powerful, God could have created any world he chose; being all-good, God must have chosen the best world possible. Voltaire found this argument repugnant; for if ours were the best of all possible worlds, it was plainly nonsensical to strive for a better. Optimism, he wrote, is a cruel philosophy under a consoling name.

Alexander Pope, whom Voltaire had known during his enforced stay in England and whom he continued to admire (with reservations), had translated Optimism into superlatively witty and consistently shallow couplets. The most famous lines of the *Essay on Man* (1733 - 1734) summarize its thesis:

> All Nature is but Art, unknown to thee;
> All Chance, Direction, which thou canst not see;
> All Discord, Harmony not understood;
> All partial Evil, universal Good:
> And spite of Pride, in erring Reason's spite,
> One truth is clear, Whatever Is, Is Right.

Voltaire's first published reaction to the Lisbon earthquake and the several theological explanations that came tumbling after it was a poem, "On the Lisbon Disaster" (1756). A pointed rejoinder to Pope, it is charged with indignation rather than wit, perhaps because Voltaire had once been an apostle of Pope's creed, even imitating the *Essay on Man.* Do men say partial evil yields universal good? Voltaire asks. The tragic circle of destruction which the universe traces gives them the lie. To say all is well—that is folly and illusion. To say one day all will be well—that is at least plausible, that remains our fragile hope.

Candide, written two years later, attempts no formal, reasoned argument. Voltaire does not refute Leibnitz—he mocks his doctrine. Nevertheless, after being leveled by Voltaire's versatile satire, Optimism no longer remained a credo to which a discreet man might confess. Voltaire arranges, condenses, and personifies the long unhappy record of man's stupidity. In process of revising the *Essay on Manners* (1753 - 1756), which delineated man's tentative emergence from savagery to civilization, Voltaire rarely needed to search for instances with which to furnish *Candide*. Though logically inadmissible, the particular concrete situations he reduced from history add up to a denial at once comprehensive and incisive of the theory of the benign universe.

Despite the brevity of *Candide*, Voltaire found ample room for launching a variety of other attacks. Despising the false sentiment, precious language, and impossible adventures of the shapeless romantic novels of the 17th century (still popular in his day even after a century of duplicated plots), he allows their staple calamities and reversals, wrenching separations and absurd reunions, to occur in *Candide*—but with farcical frequency. Always ready to pay off personal enemies, he lampoons a dozen of the legion: a Dutch publisher, French Jesuits, German courtiers, a mathematical philosopher, a sentimental advocate of primitivism. Only the last personage, Jean Jacques Rousseau (who had courted derision not only by insisting on the idyllic situation of primitive man but also by repudiating Voltaire's persistent "doubt"), has any significance for us today. Yet, remarkably, the satire remains fresh and vivid.

Candide is an ironic anthology of man's disjointed, frequently monstrous behavior. Does Voltaire tell us how we can reform our ways? He says: "Behave reasonably." Yes, but again, how? "Adopt Candide's solution: cultivate your garden." Readers, however, have interpreted that counsel very differently. The three principal interpretations might be called the pessimistic, the opportunistic, and the melioristic.

The first holds that *Candide* ends on a sustained note of pessimism, that Martin has won the dialectical contention with Pangloss, that "we must cultivate our garden" means we must divorce ourselves from the world in which everything seems designed for the unhappiness of mankind. This seems to discount Voltaire's career as a champion of social progress, his ceaseless guerilla warfare with *l'infâme*, his total immersion in the world—his "hundred volumes," in fact. But reformers enjoy no immunity from fits of depression, and Voltaire wrote *Candide* during one of his low periods. Mme. du Châtelet had died (bearing another man's child), he had broken with Frederick, the Seven Years' War raged (Prussia and England combined against Austria, France, Russia, Sweden, and Saxony), the *Encyclopédie* had been suppressed, the Church had become more militant in its persecutions. Overcome by the blackness which may descend on the brightest spirits, Voltaire believed—briefly, it may be—that distance from the bad, stupid world was an enchanting prospect. So, at least, the text, if not the commentators, seems to say.

The second theory insists that Voltaire has created Martin as a foil to Pangloss, that Voltaire permits neither to act as his spokesman, that he himself is neither optimist nor pessimist but meliorist. In his correspondence with Diderot and other Encyclopedists, he had with progressive frequency iterated the counsel "tend your garden." He had not been cryptic. It was the essential counsel that he offered to all men: do the work within your capacity, whether crushing the infamy or growing vegetables—but work. After their debilitating experiences, Candide and his crew would live more happily and productively as vegetable growers than as infamy crushers. But not Diderot or Voltaire.

The third view is that Candide advises an enlightened opportunism. Voltaire suggests we discard the larger hypothesis about the putative workings of the universe and abandon fruitless metaphysical discussion about whether God intends well or ill. Instead, we ought to do the good nearest at hand. Thus Voltaire himself dealt with no abstractions but came vigorously to the aid of men and women who suffered persecution. Thus he defended the English Admiral Byng who had been sentenced to death for permitting himself to be defeated by a superior fleet. Thus he established a colony of weavers and watchmakers at *Ferney*, building a small utopian city.

Ambiguity shadows only the conclusion of *Candide*; the tactics and the objectives of the satire are luminous. Dazzling, rather; for sometimes the rapidity with which one facet after another of human folly and vice is held to the light, the flashing kaleidoscopic narrative, the corruscating wit generate an unreasonable effect: Voltaire's pyrotechnics may impel us to say "Yes" to propositions we regularly deny. Still that does not lessen our delight in *Candide*. And until all men are truly reasonable it will continue to delight the large number who suppose they are. That is likely to be a great while.

II. Questions for Study and Discussion

1. What is the theme of *Candide?* Discuss the subtitle.
2. What is the predominating tone of *Candide?* Is Voltaire less or more angry than Swift? Discuss.
3. What has Voltaire gained by the rapidity and compression of his narrative? What has he lost? If a realistic novelist (Flaubert, Tolstoy) were to treat of Candide's adventures, how would his novel affect readers?
4. *Candide* might be used as a textbook in satiric method. Point out examples of overstatement, understatement, logical absurdity, sudden contrast, irony.
5. What is Voltaire's most pervasive satiric tactic? How effective is it after fifty or so pages?
6. Point out some farcical situations that seem to have been imitated from the romantic novels of adventure so popular in Voltaire's time.
7. How is the form of *Candide* related to its content?
8. What institutions does Voltaire attack? What are the grounds of his attack? Would it be less extensive today?
9. What things other than institutions does he attack? On what grounds?
10. How fair is Voltaire to his philosophical (or other) opponents? Discuss, for example, his attack on Rousseau's primitivism in the chapter, "The Savages Named Oreillons."

11. What vices does Voltaire chiefly abominate?
12. The names in *Candide* are often significant. Cunégonde, for example, is the name of a saint "who was canonized," George R. Havens comments, "for having . . . successfully proved her chastity by walking unharmed over red-hot ploughshares." Additionally, in French the name has indecent connotations. What do you make of the names of Pangloss, Candide, Martin, Cacambo, Pococurante? (An unabridged dictionary will help in the deciphering.)
13. What makes Candide an appealing character? Do you "identify" with him? If so, how and why?
14. Discuss Voltaire's technique of characterization. How individual or how typical are his central characters?
15. Voltaire exaggerates the extent and evil of some aspects of existence. Why? Does this in part vitiate his satire?
16. The existence of prostitutes and the prevalence of syphilis indicate that the world is not yet perfect. But why does Voltaire introduce syphilis and prostitution so often?
17. As Dr. Pangloss is a disciple of Leibnitz, so Candide is a disciple of Pangloss. What danger does Voltaire reveal in discipleship? What is the relation between discipleship to a great idea and the very institutions that Voltaire attacks?
18. What is Voltaire's attitude toward women? Compare his view with Vergil's, Dante's, Cervantes', Shakespeare's, Milton's.
19. Characterize the universe in which Candide lives. What does it suggest about Voltaire's world view?
20. Discuss the pessimistic, the opportunistic, and the melioristic interpretations of Candide's final counsel. Which view do you hold? Why? Which character is Voltaire's spokesman, from your point of view?
21. Summarize Voltaire's social views.
22. What do Voltaire's religious convictions seem to be?
23. What does Voltaire consider the human condition to be? Compare his views with those of Lucretius and Montaigne.
24. Which great books that you have read give support to Voltaire's position? Which run counter to it?
25. What significance has *Candide* for the contemporary reader?

III. Readings in Background and Criticism

Auerbach, Erich, *Mimesis* (Doubleday Anchor Books, 1957). The first half of Chapter 16 is an acute analysis of Voltaire's style. Basing his comments on a passage from *Candide*, the critic illuminates Voltaire's "method of presenting reality."

Bottiglia, William F., "Candide's Garden," *PMLA*, LXVI (Sept. 1951, 718-733). An interesting scholarly investigation of the intent and bearing of Candide's final response to Pangloss. The author argues for the meliorist interpretation.

Havens, George R., "Introduction," *Candide* (Henry Holt, 1934). A superlative study of the background, composition, and satire in *Candide*—the best and fullest treatment in English.

Hazard, Paul, *European Thought in the Eighteenth Century* (Yale University Press, 1954). A valuable intellectual history of Europe in Voltaire's century. Chapter 3 of Part III, "Nature and Goodness: Optimism," is especially relevant to *Candide.*

Martin, Everett Dean, *Liberty* (Norton, 1930). Chapter 5 estimates Voltaire's place in the continuing war against illiberalism.

Morley, John, *Voltaire* (Macmillan, 1903). Really an extended essay. Though the Victorian prose and prejudices sometimes exasperate, Morley's is a classic study, still important in understanding Voltaire.

Redman, Ben Ray, "Editor's Introduction," *The Portable Voltaire* (Viking Press, 1949). A long, very readable essay on Voltaire—his life, philosophy, writings. Occasionally the author settles doubtful matters too positively, but he is generally sound and always stimulating.

Sainte-Beuve, Charles Augustin, *Portraits of the Eighteenth Century* (Putnam's, 1905). An intimate portrait, drawn in part from Voltaire's letters; unsympathetic but not unfair.

Strachey, Lytton, *Books and Characters* (Harcourt, Brace, 1922). Three essays on Voltaire catch something of his special quality. Strachey admires Voltaire's strengths but does not on that account excuse his failings.

Tocqueville, Alexis de, *The Old Regime and the French Revolution* (Doubleday Anchor Books, 1955). The nearly definitive study—learned, sane, balanced. Important for understanding Voltaire's background.

Van Doren, Mark, "*Candide,*" *Invitation to Learning* (Columbia University Press, 1940). A symposium—disappointing because the stature of the participants augured something much better, but useful because they make some perceptive incidental comments.

IV. Translations and Editions

Voltaire translates well: the sharp images, the lucid sentences, the energetic movement of the prose—these make him easier to translate into English than almost any other writer included in this volume. The anonymous translation in Crofts Classics, Richard Aldington's (Viking Portable), and John Butt's (Penguin) are all first-rate—and all inexpensive. Cautionary note: some translations are expurgated or abridged. Cutting a text is always a dangerous practice; cutting Voltaire (for whatever reason) is murderous.

22

Goethe:

FAUST [PART I]

I. Background of Goethe (1749 - 1832)

"I am fortunate," Goethe told Eckermann, his secretary and ever-intent audience, "that I was born at a time when major events were the order of the day and that they continued to occur through all my long life." Goethe was fourteen years old at the end of the Seven Years' War (1756 - 1763), which established the Prussian power; forty when the French Revolution appalled the chancelleries of Europe; sixty-one when Napoleon was banished to St. Helena, the Congress of Vienna maladjusted Europe's borders, and an intense reaction, which would be supervised for fifteen years by Prince Metternich, darkened the continent. At the beginning of his life, Germany was ruled by 340 sovereign princes; before he died, 300 of the principalities had been dissolved and Prussia, through the *Zollverein* (Customs Union), dominated the remnant.

In his life, Goethe was equally fortunate: the "accelerating daimons" played all the significant roles. Endowed with versatile genius, he was wealthy and handsome as well. His cultured Frankfort family actively supported his ambitions. At sixteen, he went to study jurisprudence at Leipzig, the "miniature Paris," where he absorbed much more French literature than law. Falling ill, he returned home for a year and a half, distracting himself with alchemy and religious mysticism. In 1770, he attended the University of Strasbourg, meeting and becoming converted by Johann Gottfried Herder, evangelist of the new literary dispensation exalting "strength and feeling" in literature.

After his return to Frankfort, he engaged desultorily in the practice of law, used his ample leisure more valuably in writing *Götz von Berlichingen* (1773), a historical drama magnifying a hero who spurns the shams of his society. *Götz* was an important production because it inaugurated the *Sturm und Drang* (Storm and Stress) movement, an aberration that endured till Schiller's *The Robbers* (1781). "Nature, truth, spontaneity" were the watchwords of *Sturm und Drang*, in essence a violently colored romanticism. Goethe's *The Sorrows of Young Werther*, which appeared the year after *Götz*, concentrated less on strength and more on sentimentality and stirred even greater enthusiasm. Werther loves Charlotte, a married lady, loves her hopelessly. So, as Thackery neatly abridges the rest of the story,

> . . . he sighed and pined and ogled,
> And in his passion boiled and bubbled,
> Till he blew his silly brains out,
> And no more by it was troubled.

Throughout Europe, desolate lovers are alleged to have followed Werther's example.

In 1775 the Duke of Weimar invited Goethe to his court. Weimar was a little duchy of about 100,000 people, 8,000 of whom lived in the capital. Save for a few leaves, official and other, Goethe remained there for the rest of his long life. During the first dozen years he functioned as the Duke's principal administrator, performing his heavy duties with remarkable efficiency but neglecting his creative work. Hoping for spiritual renewal, he escaped to Italy in 1788. There, amid the traces of a great vanished culture, he eagerly sought an esthetic balance, a discipline of forces. From his Italian sojourn date his abhorrence of Romanticism and his poised Classicism.

After his return to the "Cimmerian North" in 1788, Goethe threw off most of his official duties, devoting himself instead to more gratifying activities. He became director of the state theater, where he fostered a highly stylized kind of acting. He accelerated, too, those scientific researches which intrigued him all his life. He did amazingly fruitful work in several fields: both Freud and Darwin have called him an ancestor. He revolutionized the science of botany, discovered the intermaxillary bone in man (important for evolutionary theory), made salient contributions to geology and a half-dozen other sciences. He wrote several essays on art, architecture, literature, philosophy. He produced poems, novels, dramas with astonishing prodigality. And with all this multifarious activity, he still had time for a score of love affairs, some sentimental, most physical.

The Weimar edition of Goethe's works runs to 143 octavo volumes, including 50 volumes of letters! All are important to the literary historian, for they established the possibility of German literature: before Goethe, French was the language generally admired by cultivated Germans. Yet of the immense body of Goethe's writing, perhaps only *Wilhelm Meister's Apprenticeship and Pilgrimage* (1795-6, 1821-9), the autobiographic *Poetry and Truth*, a small sheaf of lyric poems, and of course *Faust*, have excited the interest of contemporary readers outside Germany.

Goethe called his works "fragments of a great confession," a baring of his life and his soul. *Faust* embodies the largest part of the confession. Goethe knew the Faust legend from childhood, through one of the puppet-play versions touring Germany. The Faust story, memorializing the career of a 16th-century "magician" frequently denounced by leaders of the German Reformation, was nearly two centuries old then, the primitive *Faust-Book* having been published in 1587. An English translation, quickly gotten up, supplied the basis of Marlowe's splendid *The Tragical History of Doctor Faustus* (c. 1589), which follows the traditional story. Marlowe's hero sells his soul to the devil for knowledge and, even more, power, lives twenty-four rather frustrating years, and then is carried screaming off to hell.

Many edifying and extravagant variations of the Faust theme followed: around Faust gathered tales of wizards and magi, part of man's heritage of legend for countless centuries. In the Protestant versions which proliferated in the late 16th and 17th centuries, however, the wonder-worker was invariably an evil sorcerer and the locus of his power the devil. The Protestant Church of the Reformation, like the Catholic, condemned purely human learning, the kind Faust lusted after, for it divorced the mind from God and vastly simplified the devil's labors.

Gotthold Ephraim Lessing, the great protagonist of the German Enlightenment, had sketched a different interpretation of the Faust story. To Lessing, Faust was a type of modern man, striving toward the light. Surely he ought not to be the devil's prize, surely he ought not to be damned through eternity? Rather, Faust is a heroic figure who deserves and who must attain salvation. Between 1759, when Lessing published a scene from his projected *Faust*, and 1808, when Goethe published *Faust, Part I*, twenty-nine different variations of the theme were delivered, both "traditionalist" and "salvationist." Goethe, once given his direction by Lessing, seems to have been little influenced by any of them, nor by Marlowe's *Doctor Faustus* or Calderon's *The Prodigious Magician*—neither of which he had read before 1808.

Faust spans Goethe's creative life. He conceived it as early as 1770; he completed Part II in 1831, seven months before his death. He worked on it fitfully, however; without the sympathetic encouragement between 1794 and 1805 of another great poet and dramatist, Friedrich Schiller, *Faust* might never have been completed; certainly it would have taken a different form. In *Faust* Goethe condensed his youthful storms and stresses, his experiences and speculations, his reading and love affairs. If sometimes it seems discontinuous, if there are gaps and even chasms in the narrative, if Faust and Mephistopheles himself suffer personality dislocation in the course of the action, the plain explanation is that Goethe's ideas evolved and his stance toward life altered during the sixty years over which he elaborated his Faustian outline. The romantic "subjectivity" that he had cherished came under firm classic control; the shaping imagination checked the incursions of "spontaneity and passion."

Save by an occasional critic, *Faust, Part I* has always been considered Goethe's ultimate achievement. It deals with deeper issues than Part II, and deals with them more humanly as well as more vividly. It is Part I rather than Part II (brilliant and bloodless as a star, a tangle of erudition and a wilderness of symbols) that has been the source of so much music, so many paintings, so much imitation. When *Faust* is presented on the stage, Part II is rarely included—and, because of its complexity and, still more, its distance from reality, almost never successfully. Part I, on the other hand, has real dramatic values and even dramatic structure. It treats of the "little world," the world bounded by personal experience. Basically it consists of the Prologue in Heaven (modeled on the *Book of Job*) and two dramas: a morality play, The Temptation and Compact; and a love tragedy, Gretchen.

But to understand Goethe's whole intention, to discover the outcome of the wager in heaven and the pact below, the reader needs at least an elementary knowledge of Part II, which explores the "Great World," the world of Institutions and Governments (actually, of Art and Philosophy, too). Faust has come to the court of the Emperor Maximilian and with Mephistopheles' collaboration performed a variety of services for him—ranging from producing a fireworks display to solving his fiscal problems and routing his enemies. After some harrowing journeys, he marries Helen of Troy, the symbol of Classical Greece as Faust is the symbol of Romantic Germany, and fathers a son, Euphorion, the spirit of modern poetry (a portrait modeled on Byron). Faust loses both wife and son, however, and the Faustian quest for fulfillment, the pursuit of the consummate moment, must go on.

In the last stage of his life, Faust turns his efforts to benefitting mankind. He is engaged in a huge project, draining a pestilential swamp. In a moment of vision he sees the community of free people who will flourish on the reclaimed land. Then, swept up by his imagination, he speaks the words that he has agreed will make him the devil's prize: to the "passing moment" he says, "Ah, still delay—thou art so fair!" But Faust employs the conditional future: he says "delay" to no actual moment, merely to the moment he envisions. Though Faust dies, Mephistopheles does not triumph. Angels defend him, the saints intercede, Gretchen pleads for him. He is saved.

Faust will not unfold its meaning easily. Goethe rejected the notion that a life so multiform as the one he pictured in *Faust* had a simple, unitary meaning: "That the devil loses the wager and that a man continually struggling from difficult errors towards something better should be redeemed is an effective, and, to many, a good enlightened thought; but it is not the idea at the foundation of the whole or of every individual scene." *Faust* embodies Goethe's philosophy of art, science, life. It is not only autobiography; it is cultural history as well: The Temptation and Compact evokes the spirit of the Middle Ages, as the Gretchen tragedy evokes the Renaissance. It incorporates a diversity of styles, prose and doggerel and iridescent poetry.

The best way to read *Faust* for the first time may be to view it as a series of different plays, connected by characters and, loosely, by a theme, but without rigid scenic governance, without necessary sequence, without classic unity. Primarily *Faust* is a drama of experience, of education. Its hero, a divided man and consequently a just symbol for man today, tries to discover the meaning that informs life. He learns the limits and potentials of mankind, learns that there is something beyond the reason on which the reasonable devil insists, learns what imbues life with meaning for him. He learns that life is a totality, an organism, that the head is only the topmost part of man, not his whole being (an observation the 18th-century rationalists refused to make).

Through the 19th century, in England and America, Goethe was hailed as the supreme poet. Emerson and Carlyle praised him for his moral insight, Arnold for his sanity and wholeness. Today, some critics have over-reacted, tending to discount his value as either poet or seer. As Goethe warned, truth will not be found at extremes, either of abomination or of adulation. But whatever his faults, Goethe has a special importance for our age. In *Faust* he articulated the question we ask more poignantly now than ever before: in what endeavor can a man find satisfaction, justification? He illustrated the question richly, and he pointed not perhaps to but certainly toward the answer.

II. Questions for Study and Discussion

1. What is the theme of *Faust, Part I?*
2. Explain the function each scene in the play has in advancing the plot and developing the theme.
3. Into how many separate and distinct plays could *Faust* be divided? How does Goethe unify his seemingly disparate material?
4. Describe Goethe's various dramatic and poetic styles.
5. Describe Mephistopheles' wager with the Lord. What is ironic about the Lord's acceptance of the wager? Compare this wager with that in *Job*.
6. Characterize Mephistopheles. What is his function in this world? What power in man continually thwarts him?
7. Characterize Faust. Is he introduced as an exceptional or as an exemplary average man? What is his mental state when we first meet him? How does he change in the course of the drama?
8. When Faust says, "Two souls, alas, are housed within my breast," what two souls does he mean? How does the play as a whole dramatize this conflict?
9. Explain the significance of Faust's new translation from the Gospel of St. John. Why is this the psychological moment for Mephistopheles to reveal himself?
10. Explain the conditions of the pact between Faust and Mephistopheles. What does Faust want? What does Mephistopheles promise to supply?
11. In urging Faust into the realm of action, how is Mephistopheles repeating his old ironic role of willing evil and doing good?
12. What do the scenes in Auerbach's Cellar and the Witch's Kitchen symbolize in Faust's development? How does he respond to each experience?
13. How does the tragic affair with Gretchen serve as another test of Faust?
14. Characterize Gretchen. What qualities make her the ideal bait for Mephistopheles' trap? How, in the end, does she serve the Lord's purpose?
15. How does Goethe regard sensual pleasures? How would Dante rank Faust's sin with Gretchen?

16. What is the symbolic function of love in *Faust, Part I?*
17. Describe Faust's religion.
18. Why was Gretchen imprisoned? Why does she refuse to flee with Faust? Why, in the terms of the divine wager, is she saved at the end? Why is Faust not damned at the end?
19. In what sense is *Faust* a critique of rationalism?
20. Where do you find Shakespearean influences in *Faust?*
21. In what sense is *Faust* a justification of God's way to man? Of man's way? Compare Goethe with Milton on this subject.
22. What seems to be Goethe's view of human nature? Of the human condition in general? Compare and contrast his views with Voltaire's or Swift's.
23. In what respects does *Faust* explore the illusion-reality conflict? Compare *Faust* with *Hamlet* and *Don Quixote* in its treatment of this conflict.
24. How would Goethe define evil? Does his solution of the problem of evil seem adequate to you?
25. What would you surmise is Goethe's idea of the good for man? What is his view of the Christian ideal of humility and worldly renunciation?
26. What danger exists in the Faustian desire to know the full range of human experience, every kind of good and evil?
27. What is the significance of Goethe's thought for us today?

III. Readings in Background and Criticism

Atkins, Stuart, *Goethe's "Faust"* (Harvard University Press, 1958). A scene-by-scene explication of the text. An extensive effort—the most convincing yet published—to prove that *Faust* has organic unity.

Barzun, Jacques, "Introduction," *Faust, Part I,* tr. by Alice Raphael (Rinehart, 1955). An interesting discussion of Goethe's conception of Faust, which the critic values as "a complete presentment of man's doubts and aspirations."

Bergstraesser, Arnold, ed., *Goethe and the Modern Age* (Henry Regnery, 1949). In this collection of the Aspen Goethe Bicentennial lectures, leading scholars probingly examine aspects of Goethe's work and personality, his impact on world literature, and his relevance to man's situation today.

Butler, E. M., *The Myth of the Magus* (Cambridge University Press, 1948). An illuminating study of Faust's origin and ancestry.

Carlyle, Thomas, *Essays on Goethe* (B. Tauchnitz, 1916). Nine important essays on Goethe and his work; though overstressing his moral objectives, they help one to understand him.

Eliot, T. S., "Goethe," *On Poetry and Poets* (Farrar, Straus and Cudahy, 1957). Certain to be influential on modern criticism, Eliot's essay is a tissue of *aperçus:* the critic prefers *Faust, Part II* and he considers Goethe's prodigality the clue to his greatness.

Enright, D. J., *Commentary on Goethe's Faust* (New Directions, 1949). A querulous but often acute scene-by-scene explication of the drama. Useful for the beginning student of Goethe.

Fairley, Barker, *A Study of Goethe* (Oxford University Press, 1947). A provocative reading of Goethe and an admirable commentary on his life and thought.

Fuerst, Norbert, "The Pentalogy of Goethe's *Faust,*" *Goethe Bicentennial Studies* (Indiana University Press, 1950). A learned, fascinating, generally successful attempt to explain the dramatic structure of *Faust* as a combination of five plays, each with a different purpose, appeal, and form.

Langbaum, Robert, "The Dramatic Lyric and the Lyrical Drama," *The Poetry of Experience* (Random House, 1957). An original and perceptive essay on *Faust's* genre and an analysis of *Faust* as "a quest for knowledge through self-realization."

Lewes, G. H., *The Life and Works of Goethe* (Dutton, 1930). Still the standard biography, though the criticism sometimes fails to probe deeply enough.

The Listener. A variety of excellent short Third Programme (BBC) talks on aspects of Goethe printed in *The Listener* from September, 1949, through March, 1950. Especially relevant: E. M. Butler, "Goethe and the Faust Legend" (December 8, 1949) and "Goethe and the Faust Tradition" (December 22, 1949); Barker Fairley, "The Universal Goethe" (March 2, 1950); Thomas Mann, "Goethe, the German Miracle" (February 9, 1950); and L. L. Whyte, "Goethe's Single View of Nature and Man" (November 24, 1949).

Mann, Thomas, *Essays of Three Decades* (Knopf, 1947). Contains four essays on Goethe by his great 20th-century analogue; written from deep understanding and sympathy.

Santayana, George, *Three Philosophical Poets* (Doubleday Anchor Books, 1953). Contains a beautifully luminous essay on Goethe and *Faust,* discounting the "official and belated moral" and emphasizing the

Spinozist insight that "the biography of Faust, seen under the form of eternity, shows forth his salvation."

Schweitzer, Albert, *Goethe: Two Addresses* (Beacon Press, 1948). A somewhat idealized version of Goethe's life and personality. In our Mephistophelean era, Schweitzer believes, Goethe's message to mankind—do not give up your personality for the magic formulas of economic and social witchcraft—assumes a new significance.

IV. Translations and Editions

Faust, Part I has been translated into English about 60 times—never with remarkable success. Translators have failed variously, but none has been able to convey to English readers the beauty and strength of Goethe's poetry; none makes Goethe seem a great poet.

Of 19th-century translations, only Bayard Taylor's, "in the original meters," is at all readable today. Diffuse and old-fashioned, it is nevertheless the best known, the oftenest quoted, and the most easily procurable (for example, Modern Library and World's Classics).

Four modern metrical versions are distinctly preferable to Taylor's. Louis MacNeice's translation of Part I and Part II is the most effective as poetry, but it is severely abridged and sometimes misses Goethe's meaning (Oxford University Press). The translation of Part I by Alice Raphael (Rinehart), while accurate and clear, never comes within reasonable distance of poetry. Philip Wayne's translation (Penguin), though modern, sound, and intelligent, is less than exhilarating. The reader will perhaps be wisest to make his acquaintance with Goethe in the lucid, sensitive version of C. F. MacIntyre (New Directions).

As Jacques Barzun suggests, however, one ought to sample several versions, for something of Goethe comes through each. A very good prose translation by Bayard Quincy Morgan (Library of Liberal Arts) will be useful as a basis of comparison.

23

Hawthorne: THE SCARLET LETTER

I. Background of Hawthorne (1804 - 1864)

A portrait of Nathaniel Hawthorne has been etched on our imaginations. We see him dark-visaged and ghost-ridden, pondering ancestral guilt till it becomes the solid reality and the violent surging world about him fades into dream.

Between model and portrait some likeness admittedly exists. After being graduated from Bowdoin in 1825, Hawthorne returned to his mother's home in Salem, Massachusetts. It was not a happy homecoming. Following the death of her husband, a sea captain, in 1808, when Nathaniel was four years old, his mother had gone into protracted solitary mourning. Quite without intending it, Hawthorne, too, embraced solitude—made himself a captive and put himself into a dungeon, as he wrote his former classmate Henry Wadsworth Longfellow. For twelve years he secluded himself in his "dismal chamber," reading steadily, writing much (destroying nearly as much), meditating most of all—emerging chiefly for lonely walks.

It is true, moreover, that he was haunted by the sins of his colonial ancestors. The first of them, Major William Hathorne (Nathaniel added "w" to the family name), came to Massachusetts in 1630. "Soldier, legislator, judge," he achieved his greatest distinction as a bitter, relentless persecutor of the Quakers, whom the Puritans abominated as thoroughly as they did the Papists. His son, John Hathorne, one of the "witch judges" in Salem during the last decade of the 17th century, served as conspicuously in "the martyrdom of witches." Recalling their cruelty, the pale 19th-century inheritor of their guilt breaks his narrative, in the Introduction to *The Scarlet Letter*, "to take shame upon [himself] for their sake" and entreat "that any curse incurred by them . . . may be now and henceforth removed."

The outlines of the portrait, nevertheless, need altering. For Hawthorne did at last find the key to let himself out from his dungeon. Sophia Peabody, whom he married in 1842, helped engineer the escape. A member of an intellectual Boston family, she possessed, in addition to some artistic talent and great refinement, sure sympathies and excellent sense. Her help ought not to be discounted; but Hawthorne was self-confined and ultimately self-released. By 1837 he had endured what he later came to believe was the necessary period of isolation, necessary for the strengthening of his delicate art, and he longed to go among men once again. "There is no fate in this world so horrible," he wrote Longfellow, "as to have no share in either its joys or sorrows."

He even became a shrewd practical politician, intermittently devoted to the Democratic cause—in opposition to most of the Salem gentry, who were convinced that it was a rallying point for rowdies. He wrote the campaign biography of Franklin Pierce (1852), a Bowdoin friend, and was rewarded with a consulship at Liverpool (1853 - 1856)—an eminence for which his other political offices, weigher and gauger in the Boston Custom House (1839 - 1840) and surveyor in the Salem Custom House (1846 - 1849), were certainly not adequate steppingstones.

More important, he developed into a perceptive, if sometimes wrongheaded, critic of his society. Having labored without spiritual or other gratification at Brook Farm (1841), a utopian community based a bit shakily on Transcendental idealism and Fourierist socialism, he satirized the Transcendental illusion of unremittent progress ("The Celestial Railroad," *The Blithedale Romance*). Having witnessed the delirium of the Gold Rush and the quieter but deadlier disease of land exploitation, he denounced the folly of the pleasureless accumulation of wealth, "of tumbling down an avalanche of ill-gotten gold, or real estate, on the heads of an unfortunate posterity, thereby to maim or crush them" *(The House of Seven Gables)*. Having experienced the dehumanization that follows in the wake of every fanatic course of action, no matter how well intentioned, he warned against the single-minded zeal of the scientist and the reformer alike ("The Birthmark," "Rappacini's Daughter," *The Blithedale Romance*).

No surface trace of mid-century America, however, may be discerned in *The Scarlet Letter*. Apparently the Puritan theme so solidly bounded Hawthorne's "ancestral mind" that it withstood the stress exerted by every contemporary issue. Yet Hawthorne, one might argue, never wrote a more urgently contemporary story. *The Scarlet Letter* probes the matter of sin, of individual and social evil—a reality that the Transcendental vapor did its best to obscure. In the grip of Transcendental metaphysics, for example, Emerson and Whitman were constrained to say that evil was illusion—or, if it existed at all, it was on its way to merge with good. Frequently, though, when moved by common sense rather than metaphysics, both men saw and spoke out against the evils thriving in their America.

Hawthorne rejected Puritan theology. Despite its earnestness and moral energy, it was a narrow, cruel, joyless doctrine. Yet he never shed the Puritan consciousness. While he gave his assent to none of the "points" of Calvinism, he shared the Puritan attitude toward weak and wicked mankind. Against the affirmations of the Transcendentalists he posited his negatives. They believed that man was innately good, since he held divinity within himself. Hawthorne knew that man was born with a propensity for evil, a tendency encouraged by the devil. They envisioned limitless possibilities of betterment for society. He saw that all horizons were blocked. They hoped confidently to do away with the dead weight of the past, the old errors and iniquities. He hardly hoped at all, because "so long as the human heart remains unpurified, all the wrong and miseries will again issue forth from that foul cavern."

Before *The Scarlet Letter*, in several of the tales reprinted in *Twice-Told Tales* (1837, 1842), *Mosses from an Old Manse* (1846), and *The Snow Image* (1852), Hawthorne had made preliminary explorations of its major themes. He had examined the nature of sin and its multiplying effects on the sinner, looked deeply into faceless sins, noted how they were hugged even while hated by the sinner. He had perceived the tragic distortion of personality that ensues when human beings are treated as means only and not as ends also, as objects rather than as persons. He had descried the progress of sin, increasing like a gradual stain, a slow contagion.

Moreover, he had consummated his distinctive method: first he got a "glimmering" moral idea, then "materialized" it in story. Characteristically a symbol enforces or realizes the moral idea—and, in the best tales, leads to new meanings, often deliberately ambiguous. Such a procedure has an obvious defect: the abstraction may never be vitalized, may remain a separate moral notation in spite of symbol and story. When Hawthorne achieves his special triumphs, however, abstraction, symbol, and tale fuse. Then the critic dissociates them only by violence, and the act wrenches life from an organic unity.

In 1844, five years before he began writing *The Scarlet Letter*, Hawthorne jotted into one of his notebooks a plot summary to be developed later, a kind of brief note to himself—a practice he had adopted some years earlier: "The life of a woman, who, by the old colony law, was condemned always to wear the letter A, sewed on her garment, in token of her having committed adultery." Three years later he made a similar, though then unconnected, entry: "A story of the effects of revenge, diabolizing him who indulges in it." How lastingly Hawthorne brooded over Puritan traditions the former notation implies: even as early as 1837, he had written "Endicott and the Red Cross," which incidentally pictures a "lost and desperate creature" who had been doomed to wear the letter A on the bust of her gown and who had "embroidered the fatal token in scarlet cloth, with golden thread and nicest art of needlework."

Such long maturation may in part explain the rapidity with which Hawthorne composed *The Scarlet Letter:* he completed it in less than six months. There are other reasons, too, for his new access of energy. First, having been discharged from his Custom House surveyorship in 1848, when the Whigs defeated the Democrats, he desperately needed to make money. Again, he had written little during the five years preceding 1849, and liberated from deadening routine, he returned to his vocation with unprecedented vigor. Finally, in *The Scarlet Letter* his emotion as well as his perception was wholly enlisted. As never before, or after, he was able to integrate the novelistic situation and the moral insight—the one was the perfect vehicle for the other.

At first Hawthorne intended *The Scarlet Letter* as the longest of several tales to be called *Old Time Legends; together with Sketches, Experimental and Ideal.* His publisher thought it deserved separate publication, and Hawthorne finally agreed. To relieve the sombre whole, he prefaced the novel with "The Custom House." Pleasantly satirical and engagingly written, it provides *The Scarlet Letter* with a frame, after the manner of the Gothic romances on which he doted. While "poking and burrowing" in a large room of the Custom House, Hawthorne alleges, he found a small package done up in ancient yellow parchment and bound with red tape. In it reposed the scarlet letter itself and some foolscap sheets that formed the basis for his tale. But the device had already worn thin by Hawthorne's day, and, as many critics have argued, *The Scarlet Letter* needs no such frame.

"The Custom House," perhaps, is Hawthorne's attempt to requite his political enemies and their toadies. He had resented being removed from his surveyorship. He had been, after all, "an inoffensive man of letters" with a "pitiful little office." Nor had he behaved with partisan ferocity—a circumstance displeasing to many good Democrats. He had refrained, for example, from decapitating Whigs when he had had power of the ax. Just the same, the victorious spoilsmen refused to spare his head. As a result, his commitment to party solidified—probably to his benefit as a writer: overdisposed to turn quietly within, he needed some of the noise and movement of politics as a check against excessive introversion. Since, additionally, the Democratic Party prided itself, accurately for the most part, on being the party of liberalism, Hawthorne's adherence tended to counteract his ingrained conservatism, a reflex of the Calvinist hostility to reform.

Had he not served his apprenticeship in the world of men and affairs, Hawthorne would probably have produced another of the "pale flowers," the anemic allegories which had become associated with his name by those who knew it at all—not *The Scarlet Letter*. In his Salem isolation he could hardly have evolved the psychological insight, the profound "knowledge of the human heart" that his dark Puritan drama evidences. Narrow in scope, subdued in color, meager in realistic detail, it nevertheless attains great tragic force by the intensity with which Hawthorne conceives his characters and the concentrated power with which he presents them. Though he projects his situations like a dramatist, Hawthorne develops them like a novelist: his evocation of character through slow deliberate analysis, the mode essentially of the novelist, gives the climactic scenes their impact. He prepares the reader carefully for each explosion; none seems accidental.

The symbolism supports Hawthorne's themes and imparts range to them—allows a dimension beyond realism: Dimmesdale's festering wound, for example, or Coverdale's gradual transformation. Rarely will the symbol be wholly "marvellous," however; Hawthorne allows multiple possibilities of interpretation. Thus, at the conclusion of *The Scarlet Letter*, the reader may argue that the A engraved on the minister's breast is a stigma, a psychosomatic branding; or the mark of the minister's long-endured self-torture; or the effect of Chillingworth's ministrations; or the reader may deny that it ever existed, save as a figment of overheated imaginations. While he does not insist on it, Hawthorne clearly prefers the first of these options.

Such an explanation—preternatural or at least "marvellous"—does not violate his philosophy of fiction. He took pains to distinguish between the "novel" and the "romance." The novel must keep faithfully to the real and probable. The romance, on the other hand, must remain faithful only to "the truth of the human heart"; the author may explore that truth under whatever circumstances he chooses to create—even if they breach literal reality. Still, as a caution, Hawthorne advised that the merest tincture of the "marvellous" is enough for the romance. By employing the technique of multiple choice, he was consequently enabled to keep within reasonable limits and yet to lead far beyond.

The Scarlet Letter has a virtue surpassing realism. Whether we translate into the language of the 20th century and speak of delusions, obsessions, fixations, neuroses, and psychosomatic disorders, or retain the Puritan diction and refer to sin, depravity, and reprobation depends on our predilections. What is most salient is that, surpassing forms of narrative and fashions in language alike, *The Scarlet Letter* creatively, poetically explores the confused motives, the destructive passions, the wicked imaginings, the discordant impulses, even the latent nobilities that make up man—man as he was, man as he is.

II. Questions for Study and Discussion

1. What is the theme of *The Scarlet Letter?*
2. Three dramatic scenes take place on the scaffold—in Chapters I, XII, and XXII. What structural effect does the placement of these chapters produce?
3. What does the scaffold symbolize? Does it connote the same thing in each of the three great scenes?
4. Supply at least two instances of Hawthorne's "technique of multiple possibilities," other than the ambiguity involved in interpreting the letter A.
5. A symbol may be suspected when an image occurs with frequency, density, or intensity. One would suspect the scarlet letter of being a symbol because it is referred to about a hundred and fifty times. What do you think it symbolizes? Search out at least five other symbols of some importance.
6. Why does Hawthorne introduce Mistress Hibbins, the witchly sister of Governor Billingham, into his narrative?
7. Characterize Hawthorne's style. What varied effects does he achieve?

8. To what extent is local color (particular details of time and place) infused into *The Scarlet Letter?* Why does Hawthorne use such details where he does?
9. What does Pearl symbolize? Support your answer. Is she a wholly satisfying character? Why?
10. Why does Pearl reform her elf-ways after the minister's confession?
11. Characterize Dimmesdale, Chillingworth, and Hester. What is the key to the character of each?
12. What are the sins of each central character? Which sin does Hawthorne seem to regard as the most grievous?
13. "Hawthorne correlates inner evil and outer manifestation." Support or attack this statement.
14. Hester says to the minister: "What we did had a consecration of its own." Do you think Hawthorne agreed or disagreed with Hester's assertion? What evidence supports your position?
15. Sin yields suffering in *The Scarlet Letter*. Does sin lead to any good as well? To what extent does Hawthorne regard suffering as valuable?
16. Compare Hawthorne's attitudes toward sin and suffering to those of Aeschylus, the Old Testament, and Dante.
17. Why does Dimmesdale not confess his sin?
18. Why does Chillingworth try to prevent the minister from ascending the scaffold in Chapter XXV?
19. To Hawthorne, what is the fundamental defect of character? Compare his view with those of Sophocles, Christ, Montaigne, and Melville.
20. What irony is implicit in the townspeople's attitude toward Dimmesdale as he comes closer and closer to death?
21. What function does the conversation of the townspeople, which we overhear from time to time, serve?
22. Hawthorne, critics have said, had a weakness for the abstract. Does it intrude into this tale? If so, where, and to what effect?
23. What religious convictions of Hawthorne emerge from this novel?

24. Summarize Hawthorne's philosophy of life.
25. Compare and contrast the views of Aeschylus, Goethe, and Dostoevski with the views of Hawthorne on crime and punishment.

III. Readings in Background and Criticism

Arvin, Newton, *Hawthorne* (Little, Brown, 1929). A critical biography attempting to probe the guilt manifest in Hawthorne's fiction, and, more successfully, to discover the source of its power.

Brownell, W. C., "Hawthorne," *American Prose Masters* (Scribner's, 1909). While exempting *The Scarlet Letter* from his strictures, Brownell analyzes Hawthorne's allegories with destructive brilliance.

Feidelson, Charles, Jr., "Hawthorne," *Symbolism in American Literature* (University of Chicago Press, 1953). Hawthorne's use of symbols examined against the background of American symbolism. Difficult, but valuable.

Fogle, R. H., *Hawthorne's Fiction: the Light and the Dark* (University of Oklahoma Press, 1952). A cogent and rewarding study of Hawthorne's fusion of "light" and "dark"—of clarity in design and tragic complexity—in *The Scarlet Letter* and other works.

James, Henry, *Hawthorne* (Harper, 1879, contained in Edmund Wilson, *The Shock of Recognition*, Doubleday Anchor Books). A long, stimulating critical essay, concentrating on how Hawthorne's "provincialism" hurt and helped him as an artist.

Matthiessen, F. O., *American Renaissance* (Oxford University Press, 1941). An important work, examining Hawthorne's fiction in its cultural, social, and literary contexts and interpreting it with sensitive understanding. Pages 275-282 discuss *The Scarlet Letter* with real acumen.

Stewart, Randall, *The American Notebooks by Nathaniel Hawthorne* (Yale University Press, 1922). Three excellent introductory essays discuss Hawthorne's sources, characters, and themes.

———, *Nathaniel Hawthorne* (Yale University Press, 1948). The best biography, detailed and accurate. Against the conventional view of Hawthorne as recluse, it demonstrates that he was for most of his life an engaged man of the world. Though uncritical, the biography summarizes important criticism.

VanDoren, Mark, *Nathaniel Hawthorne* (Compass, 1958). Contains an interesting attempt to correlate life and works, as well as sane balanced interpretations of Hawthorne's fiction.

Warren, Austin, *Nathaniel Hawthorne: Representative Selections* (American Book Company, 1934). The eighty-page introduction, scholarly but extremely readable, discusses Hawthorne's personality, theology, politics, influence, and artistry. Perhaps the best short introduction to Hawthorne.

Winters, Yvor, "Maule's Curse, or Hawthorne and the Problem of Allegory," *In Defense of Reason* (Swallow Press and William Morrow, 1948). A vigorous essay, praising *The Scarlet Letter* but reprobating most of Hawthorne's other work for "obscurantism."

IV. Translations and Editions

There are any number of satisfactory inexpensive editions of *The Scarlet Letter*. The quality of the editor's introduction will therefore determine one's choice. Admirable introductions are Newton Arvin's (Harper's Modern Classics), J. C. Gerber's (Modern Library College Edition), Gordon Roper's (Farrar, Straus), and Austin Warren's (Rinehart).

24

Melville: MOBY DICK

I. Background of Melville (1819 - 1891)

The thought of Herman Melville's age was conditioned by a zealous optimism, a facile version of Emerson's transcendentalism. This optimism is a distorted version of his idealistic philosophy, certainly, but even Emerson, his gaze fixed on the "beneficent tendency" in American life, at times succumbed to it. And from a lower level than philosophy—from President James K. Polk, for instance—came blatant assurances that America was marching inexorably to greatness, wealth, and power; indeed, that America presented "a sublime moral spectacle to the world."

Melville, who thought Ecclesiastes "the truest of all books . . . the fine hammered steel of woe," was driven to attack this entrenched optimism. Though abominating the bleak and bloodless Calvinism which he had inherited, he appreciated its residual insight, that sin and anguish were man's certain lot. Like Hawthorne, he could speak few comfortable words to his age. He saw as a vision of evil, not as a "sublime moral spectacle," the truculence of the War Hawks in the Oregon Dispute with England; the unprincipled maneuvers of the expansionists which spurred President Polk's declaration of war against Mexico; the aggressiveness of the slavocracy; the "land greed," the "gold fever," the individualism unrestrained by traditional moral sanctions. He saw them undermining the American promise, sapping the moral strength of the democracy he cherished.

While less harrowing, Melville's career had been as educative as Candide's (see Chapter 21). At eighteen, he had signed on a trading vessel for a summer's voyage to Liverpool. Aboard, the savagery of the forecastle, and, ashore, the savagery of the slums—civilized phenomena that made him more forbearing in his judgment of the barbaric natives he later met—crumbled his romantic notion of a sailor's life. But Melville's prospects on land seemed fairly hopeless, and in 1842, after five landlocked years, he sailed again, this time on the new whaler *Acushnet*. The "unmitigated tyranny" of the captain made Melville and a companion decide to jump ship at Nuku Hiva, one of the Marquesas Islands. There he was a guest of the cannibal Typees for twenty-seven idyllic days. Nevertheless, he welcomed the Australian whaler that rescued him. Conditions on the ship were normally snarled though, and off Tahiti Melville participated in a mutiny (somewhat more discreetly than he admits). Imprisoned, he engineered an effortless escape to Eimeo, where he spent a picaresque month among natives, observing conditions that strengthened his antipathy to projects for "civilizing the savage"—especially when undertaken by Christian missionaries. Beachcombing having palled, he managed to get a berth as boat-steerer and harpooner aboard a whaler cruising the South Pacific. After a six-month voyage, he was deposited in Hawaii, where he remained for fourteen weeks and then enlisted in the United States Navy for the duration of a cruise. When his ship arrived at Boston in October of 1844, his professional sailing days were over.

Though Melville had small experience in writing, no more plausible way of earning money emerged. Using his memories of life among the cannibals as a fluid base, supplementing his memory by his reading, he wrote *Typee* (1846), a captivating narrative of his sojourn among the cannibals. It was immediately successful, and he was encouraged to try another free retrospect of his experiences. *Omoo* (1847) achieved wide popularity too, in spite of Melville's sharp criticism of the missionaries determined to impose a repugnant civilization on a charming culture. *Mardi* (1849), which at the outset follows in the wake of Melville's southern Pacific and Polynesian experiences, but shortly veers into fuddled allegory and clogged if often penetrating satire, failed decisively—almost catastrophically. He managed to recover some of his reputation with the dark-shadowed *Redburn* (1849), a quasi-autobiographical account of his maiden voyage to Liverpool. And *White-Jacket* (1850), based on his last voyage before the mast, stirred more commotion than any of his other narratives because of its vivid account of the cruelty prevailing on American naval vessels.

None of these five books was really a novel—if by "novel" we mean, among other things, an ordered progression of episodes upheld by suspense. Only exceptionally did Melville design. Instead he added incident to incident, until tact suggested that he bring his book to a close. As a consequence, all the narratives were written easily and rapidly, even *Typee*, his first venture, and *Mardi*, his most complex.

Moby Dick (1851) demanded different treatment and greater effort. Though Melville had been broiling his whale in hell-fire for more than a year, he wrote his neighbor Hawthorne in 1851, the tail was not yet cooked. There were reasons. Most important, Melville seems at first to have contemplated another story flowing from his experiences at sea, a "romantic and literal" representation of the Whale Fishery. But before the narrator, Ishmael, and his bosom companion, the head-hunting Queequeg, embarked, Melville's conception deepened and widened. The chase for whales became a quest for ultimate meanings—an attempt to reach where the vast Leviathan sleeps.

What motivated the revised purpose? Not, certainly, Melville's cetological researches; he had always grubbed in libraries to fill out his narratives or to reinforce his impressions. For *Moby Dick* he read Frederick Bennett's *Narrative of a Whaling Voyage* (1840), J. Ross Browne's *Etchings of a Whaling Cruise* (1846), William Scoresby's *An Account of the Arctic Regions* (1820), and a score of other source books, all interesting factual works but hardly inspirational.

For some time Melville had been looking unhappily at his published volumes—"*Peedee, Hullabaloo,* and *Pog-dog,*" he called them derisively. To Hawthorne he wrote of his depression over what seemed a likely destiny, to go down to posterity "as a 'man who lived among cannibals.'" It was Hawthorne's contemporary example chiefly that roused Melville's dissatisfaction with his own works—with all works that did not dive, that were not charged with the "power of darkness"—and wrought his new sense of creative potential and purpose.

The purpose was quickened by the reading in which he immersed himself: Shakespeare's plays especially (and *King Lear* beyond the others), Carlyle's *Sartor Resartus*, Milton's *Paradise Lost*, Burton's *Anatomy of Melancholy*, the Book of Job, Byron's *Manfred*. All were books "to make a man swim for his life." But other men had read them—Melville himself had read most of them—without such spiritual release. Now, though, after his novitiate as author, his friendship with Hawthorne and other literary men, and his steady maturation, he read them with singular receptivity, with a total sympathy. And mysteriously, for all creativity is ultimately shrouded in mystery, they worked to liberate his genius. "Until I was twenty-five," he told Hawthorne in one of his splendid exuberant letters, "I had no development at all. From my twenty-fifth year I date my life. Three weeks have scarcely passed between then and now, that I have not unfolded within myself. But I feel that I am now come to the inmost leaf of the bulb, and that shortly the flower must fall to the mould."

Though *Moby Dick* is more nearly a novel than any of his previous books, it bursts all forms; compounded of tumult, it refuses to be cabined. The incidents and points of view pitch and tumble like a drunken whaleboat. Ishmael is ostensibly the narrator: he opens the tale by saying, "Call me Ishmael," and, about six hundred pages later, closes it by quoting Job, "And I only am alive to tell thee." Yet soliliquies which he could not have heard and dramatic dialogues which he could not have overheard are set down without apology.

The language leaps and spirals, only rarely flounders. There is broad folk humor, perhaps too broad in a few of the shore-based scenes. There are passages of soaring prose that often need only typographical rearrangement to be recognized as poetry. There are chapters of cetological exposition, sometimes grave, sometimes playful, sometimes, as in "The Whiteness of the Whale," plunging to Melville's deepest meanings.

All the lines of *Moby Dick*, no matter how far-flung, converge at Ahab and his quarry. They are real beings, the obsessed sea captain and the great whale, but also they are symbolic creations. While first and last they mean themselves, they have, too, a meaning beyond themselves.

It is the attempt to fathom their symbolic meaning that has spawned so many and such diverse interpretations. Is Ahab arrogant man in revolt against God? Or irresponsible man striving to penetrate the universal mystery? Or heroic man resolved to assert his human status against the demonism of the universe? Or lunatic man bent on a futile mission? Or hubristic man seeking to become God? To set down an "approved" answer, as to a problem in algebra, would be presumptuous—and, besides, some problems have no approved answers. Each reader must himself try to hoist Leviathan, "that crooked serpent."

But even if we choose not to penetrate the huge cloudy symbolism (as many readers have chosen), the profound contemporary significance of *Moby Dick* looms through. To us, it speaks with greater authority than it could to Melville's generation; for though evil is "a permanent fact of the universe," surely we have experienced it more intensely. We have intimately known the baleful force that brooded over the *Pequod*. We have shared Ishmael's awareness of impending doom. We have watched horrified the progress of fanaticism figured in Ahab. Time has vindicated Melville's tragic meaning.

II. Questions for Study and Discussion

1. What is the theme of *Moby Dick?* Justify your answer.
2. Would *Moby Dick* be improved by judicious cutting? Where?
3. Why does Melville delay Ahab's entrance?
4. What is the significance of Father Mapple's sermon to the theme of *Moby Dick?* How is the sermon dramatically functional?
5. What is Fedallah's function in the novel? Is he a satisfactory character? Why?

6. Discuss the varieties of prose used in *Moby Dick*—expository, dramatic, poetic, humorous—and comment on the use of each.
7. Does the setting, a whaling ship on a whaling cruise, advance Melville's theme? Would another setting be quite as good? Discuss.
8. What does the sea mean to Ishmael? What does the land mean to him?
9. To what extent is *Moby Dick* an allegory? How can the realistic elements be explained figuratively?
10. "In *Moby Dick* we see the world in microcosm." Discuss.
11. Ahab, Ishmael, Elijah, Flask, Stubb, and Bildad have biblical names. What is the significance of these names?
12. What is the symbolic significance of the doubloon Ahab nails to the mast? Discuss the reactions of the crew and the interpretations they propose. How do these reactions and interpretations evince character?
13. Select at least three other important symbolic scenes. What significance has each for Melville's theme?
14. What is the significance of Ishmael's escape from disaster on Queequeg's coffin?
15. Are Ishmael, Ahab, Queequeg, and Fedellah "round" or "flat" characters—that is, are they drawn from life or are they merely symbolic projections?
16. Starbuck, Stubb, and Flask are obviously foils for Ahab. How? What other roles do they play?
17. Does Ahab's fanaticism make him a case for the psychiatrist, the moralist, or the metaphysician? Explain.
18. Characterize Ahab and Ishmael. Contrast them. What makes one the more human character, the other the more heroic? Which represents mind, which will?
19. Compare and contrast Ahab with Job, King Lear, Satan and Faust.
20. What purpose does each gam serve in the action of the novel and the development of its theme?
21. Compare Melville's main characters in *Moby Dick* to Tolstoy's in *War and Peace* and to Hawthorne's in *The Scarlet Letter*.
22. What is Pip's function in the novel? Compare him to the Fool in *King Lear*.

23. One writer, with Moby Dick in mind, quotes:

    The animal is very wicked:
    When one attacks it, it defends itself.

    Is the verse appropriate? Why or why not?
24. What reasons does Melville have for interpolated chapters on cetology? What is their thematic significance? Are there any analogues in Homer, in Tolstoy, in Milton?
25. From the comments of Ishmael-Melville, you may deduce his opinions of democracy, of evil, of man's function and fate, and of the nature of the universe. What are these views?
26. Comment on one critic's description of *Moby Dick* as "an economic epic of nineteenth-century America."
27. In what sense is *Moby Dick* an epic? Compare it to the *Iliad* or the *Odyssey* with regard to conception, language, characters.
28. Which problems raised by the novel are resolved at the end? Which are not?
29. What specific importance has *Moby Dick* for us today? Who in the modern world is like Ahab? Who like Ishmael? Is it easier to think of a parallel to Ahab? Why?

III. Readings in Background and Criticism

Arvin, Newton, *Herman Melville* (Compass, 1957). A critical biography. Despite some wild and wide conjectures, the critique of the levels and language of *Moby Dick* is penetrating and as nearly satisfying as any.

Canfield, F. X., "*Moby Dick* and the Book of Job," *Catholic World* (January, 1952, 254-260). Argues concisely and persuasively that the theological key to *Moby Dick* is the Book of Job.

Feidelson, C. N., *Symbolism in American Literature* (University of Chicago Press, 1953). Chapter 5, "The Fool of Truth," is a luminous essay on Melville and the American symbolist background.

Howard, Leon, *Herman Melville* (University of California Press, 1951). The best and fullest biography. Though hardly a portrait in depth, it is, at least for the time being, definitive. Complements Leyda (see below).

Lawrence, D. H., "Herman Melville's Moby Dick," in *The Shock of Recognition*, ed. by Edmund Wilson (Doubleday Anchor Books, 1955).

A very personal, very provocative interpretation in terms of "blood-being." Often weird, but brilliant and extremely influential.

Leyda, Jay, *The Melville Log* (Harcourt, Brace, 2 vols., 1951). All the documents—letters, source materials, reviews, clippings, and the like—for a Melville biography. Complements Howard (see above).

Matthiessen, F. O., *American Renaissance* (Oxford University Press, 1941). Of first importance. Contains a balanced, perceptive study of Melville's sources, background, symbolism, language, and artistry.

Millhauser, Milton, "The Form of *Moby Dick*," *Journal of Aesthetics and Art Criticism* (June, 1955, 527-532). Millhauser propounds the thesis that *Moby Dick* is an adaptation to the novel of the form and content of classical Greek tragedy.

Percival, M. O., *A Reading of Moby Dick* (University of Chicago Press, 1950). An acute, sane, helpful commentary. The author sticks to his text, rarely rides his own whale.

Stewart, George, "The Two Moby Dicks," *American Literature*, XXV (January 1954, 417-448). An important article, demonstrating as nearly as is possible that Melville's conception of *Moby Dick* changed radically after the twenty-second chapter, and that in the light of his changed conception he revised the first fifteen chapters slightly and the next seven thoroughly.

Thompson, Lawrance, *Melville's Quarrel with God* (Princeton University Press, 1952). A brilliantly sustained wrong-headed thesis claiming that from *Redburn* on Melville attacked (though disguising his attack) religious orthodoxy. Valuable, not least as a counterbalance to conventional studies.

Thorp, Willard, *Herman Melville: Representative Selections* (American Book Company, 1938). A long, scholarly critical introduction examines Melville's background, sources, and objectives, and reviews Melville criticism.

IV. Translations and Editions

Though many texts of *Moby Dick*, particularly those published before 1940, are corrupt, none is so bad as to be unusable (save for scholarly work). The best edition is the "Leviathan" *Moby-Dick* (Hendricks House) edited (with a superabundance of annotations) by L. S. Mansfield and H. P. Vincent. Other very satisfactory—and more reasonably priced—editions are Newton Arvin's (Rinehart), Leon Howard's (Modern Library College), and Alfred Kazin's (Houghton Mifflin)—all containing excellent introductions. Avoid abridgements.

25

Flaubert:
MADAME BOVARY

I. Background of Flaubert (1821 - 1880)

In 1957 the literary world paid centennial homage to Gustave Flaubert's novel, *Madame Bovary*, and to Charles Baudelaire's volume of poetry, *Les Fleurs du Mal (Flowers of Evil)*. Avant-gardists in literary symbolism and realism, dispassionate recorders of physical and spiritual corruption, these two Frenchmen did much to shape the style and content of fiction and poetry as we know it today. Yet when their books first appeared, the 36-year-old authors were not hailed; rather they were ignominiously hauled into court to answer charges of outraging public taste and morality. Flaubert won acquittal; Baudelaire, tried a few months later and found guilty, successfully entreated Empress Eugénie to reduce his fine to fifty francs. Few people today recall the trials; they simply memorialize another of man's fitful and generally ludicrous attempts to judge great literature by law. No one who has read their work, however, forgets how these writers anatomized French society—Flaubert the country folk, Baudelaire the Parisian.

During the mid-19th century, the French *bourgeoisie* manifested extraordinary sensitivity to such clinical analysis. Since 1830 they had gradually assumed dominance in the French economy. They shared handsomely in the remarkable industrial and commercial prosperity of the Second Empire. Yet they knew that the France of Napoleon III was a "sickroom in which people spoke with lowered voices." A professed democrat but a practicing demagogue, Napoleon III, whom Victor Hugo contemptuously termed "Napoleon the Little," bartered intellectual freedom for economic progress: he stifled free speech in the press, the university, and even the parliament. But mindful of the dangers of revolutionary thought and terrified by the prospect of economic upheaval, the *bourgeoisie* acquiesced to Napoleon's new "liberalism." By their submission they became patients in the "sickroom" that was France: their malaise—smugness, drabness, mediocrity, and acute allergy to criticism.

Toward *muflisme* (their epithet for bourgeois vulgarity and muckerism) French writers manifested single-minded loathing. But they expressed their distaste variously. Some quested romantically, often sentimentally, in past and future for the heroic, the picturesque, or the ideal. Others, influenced by widespread advances in scientific thought, began to probe the mechanism of existing society and to shatter the illusions of its members. None of them, however, exemplified so fully as Flaubert in *Madame Bovary*, his first published novel, the artistic mastery needed to compel the reader's imagination or to render painfully credible the hollow elegance or the piddling, nasty lives of the *bourgeoisie*. Flaubert's achievement was especially difficult, for within him the lyric exuberance and idealism of the poet struggled against the impersonality of the clinician. The inner conflict between illusion and reality that destroyed his bourgeois heroine, Emma Bovary, was incarnate in Flaubert himself—and he knew it. Asked to identify the prototype of Emma he replied, "C'est moi" ("Me").

Until 1851, when he began to write *Madame Bovary*, Flaubert sought in romance the meaning of reality. He abhorred the dullness of Rouen, his birthplace and home. As a child, living in a wing of the municipal hospital where his father was chief surgeon, he diverted himself and terrified his family by writing and enacting grisly, corpse-ridden plays and tales. He detested the law his father intended him to study; a nervous ailment—real or pretended—freed him from this obligation and won him complete leisure. Like many youths of his time he cherished, in life and literature, the romantic and the grandiloquent. Inspired by Chateaubriand, Gautier, and Hugo, he wrote in 1848 the first of three versions (he wrote the last in 1872) of *La Tentation de Sainte Antoine (The Temptation of St. Anthony)*—a lyrical philosophical dialogue whose florid romanticism even his friends mocked. He initiated and for eight years intermittently conducted a tempestuous love affair with Louise Colet, a married woman already mistress to the head of the Academie Française. With sympathetic friends he traveled briefly to the Pyrenees and Corsica, admiring the scenery and the bandits, and later for two years toured in the Near East, drenching himself in the exotic.

At thirty, half his life already gone, Flaubert returned to Rouen to seclude himself at the family estate and revise the first draft of *St. Anthony*. Only acute consciousness of his undisciplined style—intensified by the perceptive criticism of his friend, Louis Bouilhet, a classicist—temporarily deterred him. Thus, he accepted Bouilhet's suggestion that he transmute a local scandal into a novel—but only for two reasons: to purify his style and to determine how the bourgeois temperament inevitably corrupted the romantic spirit. For the next five years, as his superb letters reveal, Flaubert struggled relentlessly to incise and drain his "abscesses of style." He strove tirelessly for *le mot juste*, for the perfectly framed sentence: "like a good line of poetry—*unchangeable*." Above all, knowing that he shared too many of Emma Bovary's romantic dreams, he sought emotional detachment: "No lyricism, no comments, the author's personality absent."

Madame Bovary has been called the first modern realistic novel. It was not of course the first novel to treat of the details of daily routine existence among the *bourgeoisie:* Stendhal and Balzac had anticipated Flaubert. Hundreds of competent writers since have portrayed "slices of life"—photographic reproductions of actual experience. To match Flaubert's standards, however, requires skill and discipline other novelists have rarely achieved; Turgenev, Henry James, Hemingway, and James Joyce are members of the small aristocracy of talent who have acknowledged indebtedness to Flaubert.

Flaubert's brand of realism demands two primary tasks: to select the indispensable episode and to communicate it in the absolutely right words. The novelist may not comment upon events or characters, whether to explain motives or to express personal sentiments. The theme of *Madame Bovary* and the vitality of its characters derive from the dramatic and psychological tension inherent in the narrative—the thrust of illusion pitted against the counterthrust of reality. A variety of techniques reinforces Flaubert's method and purpose: ironically contrasted or juxtaposed scenes, simultaneously perceived levels of individual consciousness, imagery, and symbolism. Although Flaubert himself never overtly condemns the bourgeois temperament or explicitly confesses his dismay at its effect upon the romantic spirit, his structural devices enable him to display precisely the absurdity of his characters' delusions, their vulgar avarice and lust. His perfect control of language enhances his purpose. Selecting images and symbols rigidly disciplined to his theme, he maps the narrow limits of his characters' imaginations, draws the boundaries of their empty worlds.

"The morality of art consists in its beauty," wrote Flaubert, "and I value style even above truth." Perhaps because it so completely fulfills Flaubert's standard, because it is the most perfectly styled of novels, *Madame Bovary* stirs a peculiar sort of controversy among readers. Flaubert's control seems so absolute, his detachment so complete, that some critics protest that the novel creates a world in which stupidity—*la bêtise humaine*—is all, that it denies the existence of moral values, that it lacks humanity. If such criticism is valid, then the impact of Emma's experience must be lost in disgust rather than in pity. If, on the other hand, readers feel that Flaubert probes life surgically, not sadistically, they will see Emma's life as an ironic, even tragic, symbol of man's destiny.

To those contemporaries who complained that his impersonality spoiled the novel, Flaubert had little to say: he had more immediately important things to do. *Madame Bovary* had been an exercise: "This book has served to train my hand how to do other things." He was eager to return to *St. Anthony* and to *Salammbô*, a lavish historical novel that enticed him to Carthage for a year of research. In brief, he was moved once more by the exotic, the romantic. But these works failed with public and critics alike. Nor was he more successful with the brilliant *Three Stories* he wrote toward the end of his life, though at least one of them, *A Simple*

Heart, has since won the praise it merits. Flaubert died aware that he had been most successful in the work he had least enjoyed doing —the work in which the poet had been deliberately inhibited by the clinician. That success continues, for although the *bourgeoisie* often accepts criticism ungraciously, it remains fascinated with analyses of itself. So long as *Bovarism* continues (sometimes under the name of "Babbittry"), Flaubert's novel will be read, its artistry admired, its criticism of life debated.

II. Questions for Study and Discussion

1. What is the theme of the novel?
2. What are the major divisions of *Madame Bovary?* Explain the structural function of each. How sharply does Flaubert outline the incidents? Why?
3. How would you explain the fact that the novel opens and closes with Charles, not with Emma? What dramatic function do the opening and closing chapters have?
4. What points of view does Flaubert employ in narration? Why?
5. What significance have the following scenes: the ball at Vaubyessard; the burning of the wedding bouquet; the agricultural fair; the opera; the singing beggar's appearances; Emma's meeting with the priest?
6. What dramatic techniques does Flaubert introduce during the scene at the agricultural fair? How do they point up his theme?
7. Characterize the atmosphere of Yonville. Of Tostes. To what extent does environment shape the lives of the characters?
8. Show how the following symbols illuminate character or theme: Emma's greyhound, Charles' hat, the different types of carriages (especially the diligence), the black and white butterflies, the cigar case. Which other symbols have like functions?
9. Isolate passages which illustrate Flaubert's narrative impersonality. How does he employ irony?
10. Characterize Emma. Why is she bored? What does she do to make her marriage work? Compare her attitudes toward Leon and toward Rodolphe.

11. What role does reading play in Emma's development?
12. Why does Emma commit suicide? To what extent is her death symbolic? How does she "corrupt" Charles "from beyond the grave"?
13. To what extent is Emma's death tragic? How does her death compare as tragedy with Agamemnon's death in *Agamemnon* or Margaret's in *Faust?* What universality does Emma have?
14. What is Flaubert's attitude toward Emma? Is he unduly harsh? Explain.
15. Characterize Charles Bovary.
16. Many critics regard Homais as the supreme characterization in the novel. Do you agree? Why? Characterize Homais.
17. Compare and contrast Leon and Rodolphe.
18. Characterize such secondary characters as Justin, Roualt, Mme. Bovary, Senior, Bournisien, Lheureux. What dramatic and thematic function does each serve?
19. Which characters are treated sympathetically? What light does such treatment shed on Flaubert's moral sense?
20. Flaubert acknowledged *Don Quixote* as the archetypal source of *Madame Bovary*. Detail the evidence of his indebtedness. Why do you think that Kierkegaard, the Danish philosopher, called Emma "a female Quixote"?
21. What does *Madame Bovary* tell us about the middle-class attitude (and about Flaubert's attitude) toward religion, science, sex, marriage? To what extent would you call this a sociological novel? A tragic novel?
22. If the novel is tragic, what is the tragedy?
23. In what ways does your reading of modern fiction make you aware that *Madame Bovary* is the manual of literary realism?
24. How mature is Flaubert's conception of life? Explain.

III. Readings in Background and Criticism

Auerbach, Erich, *Mimesis* (Doubleday Anchor Books, 1957). In the chapters "In the Hotel de la Mole" and "Germinie Lacerteux," Auerbach perceptively distinguishes the strategies of Flaubert's realism from those of Balzac and Stendhal. "Objective seriousness"—impersonal and impartial—marks *Madame Bovary*, the first novel to capture the formless tragedy of middle-class domesticity.

Bart, B. F., "Aesthetic Distance in *Madame Bovary*," *PMLA*, LXIX (December 1954, 1112-1126). A scholarly enquiry into Flaubert's recurrent use of Emma Bovary's convent readings. Bart reasons that Emma's literary interests orient her response to crucial events and afford the reader a vantage point ("aesthetic distance") from which to survey the results of her thinking.

Levin, Harry, "*Madame Bovary:* The Cathedral and the Hospital," *Essays in Criticism* (January 1952, 1-23). Embodying in his novel both romance (the cathedral) and realism (the hospital), Flaubert works them technically and thematically to achieve ironic counterpoint. Levin shows clearly how Flaubert achieves his effects and how they differ from those of his archetype, *Don Quixote*.

Lubbock, Percy, *The Craft of Fiction* (Compass Books, 1957). A provocative discussion of the dramatic and pictorial elements in *Madame Bovary*, especially useful for its attention to the narrative problems implicit in Flaubert's method.

Mercier, Vivian, "The Limitations of Flaubert," *Kenyon Review*, XIX (Summer 1957, 400-417). An incisive presentation of Flaubert's shortcomings as man and artist. Mercier pointedly argues with the *Times Literary Supplement's* analysis (see below) of symbolic implications in various episodes of *Madame Bovary*.

Spencer, Philip, *Flaubert: A Biography* (Grove Press, 1953). A useful though rather academic biography. In Chapter 8, "*Madame Bovary*," Spencer relates the genesis and writing of the novel and the events attending its publication. Chapter 9, "The Artist," limns Flaubert's esthetic development.

Steegmuller, Francis, *Flaubert and Madame Bovary* (Vintage Books, 1957). Strikingly original in method, superbly styled, Steegmuller's book expertly uses social history, biography, and criticism to elucidate *Madame Bovary*.

———, editor, *Selected Letters of Gustave Flaubert* (Farrar, Straus, and Young, 1953). Flaubert's epistolary style is looser, more discursive, and warmer than his novelistic prose. Beyond his letters to Louise Colet, Max DuCamp, and Louis Bouilhet—invaluable as background to *Madame Bovary*—those to Baudelaire, George Sand, Turgenev, Zola, *et al.*, illumine his attitudes toward art, social forces, and himself.

London Times Literary Supplement, "*Madame Bovary*," London, April 12, 1957. A brilliant analysis of Flaubert's symbolic imagery in *Madame Bovary*. The anonymous essayist details several instances proving that Flaubert's imagery subserves theme and structure. Unfortunately, he holds, Flaubert manipulates his characters as he does his images—makes them mere figures in a pattern.

Turnell, Martin, *The Novel in France* (New Directions, 1951). A lucid and discerning study of seven major French novelists. In his chapter on Flaubert, Turnell insists that *Madame Bovary*, though technically superb, expresses an immature, doctrinaire pessimism that vitiates much of its irony.

Wilson, Edmund, *The Triple Thinkers* (Oxford University Press, 1948). In the chapter "The Politics of Flaubert," Wilson argues tenaciously —and, some critics would add, tenuously—that Flaubert's novels exemplify a consistent, if unsystematic, body of social, almost socialistic, thought.

IV. Translations and Editions

Francis Steegmuller's recent translation (Random House, Modern Library), occasioned by the centennial of *Madame Bovary*, is the finest now available. A biographer and translator of Flaubert's correspondence, Steegmuller is more graceful and accurate than other translators. Though lacking Steegmuller's effectiveness, several other good translations are in print and available in paperback. Three are particularly recommended: that by Lowell Bair (Bantam); that by Alan Russell (Penguin); and that by Karl Marx's daughter, Eleanor Marx-Aveling (Rinehart), whose unhappy life and death oddly parallel Emma's.

26

Dostoyevsky: CRIME AND PUNISHMENT

I. Background of Dostoyevsky (1821 - 1881)

The ordinary man will generally admit that he has from time to time hankered to break the law—even to commit murder. But it would be an extraordinary man indeed who yielded to the impulse on the ground that crime—murder, particularly—was ennobling and liberating, that it brought triumphant release from the bondage of convention. Happily, most men are ordinary. They do not murder; they read murder stories. Identifying with the detective hero—the latter-day angel of retribution—they satisfy both their criminal urge and their sense of justice.

The reader of Fedor Dostoyevsky's *Crime and Punishment* (1866) ought not anticipate such easy satisfaction. The shrewd and sardonic detective, Porfiry, is not the hero. The murderer, Raskolnikov, is. And with Raskolnikov the reader's lot is cast; with him the reader must acknowledge the justice of punishment—and experience it vicariously. More significantly, while analyzing the aberrant motives that spur Raskolnikov to murder, he is shocked to recognize that something of Raskolnikov's demonism inhabits *all* men. Because it probes dark, cavernous places where the light of ordinary reason cannot penetrate, *Crime and Punishment* eludes facile explanation. Raskolnikov's incentive for committing murder, for example, may at first seem neither rational nor plausible. It is wise, therefore, to keep in mind Dostoyevsky's pronouncement: "What most people regard as fantastic . . . I hold to be the inmost essence of truth . . . I am a realist in the higher meaning of the term."

Not until he was past forty did Dostoyevsky embody in his novels the "higher" realism. That he survived his hellish existence until then seems almost incredible. Disease, imprisonment, and poverty shadowed his life. The only joy in his Moscow childhood and adolescence he derived from reading. At school he was lonely; at home he was tyrannized by his father, a miserly, brutish doctor whose own serfs murdered him. At twenty-five Dostoyevsky tasted success and fame when his first novel, *Poor Folk* (1846), won him the accolade of "a new Gogol." The happy interlude was short-lived: what seemed arrogance and vanity but was really neurotic hypersensitivity alienated would-be admirers; his second novel, *The Double*, earned little favor. For three more years, penniless and ill, he struggled on, writing sketches and stories. But critics now either ignored or ridiculed his compassionate studies of the oppressed and the humiliated.

Like many Russian intellectuals of the 1840's, Dostoyevsky burned with the European fever of reform. Some of these men—the "Westernizers"—urged that Russia emulate the liberalism and rationalism of the more enlightened European nations; others—the "Slavophiles"—wanted orthodoxy, aristocracy, and hypernationalism to prevail, as in the days of Peter the Great. Toward both groups Czar Nicholas I was implacable. By execution and exile he tried to extirpate any effort to free the serfs or to ameliorate the widespread social injustices of the age. Influenced by V. G. Belinsky, a noted critic, socialist, and atheist who furthered his literary career, Dostoyevsky became an enthusiastic Westernizer. He joined the Petrashevsky Circle, a group of utopians to whom he occasionally addressed ardently liberal speeches. On a morning after one of these meetings, Dostoyevsky was arrested and imprisoned in solitary confinement. Eight months later, on December 22, 1849, he and twenty-eight others were marched to a public square to be shot. The men listened to their death sentences, then watched silently and half-frozen as three of their group were blindfolded and tied to stakes. Only a moment before the scheduled execution an officer interrupted to announced that Nicholas I had beneficently commuted their sentences to eight years of hard labor in Siberia. At that instant, it is alleged, one prisoner's hair turned white; another prisoner went mad.

In *The House of the Dead* (1863) Dostoyevsky recalls the terrors of his exile, how he was shunned as an intellectual by the murderers with whom he lived, wracked by stomach pains, rheumatism, and increasingly recurrent attacks of epilepsy. His only reading matter was the New Testament. Nevertheless, shortly after he was pardoned and released in 1854 (to begin a four-year term as a private in the army), he wrote: "The penitentiary killed many things in me and made others blossom . . . The constant concentration on my inner self, to which I escaped from reality, bore its fruit." Enlarging his sympathies, suffering gave birth to Dostoyevsky's passionate devotion to the Russian people and his mystical faith in God, themes inextricably woven into his greatest novels. The near martyr of the Westernizers, now the apostle of the Slavophiles, began to preach the gospel that Russia, inspired by the love and suffering of Jesus, would ultimately lead a corrupt world to universal brotherhood.

In Dostoyevsky's novels, as in his life, man must experience damnation before he can know salvation. Thus in *Crime and Punishment*, half-dead, half-mad souls anguish in St. Petersburg, their earthly inferno. Hell, like heaven, has its brotherhood. In the nether world of *Crime and Punishment*, men and women are linked to one another and spiritually enchained to their sins: usury, drunkenness, lechery, hypocrisy, cynicism, self-pity, and nihilism.

Because of its lurid atmosphere, bizarre characters, and tortured episodes, many read *Crime and Punishment* simply as a melodramatic murder story. To do so is to miss Dostoyevsky's "higher realism," a fervid inward search that thrusts to the source of man's behavior. With insights Freud, Jung, Adler, and others have marveled at, Dostoyevsky anatomizes man's conscious and unconscious drives: his will to power, his sense of inferiority, his sadism, his masochism. Through dialogue, reverie, and dream, Dostoyevsky scrutinizes man's motives and then raises questions that defy final answer: Why must man suffer? What law of man or God sanctions his misery? And why, if none can answer, are not all things lawful—drunkenness, prostitution, murder? In *Notes from the Underground*, written the same year as *Crime and Punishment*, Dostoyevsky created an "underground" man, the prototype of Dostoyevskian heroes—of Raskolnikov, Stavrogin in *The Possessed*, and Ivan Karamazov in *The Brothers Karamazov*—men who asked forbidden questions, frame their own answers, and resolve to act rather than be. Like Milton's Satan, Dostoyevsky's "underground" man, abiding in Hell, determines to reign there free of all law but his own.

God punished Satan for his crime by casting him into Hell. To Dostoyevsky the Slavophile, punishment involved suffering but also redemption through faith. But to Dostoyevsky the man and the novelist, suffering overbalanced all. Until his very last years when he found peace, Dostoyevsky vacillated between faith and skepticism, torturing himself as he tortured his characters. He gambled compulsively and nearly always lost. To atone he wrote self-abasing letters to his wife. He starved himself while frantically writing articles and stories (even two of his greatest novels, *Crime and Punishment* and *The Idiot*) to recoup his fortune—and immediately thereafter he squandered his earnings. He exposed himself to abject humiliation by touring spas and gambling resorts with a beautiful woman who publicly scorned him and freely gave herself to other men. At home, his wife lay dying.

Alternately Dostoyevsky behaved outrageously and brooded in guilt-ridden penance. Explanations of his personal "crimes" and "punishments" have been varied and often contradictory: for example, some critics find the genesis of the guilt pervading his writings in his feelings toward his father whose death he had wished and felt he might have prevented; others, in the sexual ecstasy he derived from epilepsy, his "holy disease." It is more relevant to literature, however, that Dostoyevsky's experience taught him that punishment, like crime, involved more than a symbolic gesture. Imprisonment or exile without contrition alter the outward, not the inward man. For Dostoyevsky crime and punishment exist only as *felt* reality, a profound inner awareness that each must discover for himself.

Perhaps nowhere else in fiction are the warmth and light of faith so long withheld as in Dostoyevsky's greatest novels. Before his tortured protagonist finds inner harmony he must liberate himself from reason. As André Gide observed, "Dostoyevsky's heroes inherit the kingdom of God only by the denial of mind and will and the surrender of personality." Readers may not accept Dostoyevsky's vision of Christian fulfillment; they cannot fail to be roused by the anguished power with which he projects it.

II. Questions for Study and Discussion

1. What is the theme of *Crime and Punishment?* What structural relationship does each of the seven parts of the novel bear to the theme?
2. How does Dostoyevsky create suspense at the outset? What devices does he employ to sustain suspense? Where does the novel reach a climax? What part does coincidence play in the narrative? Can it be justified in terms of Dostoyevsky's philosophy? Explain.
3. Compare *Crime and Punishment* with any recent "whodunit." Which holds your attention more closely? Why?
4. Evaluate Dostoyevsky's skill in creating atmosphere. Compare his realism with Flaubert's. Wherein do they differ?
5. How do Dostoyevsky's physical descriptions differ from those usually found in novels? Do his characters look and sound real? Why?
6. *Raskolnick* means "dissenter." Against what forces in society does Raskolnikov voice dissent?
7. To what extent is Raskolnikov conscious throughout the novel of his real motive for murder? What other motives does he offer also? Are they equally valid? Explain.
8. What is peculiar or ironic about Raskolnikov's reactions immediately after his crime? Why does he later try to induce the police to suspect him?
9. What qualities does Raskolnikov possess that predetermine his ultimate failure as a criminal? Do these qualities strengthen or

weaken his appeal as a character? Why? What is his basic flaw? How have other writers regarded this defect in their protagonists?

10. Why have each of the following characters been called Raskolnikov's "doubles": Luzhin, Svidrigailov, Sonia, Porfiry?
11. How do these characters illumine certain facets of Raskolnikov's personality: Marmeladov, Razumihin, Dounia?
12. Compare Porfiry with other famous detectives of fiction.
13. Compare Svidrigailov and Luzhin. Why is Svidrigailov developed more sympathetically?
14. Why is Sonia made a prostitute? Why does Raskolnikov both love and hate her? Why does he confess to her before he surrenders to Porfiry?
15. Who is the ultimate victim of Raskolnikov's crime? Why?
16. In his *Notebooks*, Dostoyevsky expresses dissatisfaction with the "Epilogue." Evaluate the "Epilogue" structurally, psychologically, and thematically.
17. Detail the steps of Raskolnikov's punishment. In which phase of human experience, in crime, or in punishment, do you find Dostoyevsky's insights more profound? Justify your choice.
18. Discuss the symbolic meaning of each of Raskolnikov's three dreams. Of Svidrigailov's.
19. How is Raskolnikov's sickness related to his social philosophy? To the central conflict of the novel?
20. What is the symbolic significance of the unintended murder of Lizaveta?
21. What symbolic meaning do you attach to Raskolnikov's tears at the end of the novel?
22. How does Dostoyevsky employ humor? To what purpose?
23. What evidence is there of Dostoyevsky's social and political thinking? Would he be a Marixst today? How do you think his reputation in the Soviet Union today compares with Tolstoy's?
24. In broad social and spiritual terms, what is Raskolnikov's tragedy? What is his triumph?
25. What similarity do you find between Raskolnikov and Faust? Between Raskolnikov and Achilles? Between Dostoyevsky's and Goethe's philosophies of man?

26. What is Dostoyevsky's attitude toward women and love? What is the symbolic role of sex in the novel? In what other authors have you found similar ideas?
27. What significance does Dostoyevsky's thought have for us today?

III. Readings in Background and Criticism

Beebe, Maurice, "The Three Motives of Raskolnikov," *College English* (December 1955, 151-158). An ingenious argument that *Crime and Punishment* achieves thematic and dramatic unity by interweaving Raskolnikov's "triple" personality with its alter egos; Luzhin, the intellectual; Svidrigailov, the sensual; and Sonia, the spiritual.

Blackmur, R. P., "Crime and Punishment: A Study," *The Chimera* (Winter, 1943, 7-29). A provocative essay suggesting that Raskolnikov's crime—symbolic of mankind's compulsion to be "extraordinary" —is implicit in life itself, not merely in the act of murder. Effective punishment, therefore, requires that mankind, like Raskolnikov, be transformed rather than reformed.

Freud, Sigmund, *Stavrogin's Confession* (Lear, 1947). In a brief psychoanalytical study of Dostoyevsky, Freud argues that Oedipal attitudes towards his father led Dostoyevsky to sadistic and masochistic drives expressed in his own as well as in his character's morbid inclinations to inflict pain and to be punished.

Fuelop-Miller, René, *Dostoyevsky* (Scribner's, 1950). A slender but useful introductory volume. Chapter 6 studies in detail how Raskolnikov's and Svidrigailov's dreams anticipate Freud's theories of dream analysis.

Gibian, George, "Traditional Symbolism in Crime and Punishment," *PMLA*, LXX (December 1955, 979-996). An engrossing scholarly essay pointing up Dostoyevsky's use of traditional Christian symbols (the resurrection of Jesus and Lazarus) and pagan symbols (water, vegetation, earth, etc.) to expose and attack the evils of rationalism.

Gide, André, *Dostoyevsky* (Knopf, 1926). In this short book the famous French novelist limns Raskolnikov as a "miserable worm" whose intellect and will must be destroyed if he is to earn salvation. Dostoyevsky's greatness, Gide maintains, lies in teaching all men to achieve personal fulfillment without imposing their physical or psychic will on others.

Lavrin, Janko, *Dostoyevsky* (Macmillan, 1947). In the chapter, "The Bankruptcy of the Superman," Lavrin, a Christian Socialist, describes Raskolnikov as an aspiring Napoleon who suffers the doubts of Hamlet.

According to Lavrin, the novel anticipates Nietzsche's doctrine of the *ubermensch*—the superman.

Lloyd, J. A. T., *Dostoyevsky* (Scribner's, 1947). Lloyd denies Lavrin's notion, asserting that Nietzsche would have rejected Raskolnikov as a superman because of Raskolnikov's deep sense of obligation to others.

Mirsky, D. S., *A History of Russian Literature*, ed. by F. J. Whitehead (Knopf, 1949). An abridgement of a classic literary history. Chapter 8, "The Age of Realism," a discussion of the major writings of both Dostoyevsky and Tolstoy, meaningfully contrasts their literary attitudes and methods.

Simmons, Ernest J., *Dostoyevsky: The Making of a Novelist* (Oxford University Press, 1950). The best full-length biography. Simmons' criticisms of the novels are also lucid and informative.

Slonim, Marc, *The Epic of Russian Literature* (Oxford University Press, 1950). A superb history of Russian literature from the 18th century to Tolstoy (a second volume carries on to the present). Chapter 14 contains what is perhaps the best general biographical and critical essay available in English about Dostoyevsky.

———, *Three Loves of Dostoyevsky* (Rinehart, 1955). A suspenseful biography that stresses the impact on his life and work of Dostoyevsky's three love affairs. Unfortunately, the book highlights Dostoyevsky's pathology at the expense of his creativity, often missing the element of genius which enabled him to transcend his psychic agonies.

Troyat, Henri, *Firebrand: The Life of Dostoyevsky* (Roy, 1946). An intensely written, almost novelized study; yet accurate and critically perceptive. The chapter, "Notes from the Underground," examines *Crime and Punishment* in the light of pervasive drives in Dostoyevsky's life and work.

IV. Translations and Editions

David Magarshack's recent translation (Penguin) surpasses all others in its readability. Constance Garnett's version (Bantam, Modern Library) is satisfactory but rather stiff and formal. Avoid abridgements.

27

Tolstoy:
WAR AND PEACE

I. Background of Tolstoy (1828 - 1910)

"I consign all my artistic productions," Count Leo Tolstoy wrote in 1898, "to the category of bad art, except 'God Sees the Truth' and 'The Prisoner of the Caucasus' "—two brief moralities of the utmost simplicity, composed for the third and fourth of a graded series of Russian primary readers. By then his theory of art, an extremely important theory in literary history, had solidified. Art, he affirmed, is effective in proportion as it "infects." In this era, he thought, good art infects with Christian feelings, with love and compassion. And the greatest art is accessible not merely to a small group of cultivated, idle men but to all men, including the poor and uneducated peasant—perhaps especially to him, for he has been saved from the viciousness of the effete trifler, the "cultured" man without values.

Rousseau, who had raised the "natural man" from simple savage to secular saint in the modern imagination, deeply influenced Tolstoy. The theory, none the less, grew intimately from Tolstoy's character and experience. In 1876 he had suffered a spiritual crisis. Appalled by his meaningless existence, by the sterility of his art, by the steady misery of a life dedicated to self, he came almost to the verge of suicide. Neither Russian Orthodoxy nor any of the philosophies of the West seemed to offer solace. Then, through a verse from Matthew (5:59), he saw the way illumined: "that ye resist not evil." From that verse Tolstoy wrought his new dispensation; new, for though it rested on the essential teaching of the Sermon on the Mount, it had been obscured through the generations by Pauline mysticism. In Tolstoy's plain restatement, according to the spirit of Jesus (supplemented by Buddha and Lao-tse), these are the ethical imperatives that can rescue man from the sickness of his civilization: Live in peace with all men. Do good to all men, renouncing distinctions of nationality. Abandon libertinage and divorce. Never take an oath for service of any kind. Refuse to employ force for any reason whatever.

Among the artistic productions Tolstoy renounced in the wake of his late conversion were *War and Peace* (1865 - 1869) and *Anna Karenina* (1875 - 1877), which many critics regard as the ultimate achievements in the novel. If the renunciation evinces humility, it must nevertheless be condemned for zealotry—and in a mistaken cause. For there is a continuity between the later and the earlier Tolstoy, the continuity of conscience. In *War and Peace* and *Anna Karenina*, as well as in the stories that received Tolstoy's imprimatur, one finds (though muted in the novels) the same disgust at worldliness, the same despair in the face of a world where greed, lust, and anger govern. In the former novel, Prince André Bolkonsky and Pierre Bezuhov, who divide among themselves the salient aspects of Tolstoy's personality, react to the stupidity of things much as Tolstoy later over-reacted. After meeting the noble peasant Platon Karateyev, Pierre even sees in his nearsighted fashion, glimmerings of the kingdom of Heaven which is within. And in *Anna Karenina*, Levin, another image of Tolstoy, similarly finds release from spiritual agony in the words of one of his peasants, that man discovers his meaning only through living by the rule of God, of the truth.

From his earliest diaries, begun in 1847, one glimpses Tolstoy's dissatisfaction with a purely sensual order of existence. Having been bored at the University, experimented with the normal dissolute pleasures of the nobility, enlisted in the army and seen service at Sevastopol, tried writing and tasted glory as the result of his first published novel (the autobiographical *Childhood*) and his Sevastopol sketches, toured Western Europe and been repelled by its rampant materialism, he returned in 1861, at the age of thirty-three, to the family estate, *Yasnaya Polyana* ("Clear Fields"). There, at the school for peasant children that he had set up twelve years earlier, he flung himself wholeheartedly into teaching. For the time, at least, he had to seek no further; the school became his "life and refuge." He seems to have been a superbly gifted teacher, and his educational theory, based on Rousseau's, startles through its modernity. Like Dewey, he regarded the "life needs" of the child as primary, insisted that each child ought to learn anything only when he wanted to, when he felt its value. In other ways, too, Tolstoy labored for Russian elementary learning, writing articles, publishing *A New Primer*, editing the enormously popular *Azbuki* (ABC books).

But the sense of futility once more reasserted itself. His students could not appreciate Beethoven or Pushkin. Perhaps they needed to be prepared? Not at all, Tolstoy maintained: who requires preparation for appreciating true, essential beauty—the beauty of the sun, of a face, of a folk song, of an act of self-sacrifice and love? Because cultivated people have been corrupted and because Beethoven or Pushkin appeal to their corrupted sensibility, cultured people adore them. What then must be done? Tolstoy decided he did not know and consequently could no longer teach.

Here Tolstoy was clearly poised on the brink of crisis. It was, however, delayed for fifteen years. In 1862 he married Sophia Behrs, who proved, until Tolstoy attempted to act on his detestation of property and money, a completely devoted wife. Moreover, between 1865 and 1869, *War and Peace* consumed his energies: he had hardly enough left for crises.

At first, he had planned a novel about the Decembrists of 1825, the gallant, futile band of aristocrats who attempted a palace revolution at the beginning of Nicholas I's reign. It was an intriguing theme, and it continued for many years to intrigue Tolstoy. But he began to wonder—as a novelist he was forced to wonder—what his characters had been like when they were much younger; and he ended by setting his novel during the years 1805 to 1812.

Although prudence was not his motive, Tolstoy acted prudently in shifting the time of his narrative. The extant fragments of his Decembrist novel suggest that he intended to treat the conspirators sympathetically: Pierre Bezuhov, the hero of the uncompleted novel as of *War and Peace*, having enlisted in the doomed conspiracy, is exiled to Siberia, whither Natasha follows him. When, in 1856, they return to Moscow, Pierre has been purified by suffering, Natasha ennobled by love. Beyond question, the glowering censor would have found Tolstoy's attitude toward his characters repugnant.

For though liberalism broke over the Russian landscape with the accession of Alexander II in 1855, those pessimists who suspected a false dawn were ultimately justified. Nevertheless, for a while at least, Alexander seemed to overhear the muffled cries of "Freedom, Progress, Reform!" issuing from the westernized liberal intellectuals, just as his predecessor, Nicholas I, had hearkened (much more appreciatively) to the shouts of "Autocracy, Orthodoxy, Nationality!" rising from the Slavophiles, the dedicated reactionaries who were convinced that Holy Russia had been chosen among the nations to guide mankind to a higher and nobler civilization. Nicholas' program, domestic and foreign, had been ruthlessly reactionary; it had been based on an elementary principle, that he was God's agent on earth—and to be anti-czar in any particular was also to be anti-God. His theory was violently challenged—by the Decembrists, by the Liberals, by the Socialists and Anarchists (who had organized in 1848, the former under Herzen, the latter under Bakunin); and ultimately, when he tried to make his theory prevail beyond his borders, by the alliance of England, France, Turkey, and Sardinia.

Following the death of Nicholas soon after Sevastopol, the climactic battle of the Crimean War, Alexander II realized that the old godly order of things had passed. Hoping to escape the troubles that had besieged his father, he formulated a variety of constitutional reforms. Some of them, like the abolition of serfdom (1861), he actually carried through. Troubles nevertheless continued to harass him; and by 1865 he had exhausted most of his reforming zeal. After an unsuccessful attempt on his life in 1866, he concluded that liberalism was not only a useless but an ungrateful creature, and he embraced reaction with almost the fervor Nicholas had displayed. But throughout Alexander's regime, whether his tendency was liberal or reactionary, the censor flourished. Russian liberalism has always looked much like despotism elsewhere.

When he left the army in 1855, Tolstoy formed, briefly, some uncomfortable friendships with liberals in St. Petersburg. Later he cherished, more lastingly, the Slavophile delusion concerning the genius of Primitive Russia. Extricating himself from both factions, however, he proceeded to develop his special kind of Christian Anarchism. How far he had come from the political realities may be deduced from his plea to the new czar in 1881, following the assassination of Alexander II. Neither reform nor repression, Tolstoy pointed out, had helped stabilize the government or end terrorism. Since political means had thus far failed, he urged a moral expedient, returning good for evil. By pardoning the revolutionaries who had blown up his father, Alexander III would set the world an example of Christian forgiveness. Such a policy, Tolstoy argued, had never been tried. Alexander III chose not to be the first to try it.

By relocating his novel in the years 1805 to 1812, Tolstoy evaded the censor; but more, he enlarged the scope of his action. For these were the Napoleonic years which culminated in the invasion of Russia. A half million men from seventeen nations, *La Grande Armée*, marched eastward in scrupulous order, ravaged the Russian land and slaughtered the stupidly led Russian soldiers by the hundred thousand, occupied the ancient capital, Moscow, without doing battle for it—then, turning, fled westward, retreating without a semblance of discipline, devastated by hunger, cold, the enemy, and, most of all, panic.

Books have been written to prove that Tolstoy violated the history of the campaign. Historians, generals, diplomats have amply demonstrated that he was wrong about the number and disposition of forces, about the objectives and results of battles, about the personalities and capabilities of commanding officers. He veils Alexander I's treachery and truckling. He discounts Napoleon's military "genius." He overvalues Kutuzov's strategy—more accurately, invents it. These objections may be sustained; but they weigh little in judging *War and Peace*. Tolstoy does not retell history; he creates an epic account of a great national struggle. What criticism engages itself with auditing Homer's catalogues or checking Milton's rolls?

Tolstoy's distortions of history flow largely from a debatable theory of history. That theory invades *War and Peace* from the first chapter of Book III, but it is pressed most vigorously and comprehensively in the second part of the Epilogue. From his dense but vague argument, we come away convinced that the prime force of history is "the ferment of peoples," not the will of heroes. (Someone like Kutuzov, who senses the direction of history and willingly submits to it, most nearly approaches the status of hero.) What motivates the ferment of peoples, however, Tolstoy cannot tell us. Once in the third book and again in the fourth, he tentatively suggests that events are "predetermined from on high." But he never pursues the suggestion, and in the Epilogue dismisses it.

Tolstoy wrote the Epilogue because he felt the need to marshal his speculations formally. But his readers have no answering need. To most the Epilogue adds only an anticlimax. Because Tolstoy persists in arguing after the vitalizing scene has faded, his arguments remain inert. The intercalary chapters dealing with history and the theory of history, on the contrary, not only are quickened by the narrative but quicken it as well. While reading, at least, one quarrels with them no more than with Homer's or Milton's theology.

Moreover, they contribute to the epic amplitude of *War and Peace*. Its amplitude, its prodigality, will impress the reader first. In addition to three emperors, a host of ministers, marshals, and generals, and several armies, more than 500 characters figure in the narrative, 100 of them importantly. The action sweeps across Russia. The tableaux shift ceaselessly. The moods range human emotion. The characters have the pulsing diversity of life.

Yet in spite of his vast panorama—wars, movements of peoples, issues of empire—Tolstoy sharply individualizes every character who enacts a significant role: the tilt of this one's head, the timbre of another's voice, the bearlike gait of a third. Tolstoy's graphic power so absorbs and convinces the reader that he often forgets he is reading; he seems immediately in the presence of the character. Though the plot is magnificent, the characters interest Tolstoy—and the reader—beyond it.

Mainly *War and Peace* threads its scenes upon the annals of three families—the Bolkonskys, the Rostovs, and the Bezuhovs (if Pierre and Hélène Bezuhov may be called a family). The Rostovs are modeled upon the Tolstoys, the Bolkonskys upon the Volkonskys (the family of the author's mother). But Tolstoy combines, adapts, shapes. Just as he split himself into André Bolkonsky and Pierre Bezuhov (and perhaps Platon Karateyev, the peasant soldier whose simple goodness is Tolstoy's ideal), so he "pounded up" his wife and sister to compose Natasha Rostov. All of his people are formed from life, none is copied from it; each evolves according to the laws of his being.

This fusion of novel and epic makes *War and Peace* a monumental work. It sets the individual against the background of destiny. It chronicles family affairs as it tells of the course of empires. It creates live people while revealing an epoch. It does even more: it shows men how basely and foolishly they behave, and it points out how they may become wise and good.

II. Questions for Study and Discussion

1. What is the theme of *War and Peace?*
2. What is Tolstoy's attitude toward war? How directly and clearly does he state it? Compare his attitude with Homer's, Vergil's, Machiavelli's, Voltaire's.
3. To what extent do Tolstoy's characters develop? Is Natasha, for example, the same person at the beginning, in the middle, and at the end of *War and Peace?*
4. Does Tolstoy describe his characters before they speak, while they speak, or both? Examine his method as applied to a secondary character (for example, Prince Vasili) and a primary one (for example, Pierre).
5. A Russian critic remarked that even Tolstoy's dogs were individualized. Did he exaggerate? Identity the individualizing traits of several minor characters, of several central characters.
6. Are Tolstoy's symbols integral or added? What is the symbolic

import (in Part I of the Epilogue) of Natasha's striding joyfully from the nursery to display a diaper stained yellow instead of green? What other comparable symbols can you find?

7. Matthew Arnold says that Tolstoy introduces people and incidents that have nothing to do with the main action of the book —that Tolstoy introduces them simply because he saw them with his inward eye. Comment on Arnold's observation. If it is accurate, cite some examples that sustain it.
8. Thomas Wolfe remarked to F. Scott Fitzgerald that there are two kinds of writers: the putters-in and the leavers-out. To which category does Tolstoy belong? Among 19th-century novelists you have read (Hawthorne, Melville, Flaubert, Dostoyevsky, Mark Twain), whose method contrasts most plainly with Tolstoy's? Who—Tolstoy or the other writer—is the greater artist? Why?
9. What are the essential differences between Tolstoy's style and Dostoyevsky's?
10. Is there anybody like Achilles in *War and Peace?* If so, who? If not, why not?
11. Characterize each of the important women in *War and Peace.* What is Tolstoy's attitude toward women and marriage?
12. How does Tolstoy's interpolated history and theory of history add to or subtract from the novel?
13. To what extent does Tolstoy allow for the possibility of a "science" of history? What weaknesses do you note in his understanding of historical process?
14. Is Tolstoy fair in his treatment of Napoleon? Explain.
15. Why does Tolstoy make Pierre a Freemason? What is Tolstoy's attitude toward Freemasonry?
16. What are Prince André's failings? What are his virtues?
17. What are Pierre's failings and virtues?
18. Who are the "bad" or vicious characters in the novel? What makes them bad?
19. What does Platon Karateyev represent? Is he believable? How convincing is Pierre's new insight as the result of knowing him?
20. Explain Tolstoy's social views. Does he admire the Russian

nobility? What are their virtues and vices? How does he regard the peasants?

21. What pleasures would there be for the average sensual man in the life of a Russian aristocrat? When he wrote *War and Peace*, which did Tolstoy approve, which tolerate, which abominate?
22. Summarize Tolstoy's philosophy of life as expressed in *War and Peace*.
23. What is the attitude of present-day Russian critics to Tolstoy? Why?
24. What, if anything, do you find lacking in *War and Peace*? What are its great strengths?

III. Readings in Background and Criticism

Arnold, Matthew, "Count Leo Tolstoi," *Essays in Criticism, Second Series* (Macmillan, 1889). Granting Tolstoy's genius, Arnold says the novels lose in art what they gain "in reality." An interesting early critique of Tolstoy's method and philosophy, though based too largely on *Anna Karenina*.

Berlin, Isaiah, *The Hedgehog and the Fox* (New American Library, 1957). A masterly, lively essay which critically examines Tolstoy's search for a unifying philosophy of history.

Chesterton, G. K., Perris, G. H., and Garnett, Edward, editors, *Leo Tolstoy* (Hodder and Stoughton, 1903). Fascinating, not because of the several contemporary opinions it includes, but because of the diverse illustrations.

Farrell, James T., "Tolstoy's *War and Peace* as a Moral Panorama of the Tsarist Feudal Nobility," *Literature and Morality* (Vanguard Press, 1947). An acute sociological study, based on the idea that *War and Peace* diagnoses a class and epoch, summarizes the moral consequences of a system.

Garrod, H. W., *Tolstoi's Theory of Art* (Oxford University Press, 1935). An ironical critical exposition of Tolstoy's esthetic theory—perhaps too much critical and too little expository.

Gorky, Maxim, *Reminiscences of Leo Nikolaevich Tolstoy* (L. & V. Woolf, 1920). Warm and discerning, Gorky's memoir beautifully evokes Tolstoy, the "godlike man."

Lenin, Nikolai, "Tolstoi and His Epoch," *Labour Monthly* (October 1928). A brief statement, significant because of Tolstoy's ambiguous status in contemporary Russian criticism: Tolstoy's teaching is utopian, its tendency reactionary, its conception oriental, its socialist elements no longer pertinent.

Mann, Thomas, "Goethe and Tolstoy," *Essays* (Vintage Books, 1957). A long discursive essay, comparing the ideas and background of two "natural noblemen"; a rare combination of charm and insight.

Maude, Aylmer, *The Life of Tolstoy* (Oxford University Press, 1930). Overcommitted to defending Tolstoy; nevertheless an important biography by his friend and translator.

Noyes, G. P., *Tolstoy* (Duffield and Co., 1918). Superseded as biography, but still valuable for its analysis and criticism of Tolstoy's works and ways.

Ségur, Philippi-Paul de, *Napoleon's Russian Campaign* (Houghton Mifflin, 1958). A vivid chronicle, a principal source-book for Tolstoy, and a tonic contrast to his account of the invasion.

Simmons, Ernest J., *Leo Tolstoy* (Little, Brown, 1946). The definitive biography in English.

Zweig, Stephen, "Tolstoi," *Master Builders* (Viking Press, 1939). A portrait in depth; graphic writing but at times dubious interpretation.

IV. Translations and Editions

War and Peace has been competently translated by Leo Weiner and by Constance Garnett (Modern Library)—which is to say that the words are there but the tune is lost: the vibrancy and movement appear only fitfully. The best translation, so good that it sometimes seems no translation at all, has been made by Louise and Aylmer Maude and the (Simon and Shuster) edition, complete with maps, cast of characters, a splendid introduction by Clifton Fadiman, and helpful, always pertinent notes, ought to be preferred. A new translation in two volumes by Rosemary Edmonds (Penguin) is extremely good, too—though distressing in the dialectal passages where Cossacks occasionally speak like Cockneys.

A warning note must be added: there are several abridgements easily available. Avoid reading them—not only because they derogate from Tolstoy, whose genius needs scope, but also because they are so jumbled as to be practically unreadable.

28

Twain: THE ADVENTURES OF HUCKLEBERRY FINN

I. Background of Mark Twain (1835 - 1910)

College English teachers rarely must answer charges that their reading lists are too simple. Yet each time they assign to their classes *The Adventures of Huckleberry Finn* some students protest that it is just "another boy's book"—as Twain himself unfortunately called it. (Sophisticated sophomores occasionally cover it in a plain wrapper.) In 1885, when the novel first appeared in the United States (it had been published shortly before in England), dissenters took exception on other grounds: several newspapers called it "coarse" and "vulgar," and Transcendentalists in Concord, Massachusetts, condemning the book as inappropriate for the young, collaborated to ban it from the shelves of the public library. But neither undergraduate snobbism nor genteel morality has diminished Twain's reputation. He remains the most widely read American man of letters. And *Huckleberry Finn*, his most popular novel, has been rightly called "one of the central documents of American culture." As Huck journeys along the

Mississippi, he looks at the American world of his time and judges what is good about it and what is bad.

The expanding mid-19th-century American democracy in which Samuel Langhorne Clemens lived for almost seventy-five years churned with the energy of change. Boundaries of space and thought altered as the nation pressed westward beyond the Mississippi, underwent an industrial revolution, and struggled through a tragic Civil War and turbulent Reconstruction. During the restless early years of the Frontier, the dynamism of life and letters was the present and tangible. There was little interest in abstract morality or metaphysics: neither Hawthorne's analyses of the consequences of sin nor Melville's probings into the nature of evil commanded wide attention. Broad humor, local color, and sentimentality charmed the frontiersman. Naive and optimistic, he ignored the implications of widespread land speculation, of conflict between the new industrialism and the old agrarianism—harsh realities that would tarnish his bright dreams of quick wealth in "the garden of the world" and waken him to the nightmare of bankruptcy and social exploitation. The ingenuous but illusory world of Tom Sawyer was destined to give way to the knowing and realistic one of Huck Finn.

The dream pattern lay as deep in Twain as it did in America. Like his Virginia-born father, Clemens hoped for but never gained easy wealth: his most successful years as an author were marred by financial problems resulting from impractical investments. As a boy in Hannibal, Missouri, however, Clemens suffered little from his family's straitened circumstances. Everywhere about the Middle Border lay materials for romance—rivers, forests, caves. Slave caravans were a common sight. Although the romance was disrupted by frequent episodes of violence—feuds, brawls, shootings—it surrounded him plentifully. But Hannibal was not the Wild West; unlike Huck, it wanted to be "sivilized." Schools were good, libraries well-stocked, and before he was twelve, Clemens had read the Bible (chiefly at the insistence of his Presbyterian mother), *Pilgrim's Progress, Don Quixote, Ivanhoe*, and had assimilated much of the available frontier humor and folklore. His boyhood experiences—social and cultural—formed the matrix of Twain's greatest fiction. A half-century later he returned in memory, seeking to reconcile in *Huckleberry Finn* the romance and realism, the humor and poignancy of his youth.

From the time he went to work at thirteen as an apprentice printer until at thirty-five he married Olivia Langdon and settled in Hartford, Connecticut, to pursue a literary career, Clemens roamed the world. His experiences as printer, river pilot ("Mark Twain" is a riverman's expression), prospector, and reporter stocked his memory for the creative years ahead. But in most of his writing Clemens evaded the seamier sides of reality; a man of his age, he dreaded the stark testimony of truth. Instead he delighted the Babbitts of the Gilded Age (and of ours) with humorous and gently satiric sketches about mining camps or with hilarious spoofs of greenhorns and intellectuals. None of these works prove his greatness. At their best they are funny because of their style rather than their content—marvelously picturesque language and a deliberately guileless tone. At their worst (and they are more often at their worst than at their best) they are crude and tasteless, their humor transparent and ephemeral. Most important, they never pierce the surface to reveal genuine insight into human experience. Not until his late years did Twain face life squarely, and then, anguished and embittered by financial reverses and family illness, no longer able to discover solace in memory, he lapsed into hopeless pessimism. Works like *What is Man?* (1906) and *The Mysterious Stranger* (1916, published posthumously) indict the "damned human race" as wicked, pity it as the victim of a malevolent universal force.

Twain's greatest writing, however, preceded his final despair. *Tom Sawyer* (1876) won immediate and widespread acclaim. He wrote it rapidly and lovingly, for it told the truth as Twain wished it were: tender and sentimental, joyous and romantic. Shortly after *Tom Sawyer* appeared, Twain began work on a sequel, *The Adventures of Huckleberry Finn;* he delayed its completion for seven years, filling the interim with plays, travel sketches, and a novel. Scholars still debate the reasons for the long postponement. Was Twain shunning the truth that adolescent experience may be grim as well as gay? Was he still afraid to see deeply into things because the insights might be painful? Was he intent upon sustaining the image of an eternally young America (his wife always called him "Youth") —a Tom Sawyerish world in which neither Twain nor America need change?

Huckleberry Finn was a painful book for Twain to write, and it is often a painful book to read. Feuds, murder, mob temper, and fraud fill its pages; there is enough violence and death to make the reader as well as the twelve-year-old hero ashamed of the human race. But *Huckleberry Finn* does more than catalog human degradation; and more, too, than glamorize a fugitive slave's escape to freedom. On one level the adventure of Huck Finn may profitably be read as a realistic moral adventure: the profound inward experience of a boy who forswears the only ethical tradition he has inherited and adopts one born of his adolescent conscience. A great-spirited boy among mean-spirited men, Huck stands alone and ponders a decision usually left to those much older and more experienced—the reconciliation of inherited piety with human decency.

The men, women, and children who share in Huck's adventure flesh the moral framework of the novel. Drawn from every stratum of Southern society, they are realistically etched in their Middle Border setting. Usually prone to oversimplify people and problems, Twain wisely disengaged his own passions and deftly made Huck his narrator. Critical and perceptive but also tolerant and humble, Huck allows lovable and rascally characters alike to gain dimension and earn compassion. Some have even argued—questionably—that Jim, the enslaved Negro, actually becomes the true protagonist, a father-image whom Huck merely emulates. Unquestionably, Jim's presence on the raft adds immeasurably to the drama of the novel and to Huck's growth.

One other character deserves notice—the Mississippi River. Its function in the novel has been much discussed. Some critics suggest that the river gives form and definition to the story—that the incidents stem from it rather than from Huck's flight from his father and Jim's from slavery. So interpreted, the Mississippi unifies an otherwise discontinuous, episodic story; for it is to the river that Huck inevitably returns after each harrowing experience on land. Other critics insist that the Mississippi serves a further purpose. Perhaps

Huck's return to the river indicates an escape from the harsh reality of the land. Or his journey may symbolize the rites of passage practiced among primitive cults and frequently rehearsed in modern literature, rites in which a young man journeys to a secret place where he undergoes a painful initiation (he may even symbolically die to exorcise evil spirits) before he is "reborn" as a man. Certainly the Mississippi—"the strong brown god," a fellow Missourian, T. S. Eliot, called it—endows the novel with myth creating power. Detached and impassive, its presence nevertheless influences and integrates the lives of those who, like Twain and Huck, dwell near its shores or navigate its muddy waters. Even if it is considered only a metaphor, the Mississippi helps direct attention not only to the obvious central issues of the book but also to more universal ones.

Twain's language, natural and energetic, seems appropriate to his Mississippi River setting. His masterly handling of the vernacular (he boasts in the preface of seven dialects) helps him steer clear of formalism, keeps him simple and lively. Spurning the easy tricks of comic speech, he lets the reader *hear* the speech of his characters, not merely read humorous misspellings. Among other debts to him, American writers of the 20th century number Twain's language. Hemingway had it in mind when he called *Huckleberry Finn* "the best book we've had."

Humorous, moral, and symbolic, *The Adventures of Huckleberry Finn* continues to stir controversy wherever it is read—and it is read almost everywhere. Twain once referred to the novel as "that abused child of mine who has had so much unfair mud flung at him." Nowadays, the mud smears only the negligible few who deny *Huckleberry Finn* its place among the world's great books.

II. Questions for Study and Discussion

1. What are the main themes of the novel?
2. Is the novel rambling and episodic or essentially unified? Explain. Why is its structure effective or ineffective?

3. What is the climax of the novel? How does it illumine the theme?
4. Some critics believe that Tom Sawyer's appearance in the latter part of the book seriously damages its design and orientation. What is your opinion?
5. What effect does setting have on the total impact of the novel? Evaluate Twain's ability to write about nature.
6. To what extent does Huck's background make him a good choice as the central figure in the novel? Why does he narrate?
7. Characterize the relationship of Huck and Jim. To what extent does Huck depend on Jim? Jim on Huck? What significance do you find in their spending time together naked? How does this nakedness relate to comments on clothing made throughout the book?
8. Compare Huck and Tom as personalities.
9. What changes occur in Huck in the course of the novel? What are the stages of this process?
10. Detail the levels of society represented in the novel. Which characters represent these levels? Why has Twain attempted such extensive coverage? What authors have you read who do likewise?
11. Who are the good people in the novel? Is there a villain? Who is the noblest character? What significance do you attach to Twain's selection of his noblest character?
12. To what extent does the word *pragmatic* suffice to describe Huck's philosophy of life?
13. What are the major social, religious, and philosophical conflicts explored in the novel? Describe how Miss Watson, Widow Douglas, Huck's father, and Jim help illustrate Huck's basic moral conflict.
14. Contrast Huck's rebelliousness with that of his father.
15. What ultimately is Huck's attitude toward the Negro? What position on desegregation would you expect Twain to take today?
16. What specific things does Twain satirize? What is his attitude toward: democracy, money, Christianity, loyalty, sex, juries, human nature in general?

17. To what extent does the novel resolve Twain's ambivalent attitude toward realism and romance?
18. What is your understanding of the function of the Mississippi River in the novel? In Huck's total journey? Explain.
19. Which are the funniest scenes? How does Twain achieve his comic effects? To what extent does he use irony? To what extent does his humor minimize the serious purposes implicit in the novel?
20. What similarities do you find between Huck and Telemachus (the *Odyssey*)? Between *Huckleberry Finn* and *Don Quixote?* Between the humor of Twain and Swift?
21. What is the significance of Mark Twain's novel for us today?

III. Readings in Background and Criticism

Bellamy, Gladys C., *Mark Twain as Literary Artist* (University of Oklahoma Press, 1950). A perceptive study that argues convincingly that Twain is a serious artist, painstakingly conscious of artistic form. Chapter 19, "Acceptance vs. Rejection," examines the interrelationship of character, structure, and theme in *Huckleberry Finn*.

Brashear, Minnie T., *Mark Twain, Son of Missouri* (University of North Carolina Press, 1934). Valuable because it analyzes the central influences in Twain's formative years: his family environment, his adolescence in the thriving town of Hannibal, and his reading in 18th-century radical thinkers and humorists.

Brooks, Van Wyck, *The Ordeal of Mark Twain* (Meridian Books, 1956). In perhaps the most controversial of all books about Twain, Brooks argues that "something was gravely amiss with his [Twain's] inner life." The causes: the staid proprieties of eastern social and literary life; his wife's "exquisite sense of decorum." Thus, Huck Finn's escape to the raft and the river is also Twain's declaration of independence from the bonds of eastern America's conventions which restricted his rebellious spirit.

College English. In its issues of October 1955 and November 1956, appears a lively exchange of a half-dozen essays debunking or defending the greatness of the novel. Structure, characterization, tone, and theme are earnestly—often angrily—debated.

DeVoto, Bernard, *Mark Twain's America* (Little, Brown, 1932). An irritable but always lively writer, DeVoto uses hitherto unpublished materials to explain the cultural influences of the Frontier which affected Twain.

———, *Mark Twain at Work* (Harvard University Press, 1942). In the chapter "Noon and Dark" DeVoto reconstructs from Twain's notebooks the actual writing process of *Huckleberry Finn*. Long delayed while Twain labored at other tasks, the novel, argues DeVoto, lacks continuity and suffers from some bowdlerization. Nevertheless, DeVoto considers it a major representation of American democracy and a serious judgment of the limits of that democracy. See also DeVoto's excellent introduction to *The Adventures of Huckleberry Finn* in *The Viking Portable Mark Twain* (Viking Press, 1946).

Ferguson, DeLancey, *Mark Twain: Man and Legend* (Indiana University Press, 1943). Traces Twain's career as a writing man, avoiding all nonliterary problems such as business failures, marital difficulties, and the like. Most important, says Ferguson, is Twain's increasing use of himself as part of his characterization. Criticisms of individual novels —especially of *Huckleberry Finn*—are shrewd and sound.

Paine, Albert Bigelow, *Mark Twain: A Biography*, 4 vols. (Harper, 1912). A useful work, sharply limited—biographically and critically—by Paine's indiscriminate admiration for his subject.

Pattee, Fred L., *Introduction to Mark Twain: Representative Selections* (American Book Company, 1935). A strong denial of Brooks' thesis that the East ruined Twain. Pattee insists that editors like Howells at *Harpers* and others at *The Atlantic Monthly* encouraged him to produce more of the realism he had been attempting to write while out West.

Trilling, Lionel, Introduction to *Huckleberry Finn* (Rinehart, 1948). A brilliant though arguable thesis: *Huckleberry Finn* "is a great book because it is about a god"—the river god—and is therefore a *moral* book. Thus Huck, although he rebels against Christian morality, learns moral principles through his love for the Mississippi, which "seems to foster the goodness of those who love it and try to fit themselves to its ways." For a similar thesis see the introduction by T. S. Eliot (like Twain, a Missourian).

Wecter, Dixon, *Sam Clemens of Hannibal* (Houghton Mifflin, 1952). An important analysis of the impact on Twain's artistic and psychic development of Hannibal's frontier violence and budding cultural awareness.

Young, Philip, *Ernest Hemingway* (Rinehart, 1952). In the last three chapters of his acute study of Hemingway, Young analyzes in Twain's novel the stylistic and thematic qualities which appealed to and possibly influenced Hemingway. Young, unlike Trilling, sees the river not as a god but as a source of escape from the violence and anguish of human experience.

IV. Editions

From inexpensive paperbacks to costly illustrated versions, editions of *The Adventures of Huckleberry Finn* abound. Among the paperbacks the Rinehart edition is especially useful for its stimulating introduction by Lionel Trilling (see Background Readings). Other editions are published by Pocket Books, Viking Press, Harper, Penguin, and Houghton Mifflin.

29

Eliot: THE WASTE LAND

I. Background of Eliot (1888 -   )

After World War I, many young men felt that they had inherited, instead of a world made safe for democracy, a world spiritually dead, a corpse hardly worth a shroud. The brutality of the war and the failure of the peace had shattered their idealism and morality. Their commitment gave way to cynicism and their hope to hedonism. Their disillusion and bitterness carried over into the postwar world where materialism—social, industrial, and scientific—jarred the sensibilities of the genteel and the optimistic. But the imminence of cultural disintegration inspired among writers, artists, and composers a resolute determination to salvage fragments, to establish new links between past and present, to build a future.

In 1922 two works were published—a novel, *Ulysses* by James Joyce, and a poem, *The Waste Land* by T. S. Eliot—each of which has since startled, irritated, or fascinated readers of contemporary literature. Both are "difficult" reading because, structured by myth and symbol, they employ esoteric allusions and stream-of-consciousness techniques. Nevertheless, despite the demands each work makes, their audience and influence have steadily increased. The reason is that each illumines man's quest for a meaningful world.

Like Joyce, whose influence he shows, Thomas Stearns Eliot

is an expatriate. Born in St. Louis, Missouri, in 1888, of distinguished New England parentage, he became a British subject in 1927. Though nurtured there, Eliot's art could not take firm root in native ground. At Harvard he studied philosophy with George Santayana and Bertrand Russell; then, after a year at the Sorbonne, he returned to Harvard for three more years of graduate study in philosophy and linguistics. But the strains in Eliot's background, as he has admitted, were discordant: "I had always been a New Englander in the Southwest and a Southwesterner in New England." Not until 1914, when he won a traveling fellowship which he used to go abroad, did Eliot find congenial soil for his art. After studying language and literature briefly in Germany and at Oxford, Eliot settled in London to work during the war years in turn as teacher, bank clerk, and publisher's reader. More significantly, he began to publish: in 1917, *The Love Song of J. Alfred Prufrock*, a slender volume of twelve poems, and in 1920, *Poems* (including *Gerontion; Burbank with a Baedeker, Bleistein with a Cigar*; and *Sweeney Among the Nightingales*). Both collections foreshadow his main work. Radical in rhythms and imagery, Eliot nevertheless displayed an essential conservatism in ideas, searching for a moral and esthetic order—the establishment of a meaningful "tradition," a heritage from the past of timelessly usable knowledge. Only by salvaging "the inherited wisdom of the race" could the poet survive in a society where, like J. Alfred Prufrock, men purposelessly measured out their lives with coffee spoons or, like Apeneck Sweeney, vulgarized experience in brutal and wilful ignorance of their past.

As editor of two literary quarterlies, *The Egoist* (1917 - 1919) and *The Criterion* (1922 - 1939), Eliot pursued "tradition" relentlessly. In critical prose, he denounced the individualism of the romantics and the impressionists, praising Vergil, Dante, Donne and the Metaphysicals, Dryden, and the French Symbolist poets—many of whom he echoes in *The Waste Land*. In 1927, already established as a literary dictator, Eliot announced in the preface to a volume of essays, *For Lancelot Andrewes*, that he was a "classicist in literature, royalist in politics, Anglo-Catholic in religion." Though his subsequent poetic achievement may have diminished (as many critics believe), critical acclaim has grown prodigiously; he has won the British Order of Merit and the Nobel Prize for Literature. His more recent lyric and dramatic poetry—from *Ash Wednesday* (1930) to *Four Quartets* (1943); from *Murder in the Cathedral* (1935) to *The Elder Statesman* (1958)—seems to identify "tradition" with orthodox Christianity. Looked at from the perspective of his total literary output, Eliot's notion of "tradition" is ambiguous; yet his intense moral awareness bears incontrovertibly the stamp of American Puritan thought. Not without reason has he been called "the American dean of English letters."

Initially, *The Waste Land* may seem an inordinately congested poem. Within the relatively short course of 433 lines, the reader's progress is impeded by fragmentary quotations from or allusions to thirty-five authors, and by passages in six foreign languages, including Sanskrit. Eliot's notes—possibly appended to pad the too-slim volume—provide inadequate guidance through this poetic maze. Nevertheless the wise reader will not hastily detour from *The Waste Land*, for even at first reading Eliot's poem successfully meets his own requirement that genuine poetry must "communicate before it is understood." The flat, dispassionate lines, for example, corroborate the monotonous regularity of life (or rather death-in-life) in the wasteland: when the carbuncular clerk of "The Fire Sermon" seduces his typist lady-friend, the rhythms are metronomic, the rhymes mechanized. Similarly, images persistently recur until the "auditory imagination" unfailingly creates the appropriate atmosphere of decay, drought, and sterility which shrouds the poem: in Part I "stony rubbish," "broken images"; in Part II "rat's alley where the dead men lost their bones"; in Part III "The rat crept softly through the vegetation"; in Part IV "A current under sea/ Picked his bones in whispers"; and in Part V "Dead mountain mouth of carious teeth" and "Here is no water but only rock." Read through rapidly, or better, heard in Eliot's voice on easily available recordings, the poem —through its rhythms and images—stirs genuine emotional response. And closer study breeds an awareness of Eliot's nuances that enhances the initial effect.

Despite their apparent discontinuity, the five sections of *The*

Waste Land do achieve integration. In his review of Joyce's *Ulysses* in *The Dial* (1925), Eliot observed that Joyce's use of myth was a major step "towards making the modern world possible for art" because it provided "a way of controlling, of ordering, of giving a shape to the immense panorama of futility and anarchy which is contemporary history." Eliot controls, shapes, and orders *The Waste Land* through the ancient myth of the Fisher King, a vegetation deity analogous to Greece's Adonis, Egypt's Attis, Sumer's Tammuz, and, most significantly, through the legend of the quest for the Holy Grail. The Fisher King, rendered impotent (or even killed) by a sexual wound, must remain physically sterile until a pure knight, after suffering various trials and temptations, revitalizes him by asking certain life-restoring questions. Furthermore, the curse upon the king extends to his lands, likewise blighted (perhaps sympathetically) by drought and sterility. The pagan myth of the Fisher King, like the Christian Grail legend, has both sexual and religious implications, involving such phenomena as life and death, resurrection, seasonal change, fertility and decay—all motifs central, as Eliot indicates in his notes, to an understanding of *The Waste Land*.

Upon this scaffolding, Eliot built his drama of an impotent and degenerate society. Each of the sections of *The Waste Land*, by a compelling juxtaposition of past and present, dramatizes and clarifies some aspect of the personal and social problems precipitated by sexual and, concomitantly, spiritual decay. In the opening section, "The Burial of the Dead," Eliot broadly sketches the outlines of the desolate land: in the foreground hollow voices of the living dead yearn for the past—death, retreat from reality; in the background, voices of prophecy—ancient (Isaiah, Ezekiel, Ecclesiastes) and modern (Madame Sosostris)—foretell doom. Particulars supplant the general in the next section, "A Game of Chess," as Eliot specifies in two easily comprehended episodes the futility of sexual love in the upper and lower classes: adultery and abortion rather than fidelity and fertility characterize love in the wasteland. "The Fire Sermon" details the fruitless carnality of the middle class: Sweeney visits Mrs. Porter at a brothel; Mr. Eugenides invites the poet to a homosexual weekend; the bored clerk seduces the passionless typist; and Tiresias, the ancient Greek seer who has witnessed like scenes in earlier ages, looks on helplessly at the unholy lust of the inhabitants of the wasteland. In the fourth section, "Death by Water," water, usually the rejuvenating element, fails to restore life: Phlebas the Phoenician is drowned rather than regenerated. In the final section, "What the Thunder Said," the tortured journey through the wasteland reaches its climax (recalling Christ's agony in Gethsemane and the climax of the Quest for the Holy Grail). Rain follows the dry thunder and the three injunctions from the *Upanishads*—"Give," "Sympathize," "Control"—suggest a way of restoring fertility to the wasteland or, in a broad sense, of giving our lives vitality, force, purpose. It is only a suggestion that Eliot offers, however, not a solution. By consistently subverting the conventional interpretation of the death-resurrection myth, Eliot forestalls his reader from assuming the inevitability of salvation: April, the Spring, becomes ironically the *cruelest* month; water, symbol of fertility, also causes death by drowning; fire, the purifying element, may also become the destructive element (lust). At the close of the poem, therefore, the Fisher King remains on the shore fishing, with the arid plain behind him, hoping at least to set his own lands in order. Eliot closes his poem by offering the possibility (but not the promise) of a peace that surpasseth understanding.

To order a chaotic world, to evolve a meaningful tradition, becomes for Eliot a moral problem that he best solves esthetically. Order and tradition are the machinery that operate the poem. *The Waste Land*, to paraphrase Eliot's lines, is itself a fragment shored up against the ruins: for by controlling and objectifying experience he has successfully rendered significant the "immense panorama of futility and anarchy." Ill-assorted persons, places, and times finally emerge as strangely and ominously alike. They become, in Eliot's words, "objective correlatives," each an identifiable *object* (or situation or chain of events) whose social and emotional range of meaning *correlates* with a more extensive context than may be realized on first reading. Thus, the Fisher King appears in several guises throughout the poem: as himself (or the poet) "fishing at the dull canal," as the supposedly drowned father of Ferdinand in Shakespeare's *The Tempest*, or as the omniscient but impotent and blind prophet of Greek tragedy, Tiresias. Likewise the potential sources of salvation wear different garb, yet are recognizably interrelated—among the men: the lover and the demobilized soldier of "The Game of Chess"; Mr. Eugenides and the carbuncular clerk of "The Fire Sermon"; Phlebas of "Death by Water";—among the women: Isolde and the hyacinth girl; Mme. Sosostris (who, as a modern seer, misuses and misreads the ancient prophetic cards of the Tarot pack); Cleopatra; Philomel; the neurotic mistress and the ladies at the bar; Queen Elizabeth; the typist; and the Thames maidens. All of these people represent externally the inward failure—of heart and mind, of love and idealism. All are isolated and lost in the wasteland; most important, none of them can save the Fisher King. Even the locale remains the same, though it shifts in space and time. From a beer garden in Munich to London Bridge to a brothel in Carthage; from a lush boudoir to a sleazy divan to a tawdry pub; from a canal behind the gashouse to a garden reminiscent of Gethsemane to a mountain peak in the Himalayas—always the locale is part of an "unreal" city, desolate, chaotic, sterile.

Unquestionably difficult, *The Waste Land* is far more than an intellectual exercise. If it suggests more than it solves, its readers nevertheless gain rewards from its esthetic discipline and real insights into the timeless problems of human life.

II. Questions for Study and Discussion

1. What is the theme of the poem?
2. What do the section headings mean? What is the central point established in each of the five sections? How do these points interrelate? In what ways do they satisfactorily clarify the theme?
3. How does the pagan myth of the Fisher King help to unify the poem? How does the Christian legend of the quest for the Holy Grail serve a like purpose?
4. Identify the major symbols in the poem. What does each represent? How successfully do these symbols or "objective correlatives" subserve the myth content of the poem?
5. How does Eliot use ironic contrasts of place, person, and episode to intensify the thematic impact of the poem?

6. Several of the allusions in *The Waste Land* are to works you have already encountered in this book. To what purpose does Eliot use each of the following: Sophocles' *Oedipus*, Dante's *Divine Comedy*, Chaucer's *Canterbury Tales*, Shakespeare's *Hamlet?*
7. What are the essential qualities of Eliot's imagery? What use does he make of nature?
8. Eliot frequently uses jazz rhythms. When? Why? What other variations in prosody does he employ? To what purpose?
9. Characterize the male and female characters who inhabit *The Waste Land*. How do the sexes differ in their approach to experience? Do any of the characters possess qualities which might help to rejuvenate the wasteland?
10. Some critics have accused Eliot of sex nausea. To what extent is their charge valid? What is the sex of the narrator of the poem? How do you know?
11. What chance does modern man have to endure in Eliot's wasteland? To prevail?
12. Of what value are the "fragments" that the protagonist intends to shore against his ruins?
13. To which author that you have already read among the books discussed does Eliot seem closest in his vision of human experience? From what author does he seem most remote? Explain.
14. David Daiches, a prominent British critic, has commented about *The Waste Land* thus: "Our enjoyment [of the poem] is frequently spoiled by our tripping over cultural lumber that has been deliberately left lying about by the poet." To what extent do you agree or disagree with Daiches' observation?
15. Carl Sandburg has said of Eliot: "If you wish to pray, or if you wish to sit in silent meditation in a corner . . . you will get it from this poet. But if you want clarity on human issues, he's out—he's zero." Discuss Sandburg's comment.
16. Ezra Pound blue-penciled large sections of *The Waste Land*, thus inspiring the following quip by a distinguished scholar, Douglas ing nothing." How much validity does Mr. Bush's comment Bush: "A tale told by an Eliot, full of Pound and fury, signify-possess?

III. Readings in Background and Criticism

Brooks, Cleanth, *Modern Poetry and the Tradition* (University of North Carolina Press, 1939). The chapter, "*The Waste Land:* Critique of the Myth," was one of the earliest detailed analyses to prove that Eliot had uttered more than a groan. Aware of the integral relationship between Eliot's theme and his method, Brooks argues that Eliot needed a fresh technique to revitalize time-worn notions about spiritual regeneration. Eliot's technical distortions are apparent, not real: his ironically contrasted or paralleled characters and experiences, not less than his paradoxical or intentionally ambiguous symbols, help recreate a meaningful Christian tradition.

Drew, Elizabeth, *T. S. Eliot: The Design of his Poetry* (Eyre & Spottiswoode, 1950). A Jungian analysis of the poem, centering on the archetypal death-birth pattern.

Frazer, Sir James G., *The Golden Bough: A Study in Magic and Religion* (Macmillan, 1 vol. abridged ed., 1947). Chapters 29-42 (pages 324-384) of the abridged edition of this classic anthropological study detail the symbolic and thematic parallels linking the fertility gods of Greece, Egypt, and Phrygia. Their kinship to the Fisher King myth (see Jessie Weston) illumines the method and theme of *The Waste Land.* Difficult but fascinating reading.

Friar, Kimon, and Brinnin, John Malcolm, *Modern Poetry: American and British.* (Appleton-Century-Crofts, 1951). The extensive notes constitute an excellent explication, closely attentive to individual lines. There is also a valuable analysis of musical motifs in both *The Waste Land* and Eliot's later poem *Four Quartets.*

Hoffenstein, Samuel, *Year In, You're Out* (Modern Library, 1956). The poem *The Moistland* is a delightful parody of *The Waste Land,* especially entertaining after the reader has studied Eliot's poem in detail. Among the section headings are "A Three-Handed Game of Pinochle" and "Death by Hooch."

Leavis, F. R., *New Bearings in English Poetry* (Chatto & Windus, 1950). Although guilty of serious errors (e.g., ". . . the thunder brings no rain to revive the waste land, and the poem ends where it began"), Leavis shows clearly the musical organization and thematic unity of Eliot's poem. In Chapter 3, "T. S. Eliot," he locates as the core of the poem's meaning the lack of direction of human consciousness.

Matthiessen, F. O., *The Achievement of T. S. Eliot* (Oxford University Press, 1947). A brief but brilliant account of Eliot's writing up to 1946. Matthiessen, examines Eliot esthetically rather than ideologically, but nevertheless does consider the poet in relation to his age.

Smith, Grover, Jr., *T. S. Eliot's Poetry and Plays* (University of Chicago Press, 1956). Subtitled "A Study in Sources and Meaning," this long, occasionally ponderous study painstakingly analyzes various possible meanings for almost every ambiguous line in Eliot's writing. Chapter 6 deals with *The Waste Land.*

Unger, Leonard, editor, *T. S. Eliot: A Selected Critique* (Rinehart, 1948). A useful anthology of critical essays about Eliot's poetry, prose, and drama. Included are Cleanth Brooks' and Edmund Wilson's analyses of *The Waste Land* as well as articles by more than twenty-five other critics. An extensive bibliography is appended.

Weston, Jessie L., *From Ritual to Romance* (Doubleday Anchor Books, 1957). Explores the anthropological source of Eliot's central symbol—the Fisher King. Readable for its own sake, the book has special appeal for students of *The Waste Land* because it traces the Arthurian quest for the Holy Grail to primitive fertility rituals and attempts to prove that both Christian and pre-Christian rites held sexual as well as religious meaning.

Williamson, George, *A Reader's Guide to T. S. Eliot* (Noonday, 1957). A clear, dependable analysis of each of Eliot's poems. Arranged in chronological order to match Eliot's *Complete Poems and Plays,* the volume is especially attractive to the beginning student of Eliot's poetry.

Wilson, Edmund, *Axel's Castle* (Scribner's, 1931). In a vigorous and essentially antagonistic essay on *The Waste Land,* Wilson assesses the important influence upon Eliot of two French symbolists—Tristan Corbière and Jules LaForgue. Wilson insists further—and wrongly, according to recent critics—that the poem is an expression of "emotional starvation" by a "Puritan turned artist."

IV. Editions

The Waste Land three plays, and all of Eliot's major poems are collected in *The Complete Poems and Plays* (Harcourt, Brace). More moderately priced is the paperback *The Waste Land and Other Poems* (Harvest), though it contains only a few pieces besides *The Waste Land.*

30

Joyce: ULYSSES

I. Background of Joyce (1882 - 1941)

Unlike Eliot, Joyce never formulated a capsule credo. But had he asserted, "I am an Irishman, a Catholic, and a Classicist," or "I am neither an Irishman, nor a Catholic, nor a Classicist," he could have argued cogently for either set of propositions.

Was Joyce an Irishman? By birth and compulsion, obviously—more particularly a Dublin man. Not only was he always avid for news about Dublin people and places, but Dubliners populate all his stories and novels and Dublin is their vital scene. Yet he early exiled himself from Ireland, "the old sow that eats her farrow," abjuring wholly the political activity that fevered his generation. Perhaps lasting anger at the Irish repudiation of Parnell, more likely the conviction that politics was another net to snare the artist, determined Joyce's aloofness. The course of Ireland's violent struggle for nationality—the Parliamentary maneuvers for Home Rule under Parnell's brilliant leadership, the Sinn Fein ("We Ourselves") revolutionary agitation for independence, the guerilla warfare against the Royal Irish Constabulary (the "Black and Tans") who ravaged Ireland in the attempt to suppress the Irish drive for independence, the establishment of the Irish Free State in 1921—all intrigued Joyce and permeated his work. But he gave his allegiance to no Irish cause. In *A Portrait of the Artist as a Young Man* and in *Ulysses*, each a quasi-autobiographical novel, he names his hero "Stephen Dedalus," in allusion both to the first Christian martyr and to the "fabulous artificer" who escaped from the labyrinth he had built for Minos, king of Crete, by means of the wings he had fashioned. When Joyce escaped Dublin, it was in deliberate search for liberation, for a chance to spread Daedalian wings. While he never ceased being a Dublin man, he became even more a cosmopolitan artist. No book he published is dated from Dublin.

Was Joyce a Catholic? He found Catholicism, like patriotism, a snare but not perhaps a delusion. His ultimate declaration, "I will not serve," says "No!" to the discipline, not to the dogmas, of the Church. Born a Catholic, brought up by a deeply religious mother and a father at any rate acquiescent (in spite of his Parnellism), educated at Clongowes Wood (a Jesuit school), and at Dublin University, Joyce felt Catholicism along his pulses before he was able to debate about it. The density of Catholic reference in his work, its preoccupation with theological doctrine and dialectics, more, its essentially Thomist structure, testify that if Joyce left the Church, he could never cut its tether. Nevertheless, that he consciously rebelled seems incontestable (though it has been contested). Joyce employs Catholic forms deliberately, and deliberately he perverts Catholic content. In *Ulysses*, for example, he uses the language of a scholastic, but a sniggering scholastic; or he provides a Mass, but a Satanic Mass. He concedes that Catholicism is a beautiful belief—but adds, "a beautiful lie—something at least." Though devout admirers have recently been attempting to convert Joyce posthumously, he lived without the ministrations of the Church and asked to be buried without its rites.

Was he a classicist? From Aquinas, Joyce adapted his esthetic, certainly classic in essence: the work of art, he announced, must have "wholeness, symmetry, radiance." And these qualities show forth in the hierarchy of themes and ordering of incidents as well as in the passion for analogy and "epiphany"—the revelation contained in all experience, including its symbolic disclosure. Classicism implies formal control; and in that respect no contemporary surpasses Joyce.

But, again, classicism implies an adherence to traditional literary procedures. And Joyce dislocates the traditional mode of narrative in which things happen one after another, even the flashbacks preserving a natural time-sequence, and the traditional logic of narrative, in which explicit cause leads to explicit effect. Thus in *Ulysses* he fragments the continuity of his story, shoring for the reader only those bits that flow along a character's stream of consciousness. He produces the bits, moreover, without introducing, linking, or commenting on them—merely displaying them as they drift by. The sequence, at times scarcely discernible, depends on the web of associations spun by the experience of the character (not, save accidentally, of the reader).

Both Joyce's *Dubliners* (1914), a collection of stories, and *A Portrait of the Artist as a Young Man* (1916), his first published novel, evidence his preoccupation with Dublin, with religion, and with literary form. Both supplement as well as anticipate *Ulysses* (1922). It is not merely that characters like Martin Cunningham of "Grace" in *Dubliners* or Father Flynn of the *Portrait* reappear in *Ulysses*. More important, *Dubliners*, which Joyce called "a chapter in the moral history of my country" at the center of paralysis, defines the locale and the *Portrait* reveals the emergent artist of *Ulysses*. In both, as in *Ulysses*, Joyce penetrates to the core of personality and very subtly projects it—of the several disparate characters in *Dubliners*, of the developing Stephan Dedalus in the *Portrait*.

Joyce first conceived of *Ulysses* as another story for *Dubliners*, to be entitled "Mr. Hunter." The external action might easily be accommodated in such a story, for it all takes place in eighteen hours and forty-five minutes of a single day, Thursday, June 16, 1904 (since celebrated by pious Joyceans as "Bloomsday"). But the story grew to 768 pages and took seven years to write. In part the extraordinary elaboration results from the framework, a series of intricate analogues—chief among them to Homer's *Odyssey*.

Various motives, some psychological and some esthetic, prompted Joyce's compilation of parallels. First, he needed a counterpoise for chaos, for the lack of purpose and force in the modern world. World War I had shattered the old certitudes and made the venerated codes suspect. Neither the hope of progress nor the consolations of religion seemed more than a shallow deception. Though immensely talented, Wells, Galsworthy, Bennett, and the other giants of the preceding generation had brought the novel to a dead end: their novels had not been informed by values that still appeared relevant—or, as Joyce and many of his fellow writers and artists believed, controlled by a sufficient esthetic. In the great Homeric myth, Joyce saw a design at once moving and meaningful for his time. Second, Joyce's stream-of-consciousness style disintegrates narrative, reduces it to flux. The ordering myth restores form and substance. Third, Joyce was a satirist (satire is a condition to which crypto-moralists are especially prone); he wanted to point up the diminished significance of man in this epoch of his history. *Ulysses* radiates not from the violent heroic figure of the *Odyssey* but from a timid advertising canvasser, a half-compliant cuckold, a mock-hero. Fourth, Joyce—who had rejected his father, fled his religion, and escaped his country—must have responded poignantly to the quest motif that binds the *Odyssey*. Fifth, Joyce had assimilated the allegorical habit of thought, a way of writing that has Dante for its greatest exemplar: the medieval literary tradition that consists of piling meaning upon meaning in the attempt to reach the highest truths was for Joyce a live tradition. Finally, it may be conjectured, Joyce was enchanted by intricacy for its own sake, by the complex possibilities of cross correspondence.

Some clues to the action of the eighteen chapters (or books) comprising *Ulysses* may help the reader through the Joycean labyrinth. At the end of the *Portrait*, Stephen is about to leave for Paris; there, he promises, through exile, silence, and cunning, he will forge the uncreated consciousness of his race. Before *Ulysses* opens, he has returned to Dublin, summoned by a telegram: "Mother dying." Still in revolt against family and faith, he refuses to kneel and pray at her bedside. As by a recurrent ghost, he is haunted by that refusal.

The first four books of Homer's *Odyssey*, the "Telemachiad," follow the traces of a young man, Telemachus, searching for his father. Much more closely, the first three books of *Ulysses* trail another young man, Stephen Dedalus, unconsciously seeking a surrogate father. We spy on Stephen's movements and thoughts from 8 A.M. to 11 A.M. [The parentheses in the paragraphs of skeleton summary ensuing enclose the number of each book, or episode, the time it takes place, its title—which, to signify the Homeric parallel, Joyce first prefixed to the episode and later dropped—and a notation of the episode's principal locale.]

(I. 8 A.M. *Telemachus.* Martello Tower on Dublin Bay.) Stephen breakfasts with two companions whom he cordially dislikes: Buck Mulligan, a witty, blasphemous, incurably dirty-minded medical student; and Hawes, an Englishman, consequently quite obnoxious and not quite bright. (II. 10 A.M. *Nestor.* Mr. Deasy's school at Dalkey, a Dublin suburb.) Stephen conducts a history lesson, pausing afterwards for a chat with Mr. Deasy—whose senility is more apparent than his wisdom, in spite of his paralleling Nestor, a wise old counselor—and agreeing to place Mr. Deasy's article on hoof-and-mouth disease. (III. 11 A.M. *Proteus.* Beach at Sandymount.) Stephen wanders along the beach, against an ever-changing sea and sky, thinking a thousand Protean thoughts.

In books V to XII of the *Odyssey* (the "Wanderings") Homer shifts his narrative center from Telemachus to Ulysses. Similarly, in books IV to XV of *Ulysses* Joyce shifts his from Stephen to Leopold Bloom, a Dublin Jew, a displaced person like Odysseus, but a far-wanderer only within city limits. He is married to a concert singer, Molly, who has been variously unfaithful to him; but she is a woman of emphatic sexuality, and Bloom has been impotent for ten years—since their infant son Rudy died. Molly's current manager, who doubles as her lover, is Blazes Boylan, a flamboyant, overconfident, very successful rake. (IV. 8 A.M. *Calypso.* Bloom's home.) Bloom prepares breakfast for his wife, takes his own, reads his mail, defecates. (V. 10 A.M. *Lotus Eaters.* En route to the public bath.) Bloom walks to the *poste-restante* to pick up a letter from Martha Clifford, a typist with whom he has been conducting a salacious correspondence, buys a cake of lemon soap for Molly, goes to a public bath, where, besides luxuriating generally, he contemplates his navel. (VI. 11 A.M. *Hades.* Funeral.) Bloom attends the funeral of Paddy Dignan, riding in the same coach as Simon Dedalus,

Stephen's father—whom Stephen rejects and who willingly abandons the role for tenor-singing and pub-crawling. At Glasneven cemetery, in addition to the priest, caretaker, mourners, Bloom notes the presence of an incompetent newspaperman and an unidentified "fellow in a mackintosh." (VII. Noon. *Aeolus*. Office of the *Freeman's Journal*.) Bloom returns to duty, visiting a newspaper office to arrange terms for an advertisement and narrowly missing Stephen who, lavish with severance pay, buys drinks for the editor and his cronies. (VIII. 1 P.M. *Lestrygonians*. Davy Byrne's Pub.) Bloom enters Burton's restaurant; however, repelled by the animalistic gorging, he repairs to a pub for a sandwich and glass of Burgundy.

The two episodes ensuing make a short detour: while technically part of the Bloom odyssey, one belongs to Stephen and the other to the City itself. (IX. 2 P.M. *Scylla and Charybdis*. The National Library.) Stephen proposes a theory about *Hamlet* to an assorted group of literati: Shakespeare ought not to be equated with the Prince but with the Prince's father; Ann Hathaway, Shakespeare's wife, with the adulterous queen; and the poet's brothers with Claudius, the usurping brother. (X. 3 P.M. *Wandering Rocks*. Dublin's streets.) The City prevails; along its streets the characters of the novel appear cinematically, sometimes in close-ups, sometimes in long shots.

From books XI to XV Bloom again roves Dublin. (XI. 4 P.M. *The Sirens*. The Ormond Hotel.) Bloom listens to Simon Dedalus sing—and watches Blazes Boylan enter, chat with the barmaids, and leave for his rendezvous with Molly. (XII. 5 P.M. *Cyclops*. Barney Kiernan's pub.) Bloom comes in, hoping to find lawyer Martin Cunningham in behalf of Dignan's widow; instead he finds a drunken demagogue, superpatriot, and anti-Semite, who routs Bloom, hurling a biscuit can and sicking his mongrel after him. (XIII. 8 P.M. *Nausicaa*. Sandymount Beach.) Bloom walks down to the beach, sees Gerty MacDowell, a lame eighteen-year-old sentimentalist, and, at a discreet distance from each other, they masturbate. (XIV. 10 P.M. *Oxen of the Sun*. Lying-In Hospital.) Bloom goes to visit Mina Purefoy, who is giving birth. Stephen is there, drunk, with some medical students, and, finally, Bloom encounters him. Bloom, his urge for paternity never wholly satisfied, is obscurely moved. When

Stephen invites his comrades for a drink, Bloom determines to follow. (XV. 12 P.M. *Circe.* Bella Cohen's brothel.) Bloom accompanies Stephen to the brothel, where each undergoes an extraordinary series of distorted visions and materializations: thoughts, memories, dreams, wishes, emotions are translated into fearful substantiality. Leaving, Bloom is able to save Stephen from being cheated, but not, immediately after, from being knocked down by a drunken, truculent English soldier.

Both Homer and Joyce devote the last episodes of their books to the "Return," or "Homecoming." Unlike Penelope, however, Molly dominates the scene—even when she is not on it. (XVI. 1 A.M. *Eumaeus.* Cabman's shelter.) Bloom takes Stephen for coffee, listens to some tall tales by a sailor patron, never succeeds in reaching Stephen. (XVII. 2 A.M. *Ithaca.* Bloom's kitchen.) Bloom and Stephen drink cocoa in Bloom's Kitchen. They draw somewhat closer; nevertheless, Stephen will not stay for the night. (XVIII. After 2 A.M. *Penelope.* Molly and Leopold Bloom's bedroom.) Molly, a continually unfaithful Penelope (whom we meet in bed and leave in bed), reviews her past, wonders about the possibility of acquiring Stephen as a lover and about the meaning of Leopold's request that she get breakfast the next morning, and, affirming, falls off to sleep: ". . . and yes I said yes I will yes."

Though both Joyce and his commentators insist on the Homeric parallels, these are neither comprehensive nor always exact. One cannot, for example, locate in the *Odyssey* the prototype of Martha Clifford, Bloom's romantic correspondent. And to discern Scylla and Charybdis in the critics' disputation—the rock Scylla symbolized by Dogma, Aristotle, and Stratford; the whirlpool Charybdis by Mysticism, Plato, and Elizabethan London—seems an unconvincing though commendable feat of exegesis. Nor does Stephen's inveighing against birth control, in the *Oxen of the Sun* episode, quite equal Odysseus' warning to his men against slaughtering the flocks of Helios; in any case, Bloom, not Stephen, is to be identified with Odysseus.

Still, while they can be overworked, the Homeric incidents and personages often explicate the action in *Ulysses.* A short list of

Joycean and Homeric counterparts may aid the reader bent on getting parallels straight:

Joyce	*Homer*
Parnell (statue)	Agamemnon (shade)
Leopold Bloom	Odysseus
Molly Bloom	Calypso, then Cybele (goddess of nature), then Gaea (earth goddess)
Blazes Boylan	Eurymachus
"Citizen"	Polyphemus
Father Coffey	Cerberus
Bella Cohen	Circe
Martin Cunningham	Sisyphus
Mr. Deasy	Nestor
Stephen Dedalus	Telemachus
Paddy Dignam	Elpenor
Miss Douce	Siren
Skin-the-goat Fitzharris	Eumaeus
Miss Kennedy	Siren
Milkwoman	Athena
Gertie MacDowell	Nausicaa
Mr. MacDowell	Alcinous
John Henry Menton	Ajax
"M'Intosh"	Theoclymenos
Buck Mulligan	Antinous
Daniel O'Connell (monument)	Heracles (shade)
John O'Connell	Hades
Major Brian Cooper Tweedy	Atlas

Joyce, who fused the predilections of medieval scholiast and the talents of modern novelist, would not rest content with such a simple blending. Multiplying parallels, he advanced towards greater complexity.

Thus, he insinuated an appropriate "art" into each episode—except the last, presumably because Molly represents Nature, the antithesis of art—and endows the art with an appropriate technique. The art of *Oxen of the Sun,* for example, is medicine, its technique embryonic development. Since the episode concerns the delivery of Mina Purefoy's infant, the end product of embryonic development, Joyce parodies the development of English prose from Anglo-Saxon to American Evangelistic, passing en route Malory, Lyly, Lamb, Macaulay, Dickens, Pater, and others—all the while directing a medical, particularly an obstetrical, conversation between Stephen and his friends.

Several of the episodes have a distinctive color as well, generally a liturgical color. Green, Neptune's color, predominates in *Proteus:* the sea, a protean fluid, is green by day. Blue predominates in *Nausicaa:* in the gathering evening, Mary, Star of the Sea, is ascendant.

The literary anatomist should also be able to distinguish "the cycle of the human body," Joyce says. Each episode, from the fourth to the eighteenth, is keyed to a bodily organ. In *Calypso* the fundamental organ is the kidney—Bloom eats a kidney for breakfast, employs his kidneys in defecating. In *Scylla and Charybdis,* which includes the abstruse discussion of *Hamlet* and which illustrates the art of dialectic, the brain becomes sovereign. In *Penelope,* wherein Molly lies abed, reviewing her fleshly past, the flesh has dominion.

A basic symbol correlates parallel episodes of the *Odyssey* and *Ulysses.* Circe in Homer becomes Joyce's "whore" (Bella Cohen, who also bestializes men); Nausicaa, his "virgin" (Gertie MacDowell, the young maiden whom Bloom encounters on the beach); Hades, his cemetery "caretaker" (John O'Donnell, guardian of the dead).

To run through a single episode may somewhat clarify Joyce's method. In *Aeolus,* Bloom drops by the office of the *Freeman's Journal,* a visit that corresponds to Odysseus' sojourn in Aeolus. A newspaper plant, with its roaring presses and echoing noises, obviously, makes a neat parallel to Homer's Cave of the Winds. Miles Crawford, the editor, is the counterpart of Aeolus, keeper of the winds. The bodily organ associated is the lungs—the repository of breath, the windbag. The technique is enthymemic: "enthymeme" denotes a syllogism in which a premise or occasionally the conclusion is implied rather than stated, a tactic appropriate to *rhetoric*, the art of the episode. In exemplifying rhetoric Joyce supplies not only an anthology of oratorical snatches but also a handbook of rhetoric containing about ninety-five devices, some familiar like simile and metaphor, most exotic like hepaxlogomenon and metalepsis. Furthermore, he reproduces conversations stuffed with jargon and clichés, which are burnt-out rhetoric, and divides the episode by a series of headlines, which, condensing the history of headlines since the 19th century, shout with progressive rhetorical blatancy. The predominating color is red, because, one commentator suggests (committing a paranomasia), red connotes "the blood-warming, flag-waving, red-ragging stunts of newsmongers, out to stimulate their circulation."

Of the diverse style Joyce commands, streams of consciousness has been generally considered his distinctive contribution. Though he did not invent the style (which, though it has various literary sources, probably flows most directly from Freud's and Jung's psychoanalytic technique of free association), no writer has used it with greater mastery. It enables him to achieve two supremely important literary objectives, immediacy and depth. Through stream of consciousness he can make dramatic the psychology of each hero, differentiate Bloom's thought-sequence—cheerful, erratic, a trifle masochistic—from Stephen's—quick, poetic, brooding, at times tortured. He manages the other styles dexterously too: formal catechism in *Ithaca* and informal catechism in *Proteus;* expressionism overlaid by hallucination in *Circe;* fruity pulp-love-story in *Nausicaa;* snarling monologue in *Cyclops.*

The reader who wants to penetrate *Ulysses* will find plenty of obstacles in his road: theological disputations, occult lore, private allusions, as well as the maze of correspondences. Granting Joyce's immense cleverness, he will wonder how significantly it has been directed at times. He will very likely think the route between color and art (for example, red and rhetoric in *Aeolus*) a tour de force. More important, he may decide after following some excursus (for example, the parody course of English literature in *Oxen of the Sun*) that he has come no nearer to Bloom or Stephen.

Still, Joyce's ingenuity along the way will delight the reader, even if he has to discover it with the aid of manuals—and then occasionally regards it as misguided. He need not, moreover, understand all the parallels to enjoy *Ulysses;* in fact, at first reading he would do well to neglect them. Enough remains: the style, a perfect instrument, always adequate to its purpose; the wit, the insight, the immense dexterity. There are also Bloom, one of the most splendidly achieved comic characters in world literature, and Molly, one of the most magnificently carnal.

Other personalities, too, come to pulsating, vibrant being (lacking only their Freudian censors). Yet all of them, Bloom and Stephen and Molly and Mulligan and Haines and the rest, wander in the void, their drift intensely obscure even to themselves; if they are not lost, it is because they have no direction; and the luminous formal structure, always in the background, allows us to see their futile progress more clearly. Without moralizing, just by recreating fully and movingly life as it was lived in a particular time and place, Joyce enables us to read the lesson of a wasteland, a land exhausted and, very soon now, doomed.

II. Questions for Study and Discussion

1. What is the main theme of *Ulysses?* Does the theme gain or lose force as a result of the Homeric parallel? Explain.
2. What is the climax of the novel? Does it in any way correspond to the climax of the *Odyssey?*
3. There are several motifs in *Ulysses*—that is, ideas or emotions that recur insistently. Stephen, for example, often harks back to his refusal to accede to his mother's last request—that he kneel and pray at her deathbed. Cite two others. How are the motifs relevant to the main theme?
4. The "night-town" episode *(Circe)* has been frequently termed "a Witch's Sabbath" or "Walpurgis Night" scene. Why? It is the most difficult episode in the book: is its difficulty fully justified? Why or why not?
5. Using *Ulysses* as base, write a brief analysis of Dublin. What are you able to discuss most fully? What least adequately? Does

your inability to supply some necessary data imply a fault in the novel?

6. *Ulysses* has been described as a union of Symbolism and Naturalism. Is Joyce equally successful in both modes? Or is the subjective element "allowed to invade and to deteriorate" the objective aspects of the story?
7. Does the stream-of-consciousness technique have any poetic value? Why doesn't Joyce use it throughout the novel, rather than calling other styles into play?
8. After collecting a dozen of Joyce's images, say whether they are vividly original. Without reading his poetry, do you think he would make a great poet? Why? Are the images appealing to ear and nose more frequent than in most novels? Why?
9. *Ulysses* is the story of a day. Is it, for the characters involved, an ordinary day?
10. Characterize Leopold Bloom. To what extent is he a "great comic character?" Is he *only* comic? Why did Joyce make him a Jew? Is there much distinctively Jewish about him?
11. Will Bloom, do you deduce, do anything important on June 17, 1904—the day after the events of *Ulysses?* Will Molly? Will Stephen?
12. Characterize Stephen. How does your attitude toward him change as the book progresses? Do you prefer Buck Mulligan to Stephen? Explain your answers.
13. How does his library lecture on Shakespeare cast light on Stephen's psychological state?
14. Is the Stephen we meet in *Ulysses* continuous with the Stephen who emerges from *A Portrait of the Artist as a Young Man?* How does the *Portrait* help the reader to understand the esthetic and even the technique of *Ulysses?*
15. Characterize Molly. In what way is she like Penelope? In what way like the Earth-goddess? In what way unlike both?
16. *Ulysses* has been called an "Odyssey of the sewer," a "monstrous," "cynical," "nihilistic" work. If you disagree, what positive values would you say Joyce fosters? What qualities does he admire, what despise?

17. Joyce has suggested that, had he remained in Dublin, he would have become like Gabriel Conroy, chief character of "The Dead," the last story in *Dubliners*. Read the story and decide whether Joyce's conjecture is valid. Why?
18. Joyce resembles Eliot in one way, Flaubert in another, Freud in a third. How?
19. Compare *Ulysses* with such great novels as *War and Peace* and *Moby Dick*. What are its shortcomings—in quality of action, conflict, character portrayal, plot—that become evident after such a comparison? What are its strengths?
20. To what extent has Joyce influenced succeeding novelists? What writers can you name who have adapted or imitated some phase of Joyce's method?

III. Readings in Background and Criticism

Budgen, Frank, *James Joyce and the Making of "Ulysses"* (Smith and Haas, 1934). An engaging commentary, enriched by personal reminiscences and anecdotes, by an artist friend. The beginning Joycean ought perhaps to read this study first—for its candor and enthusiasm as much as for its critical evaluations.

Eliot, T. S., "*Ulysses*, Order, and Myth," *Dial* (November 1932, 480-483); reprinted in Leon Givens, *James Joyce: Two Decades of Criticism* (Vanguard Press, 1948). A brief but important essay, pointing out the virtues of Joyce's style and the value of his mythic structure.

Gilbert, Stuart, *James Joyce's "Ulysses"* (Vintage Books, 1955). An exhaustive reading and book-by-book analysis of sources, parallelisms, and symbols. Frequently ponderous and sometimes overerudite, Gilbert's guide (produced with Joyce's aid) nevertheless is the most nearly definitive.

Givens, Seon, ed., *James Joyce: Two Decades of Criticism* (Vanguard, 1948). Ranging over Joyce's life and work, the collection includes several essays not easily located elsewhere. Especially valuable are Vivian Mercier's "Dublin under the Joyces," which limns Joyce's Dublin; Eugene Jolas' "My Friend James Joyce," which recreates something of Joyce's personality; and Philip Toynbee's "A Study of James Joyce's *Ulysses*," which asseses the novel with a novelist's insight.

Gorman, Herbert, *James Joyce* (Rinehart, 1939). The "official" and still the only adequate biography. Lacking distance and detachment, and critically deficient as well, it is nevertheless indispensable to the reader who wants to trace the details of Joyce's career.

Levin, Harry, *James Joyce: A Critical Introduction* (New Directions, 1941). A basic critical work, Levin's perceptive and learned "introduction" concentrates on relating Joyce to his great European ancestors, but provides an intelligent examination of the novel, too.

Magalaner, Marvin, and Kain, Richard M., *Joyce: the Man, the Work, the Reputation* (New York University Press, 1956). Kain's chapters on *Ulysses* are less satisfactory because they present no reasoned analysis of the novel. Magalaner's chapters on *Dubliners* and the *Portrait*, however, are the most illuminating and incisive yet published—vital for understanding *Ulysses*.

Stewart, J. M., *James Joyce* (Longmans, Green, 1957). A forty-three page pamphlet, fairly summarizing Joyce's work. Though Stewart does not reverence Joyce—he is sharply critical of Joyce's stunts, for example —he admires him intelligently.

Tindall, William York, *James Joyce: His Way of Interpreting the Modern World* (Scribner's, 1950). The author extends his inquiry further than any other listed here, emphasizing the mythic and symbolic aspects of *Ulysses*, yet remains lucid and sprightly throughout.

Ussher, Arland, *Three Great Irishmen: Shaw, Yeats, Joyce* (New American Library, 1957). In "twosome twominds" about Joyce's total achievement, the critic nevertheless regards *Ulysses* as a great comic work. Unfailingly witty, this short appraisal is also one of the most original, urbane, and just.

Wilson, Edmund, *Axel's Castle* (Scribner's, 1931). Pages 191 to 236 contain an early summary and evaluation, still useful for its clear-sighted assessment of Joyce's central virtues and faults.

IV. Translations and Editions

The Modern Library Giant edition, though retaining the misprints and typographical errors of its predecessors, is the most available edition and, in spite of its faults, quite usable.

DATE DUE
OCT 29 1982
DEMCO 38-297